RESSION

DEPRESSION

a public feeling

ANN CVETKOVICH

Duke University Press   *Durham & London*   2012

Duke University Press gratefully
acknowledges the support of the Office
of the President at The University of Texas at
Austin, which provided funds toward
the publication of this book.

For Gretchen
Twenty years isn't much, you know I want
two hundred more . . .

In writing this book I've continually felt pressed against the limits of my stupidity, even as I've felt the promising closeness of transmissible gifts.

—Eve Kosofsky Sedgwick, *Touching Feeling*

Contents

Acknowledgments

For a long time, this book's working subtitle was *A Public Feelings Project* in order to name and acknowledge the open-ended and collaborative process that enabled my writing. The collective energies of Public Feelings groups in Austin, Chicago (Feel Tank), New York, and Toronto have sustained the vision of salon-like gatherings in which thinking can be speculative and feelings both good and bad are welcome. The book's initial seeds were planted at a conference called "Depression: What Is It Good For?" partly organized by Feel Tank at the University of Chicago, and before that at gatherings on the futures of feminism and sexuality at the University of Chicago, Barnard College, and the University of Arizona that were orchestrated by Lauren Berlant and Janet Jakobsen. It grew in Public Feelings panels at American Studies Association, Modern Language Association, and Cultural Studies Association meetings, and gained critical mass at a cluster of conferences organized by our groups in 2007–8: "Anxiety, Urgency, Outrage, Hope . . . A Conference on Political Feeling" at the University of Chicago, "Decamp: A Public Feelings Toronto Project" at the University of Toronto, and "Political Emotions" at the University of Texas.

In Austin, my work has been nurtured and sustained by at least three generations of Public Feelings: an early group that included faculty and graduate students (and I'd especially like to acknowledge Deborah Kapchan and Alyssa Harad); a collective that worked toward the Chicago Political Feeling conference: Sam Baker, Neville Hoad, Ann Reynolds, Janet Staiger, and Katie Stewart; and a cohort of newer colleagues, whose members include Craig Campbell, Josh Gunn, Heather Hindman, Randy Lewis, Sofian Merabet, and Circe Sturm. I'd also like to acknowledge: in Chicago, Feel Tank Chicago (Lauren Berlant, Rebecca Zorach, Deborah Gould, and Mary Patten), as well as the organizers of the Depression conference; in New York, the leadership of José Muñoz and Lisa Duggan, and the presence of John Anderson, Nao Bustamante, Lisa Cohen, Ed Cohen, Patricia Clough, Carolyn Dinshaw, David Eng,

Gayatri Gopinath, Janet Jakobsen, Martin Manalansan, Tavia Nyong'o, and Ann Pellegrini, among others; in Toronto, Elspeth Brown, Michael Cobb, Megan Boler, and Allyson Mitchell especially, as well as Kate Eichhorn, John Greyson, Johanna Householder, John Ricco, and Dana Seitler. Integral to our meetings have been beloved fellow travelers, our term for the friends who form a larger network of conversations, events, and shared sensibilities. Among these are Miranda Joseph and Sandy Soto (who hosted numerous events at the University of Arizona), Dana Luciano, Fred Moten, Kathleen Woodward, and, especially, Heather Love, who ultimately became one of this book's most important inter-locutors. Of the many with whom I've had the pleasure of following an idea to unexpected places, I owe special thanks to Lauren Berlant, José Muñoz, and Katie Stewart, all of whom have consistently inspired and shaped my own thinking.

Live events with their performative energies have been a crucial forum. I cherish the opportunities that I've had to workshop the book at public lectures along with the informal events, especially with gradu-ate students, that were often even more productive than the formal talks. I'm grateful to my hosts for the generosity of their organizational labors: Larry Schehr at the University of Illinois, Urbana-Champaign; Vicky Hesford at SUNY Stony Brook; Laura Lyons at the University of Hawaii; Eva Cherniavsky at Indiana University; Dana Takagi at the University of California, Santa Cruz; Jila Ghomeshi and David Chur-chill at the University of Manitoba; Margot Backus at the University of Houston; Juana María Rodríguez at the University of California, Davis; Christina Zwarg at Haverford College; Sandy Soto at the Univer-sity of Arizona; Gail Lewis and Anne-Marie Fortier at Lancaster Univer-sity; Lucas Crawford and Heather Zwicker at the University of Alberta; Susan Brown at the University of Guelph; Barbara Godard and Kate Eichhorn at York University; Mary O'Connor at McMaster University; Aoibheann Sweeney at the City University of New York; and Marianne Hirsch at Columbia University.

My initial fantasy was that this project would be a small book, short enough to be written in one semester. That semester leave was a long time coming, and in the end, not long enough. For heroic efforts to get me not one but two semesters of research leave from the University of Texas, I thank my department chair, Elizabeth Cullingford, whose un-stinting dedication to faculty has made the English department a happy place in which to work. Ken Wissoker has been there from the start, and I thank him for encouraging me to follow my intuitions and then for helping make the results better. I was lucky to have the intelligent support of Heather Love and an anonymous reader. I have also had expert editorial assistance from Abe Louise Young and Laura Helper-Ferris, who worked magic behind the scenes to enhance my thinking by refining my prose, and able research assistance from Sean McCarthy, Peggy Whilde, and Hala Herbly.

For valuable readings at crucial points along the way, I thank Kimberly Alidio, Moe Angelos, Joanna Brooks, Nancy Capron, Ed Cohen, Lisa Cohen, Carolyn Dinshaw, Jill Dolan, Lisa Duggan, Heather Love, Lisa Moore, Ann Reynolds, and Jason Tougaw. Other beloved colleagues who've been part of my gang include Jennifer Brody, Mary Marshall Clark, Cathy Davidson, Avery Gordon, Jack Halberstam, Sharon Holland, Chantal Nadeau, and Chris Newfield. If I've forgotten anyone, it's only because I have needed so many. For the day-to-day support in Austin, deep gratitude to Helen Knode, Lisa Moore, and Ann Reynolds.

An earlier version of some of the material from chapter 2 appeared in Ann Cvetkovich, "Depression Is Ordinary: Public Feelings and Saidiya Hartman's *Lose Your Mother*," *Feminist Theory* 13, no. 2 (2012), 131–46. And an earlier version of some material in the introduction was in "Public Feelings" in Janet Halley and Andrew Parker, eds., "After Sex: On Writing since Queer Theory," a special issue of *SAQ: South Atlantic Quarterly* 106, no. 3 (2007), 459–68, republished as *After Sex: On Writing since Queer Theory* (Durham: Duke University Press, 2011), 169–79.

This book is about the value of process and the art of daily living, and I am honored to acknowledge the material and spiritual support of my family, especially my parents, Valerie Haig-Brown and Joseph Cvetkovich, and my aunt Celia Haig-Brown; Moe Angelos, my writing buddy; Helen Knode, who facilitated two crucial writing retreats in Carmel Valley; Annamarie Jagose, my exemplary partner in the work of editing GLQ that shadowed the book's writing; Allyson Mitchell and Sheila Pepe, for making the art that let me see and feel my ideas; Kay Turner, for intellectual and spiritual witchcraft; Liz Wiesen, for the phone sessions and the commitment to process; and my many tribes: Michfest, kundalini yoga, co-counseling, dyke artists, Austin queerdos, the cats. You know who you are. And, of course, there's Gretchen Phillips, with whom twenty years have gone by in a flash. She arrived as this story leaves off and continues to give me countless reasons to get up in the morning.

Introduction

PUBLIC FEELINGS: A COLLECTIVE PROJECT

A key inspiration for this book's desire to think about depression as a cultural and social phenomenon rather than a medical disease has been my collaborative engagement with other scholars under the rubric of Public Feelings. Begun in 2001 both nationally and at the University of Texas, our investigation has coincided with and operated in the shadow of September 11 and its ongoing consequences—a sentimental takeover of 9/11 to underwrite militarism, war in Iraq and Afghanistan, Bush's reelection, and the list goes on. Rather than analyzing the geopolitical underpinnings of these developments, we've been more interested in their emotional dynamics. What makes it possible for people to vote for Bush or to assent to war, and how do these political decisions operate within the context of daily lives that are pervaded by a combination of anxiety and numbness? How can we, as intellectuals and activists, acknowledge our own political disappointments and failures in a way that can be enabling? Where might hope be possible? Those questions stem from the experience of what one of our cells, Feel Tank Chicago, has called "political depression," the sense that customary forms of political response, including direct action and critical analysis, are no longer working either to change the world or to make us feel better.

Our meetings, whether public or among ourselves, are as likely to start with a mood as an idea; at one of our national gatherings, for example, many of us admitted to feeling exhausted and overwhelmed by our professional obligations, and we considered what kinds of projects might emerge out of those conditions and how to produce scholarship not timed to the rhythms and genres of conferences, edited collections, and books.[1] In a public event at the University of Texas shortly after the U.S. invaded Iraq, the dominant response was one of incredulity, a seemingly low-grade or normalized version of the epistemic shock that is said to accompany trauma. At another public UT event to discuss reactions to Hurricane Katrina's devastations, many participants described a sense of divided attention as the movement back and forth between the everyday business of the semester's beginning and the urgency of the disaster created a split focus that also constitutes the lived experience of race and class divisions. Although Public Feelings was forged out of the crucible of the long Bush years, its style and substance are no less relevant to the uncertain record of the Obama presidency. Hope and despair remain entwined as we track the ongoing rhythms of war (in and out of Iraq, Libya, and Afghanistan), financial meltdown, Arab springs, Occupy movements, and assaults on the university. A political analysis of depression might advocate revolution and regime change over pills, but in the world of Public Feelings there are no magic bullet solutions, whether medical or political, just the slow steady work of resilient survival, utopian dreaming, and other affective tools for transformation.

In finding public forums for everyday feelings, including negative feelings that can seem so debilitating, so far from hopefulness about the future or activism, the aim is to generate new ways of thinking about agency. The concept of political depression is not, it should be emphasized, meant to be wholly depressing; indeed, Feel Tank has operated with the camp humor one might expect from a group of seasoned queer activists, organizing an International Day of the Politically Depressed in which participants were invited to show up in their bathrobes to indicate their fatigue with traditional forms of protest and distributing T-shirts and refrigerator magnets carrying the slogan "Depressed? It Might Be Political!"[2] The goal is to depathologize negative feelings so that they can be seen as a possible resource for political action rather than as its antithesis. This is not, however, to suggest that depression is thereby converted into a positive experience; it retains its associations with inertia and despair, if not apathy and indifference, but these feelings, moods, and sensibilities become sites of publicity and community formation. One of the larger goals for Public Feelings is to generate the affective foundation of hope that is necessary for political action; hence the turn to utopia in much recent work related to its projects, but a utopia, borrowing from Avery Gordon's analysis of Toni Cade Bambara, for example, that is grounded in the here and now, in the recognition of the possibilities and powers that we have at our immediate disposal.[3] It's a search for utopia that doesn't make a simple distinction between good and bad feelings or assume that good politics can only emerge from good feelings; feeling bad might, in fact, be the ground for transformation. Thus, although this book is about depression, it's also about hope and even happiness, about how to live a better life by embracing rather than glossing over bad feelings. (In addition to drawing inspiration from the memoir, it also borrows from other manuals for better living, ranging from the philosophical treatise to the self-help book.) It asks how it might be possible to tarry with the negative as part of daily practice, cultural production, and political activism.

The Affective Turn

Public Feelings projects can be seen as one form of what is being called the affective turn in cultural criticism, which has not only made emotion, feeling, and affect (and their differences) the object of scholarly inquiry but has also inspired new ways of doing criticism.[4] The affective turn is evident in many different areas of inquiry: cultural memory and public cultures that emerge in response to histories of trauma; the role of emotions such as fear and sentimentality in American political life and nationalist politics; the production of compassion and sympathy in human rights discourses and other forms of liberal representation of social issues and problems; discussions of the politics of negative affects, such as melancholy and shame, inspired in particular by queer theory's critique of the normal; new forms of historical inquiry, such as queer temporalities, that emphasize the affective relations between past and present; the turn to memoir and the personal in criticism as a sign of either the exhaustion of theory or its renewed life; the ongoing legacy of identity politics as another inspiration for the turn to the personal; continuing efforts to rethink psychoanalytic paradigms and the relation between the psychic and the social; the persistent influence of Foucauldian notions of biopower to explain the politics of subject formation and new forms of governmentality; histories of intimacy, domesticity, and private life; the cultural politics of everyday life; histories and theories of sensation and touch informed by phenomenology and cultural geography.[5] Although each of these projects has its own specificities and reference points, their collective critical mass is considerable.

I have to confess that I am somewhat reluctant to use the term *affec-*

tive turn because it implies that there is something new about the study of affect when in fact, as the list above suggests, this work has been going on for quite some time. In a narrower sense, the affective turn has been signifying a body of scholarship inspired by Deleuzian theories of affect as force, intensity, or the capacity to move and be moved.[6] Crucial to such inquiry is the distinction between affect and emotion, where the former signals precognitive sensory experience and relations to surroundings, and the latter cultural constructs and conscious processes that emerge from them, such as anger, fear, or joy.[7] This terminology has helped to loosen the hegemony of psychoanalysis as the way to describe emotional experience, although Freud has his own version of *affect* as undifferentiated energy or feeling, especially in his early writings on the hydraulic model of psychic energy.[8] Deleuzian projects have also enabled a fuller vocabulary for accounts of sensory experience that have emerged from cultural studies of embodiment and the turn away from Cartesian splits between body and mind. But this larger project extends well beyond the rubric of one theoretical source.

Thus, although the Deleuzians are intimates and fellow travelers of the Public Feelings interest in sensory experience and feeling, my own project has not been shaped by that tradition.[9] I tend to use *affect* in a generic sense, rather than in the more specific Deleuzian sense, as a category that encompasses affect, emotion, and feeling, and that includes impulses, desires, and feelings that get historically constructed in a range of ways (whether as distinct specific emotions or as a generic category often contrasted with reason)—but with a wary recognition that this is like trying to talk about *sex* before *sexuality*. I also like to use *feeling* as a generic term that does some of the same work: naming the undifferentiated "stuff" of feeling; spanning the distinctions between emotion and affect central to some theories; acknowledging the somatic or sensory nature of feelings as experiences that aren't just cognitive concepts or constructions. I favor *feeling* in part because it is intentionally imprecise, retaining the ambiguity between feelings as embodied sensations and feelings as psychic or cognitive experiences. It also has a vernacular quality that lends itself to exploring feelings as something we come to know through experience and popular usage and that indicates, perhaps only intuitively but nonetheless significantly, a conception of mind and body as integrated. Public Feelings takes seriously questions like "How do I feel?" and "How does capitalism feel?" as starting points for something that might be a theory but could also be a description, an investigation, or a process. Terms such as *affect, emotion*, and *feeling* are more like keywords, points of departure for discussion rather than definition. We have used the term *project*, as in "Public Feelings project," to signify an open-ended and speculative inquiry that fans out in multiple directions, including new forms of writing that are "essays" in the literal sense of an experiment.[10]

In a more general way, though, the term *affective turn* does signal the cumulative force of Public Feelings projects and their commitment to new forms of cultural studies, especially those that are not just confined to ideology critique, as important as that remains. For some time now, there have been calls to think beyond the well-worn grooves of the search for forms of cultural management and hegemony, on the one hand, and modes of resistance and subversion, on the other. One of our most crucial touchstones has been Eve Sedgwick's articulation of a reparative rather than paranoid critical approach.[11] Drawing on the theoretical resources of Melanie Klein and Sylvan Tompkins, but also the model of queer aesthetic practices, Sedgwick works creatively from an eclectic range of materials, including accounts of her own feelings. We have also been influenced by the critical sensibility of our Public Feelings colleague Kathleen Stewart, who for many years has been talking about following the surfaces and textures of everyday life rather than exposing the putative realities of underlying structures.[12] The practice of criticism has not always caught up with these important invocations to alternative modes of criticism, but Public Feelings has sought to craft new critical practices through attention to feelings as both subject and method.

With its emphasis on identities and public cultures that cultivate non-normative affects, queer theory has also been a crucial resource for Public Feelings and its version of the affective turn. Especially important have been models for the depathologization of negative feelings such as shame, failure, melancholy, and depression, and the resulting rethinking of categories such as utopia, hope, and happiness as entwined with and even enhanced by forms of negative feeling.[13] The Public Feelings project resists pastoralizing or redemptive accounts of negative feeling that seek to convert it into something useful or positive, but it also embraces categories such as utopia and hope. In this respect, its work contributes to debates on the antisocial thesis that have dominated queer theory over the past decade, but it ultimately resists reductive binarisms between the social and the antisocial and between positive and negative affect, as well as paranoid critical tendencies that are on the lookout for premature forms of utopia or futurity or that presume the superiority of negative affect.[14] It rethinks distinctions between positive and negative feelings so as not to presume that they are separate from one another or that happiness or pleasure constitutes the absence or elimination of negative feeling. Depression, for example, can take antisocial forms such as withdrawal or inertia, but it can also create new forms of sociality, whether in public cultures that give it expression or because, as has been suggested about melancholy, it serves as the foundation for new kinds of attachment or affiliation. Binary divisions between positive and negative affects don't do justice to the qualitative nuances of feeling that are only crudely captured by such designations. Queer theory's focus on negative affect has created some of the same kind of sparring generated by the antisocial thesis, although such criticism sometimes seems to miss the persistently reparative and dialectical dimensions of much of this work.[15]

The queer predilection for negative affect and the virulence of debates about the antisocial owe something to the turn that mainstream lesbian and gay politics has taken toward homonormativity and queer neoliberalisms.[16] Like the social movements of the 1970s, the queer activism of the 1990s has had its own share of political disappointments, as radical potential has mutated into assimilationist agenda and left some of us wondering how domestic partner benefits and marriage equality became the movement's rallying cry. As a queer project, Public Feelings tries to reimagine a liberatory version of social and affective relations beyond the liberal versions that have come to dominate the public sphere of gay politics. Discussions of political depression emerge from the necessity of finding ways to survive disappointment and to remind ourselves of the persistence of radical visions and ways of living. Rather than a paranoid watch for how forms of resistance are ultimately co-opted, it's more about noticing and describing the places where it feels like there is something else happening, and passing on strategies for survival. Survival also involves developing a higher tolerance for the conflicts that political life invariably produces—such as those between lesbian separatist and trans communities, gay marriage and antimarriage camps, or antisocial and utopian tendencies—so that groups don't implode or splinter into factions. (But tolerance not in the liberal sense of putting up with conflict or difference, but in the sense of being receptive to them and being willing to risk vulnerability.)

The linkage between depression and political failure is relevant not just to queer politics; it also pertains to the politics of race in the wake of the incomplete projects of civil rights and decolonization. The limits of political representation and legal recognition in eliminating racism require not only new visions for the future but the affective energy to sustain disappointment. The turn to public cultures of memory that address transnational histories of genocide, colonization, slavery, and diaspora stems from the need to connect with histories of trauma that have not yet been overcome.[17] Epidemics of depression can be related (both as symptom and as obfuscation) to long-term histories of violence that have ongoing impacts at the level of everyday emotional experience. A depressive antisociality can accompany an insistence that the past is not over yet, as well as efforts to address some of the murkier dimensions of everyday racial experience for which identity politics is not always an adequate container. The Public Feelings project intersects with studies of race and ethnicity that consider how to think psychic and social life together, the use of melancholy as a historical and racialized category, and the production of hope in the face of long histories of oppression.[18] Public Feelings participates in the ongoing impact of identity politics, as well as efforts to build intersectional and comparative forms of analysis that do justice to the grief, rage, hope, and patience that attend these projects both scholarly and political. Political depression is pervasive within recent histories of decolonization, civil rights, socialism, and labor politics, and attention to affective politics is a way of trying to come to terms with disappointment, failure, and the slowness of change; it is a politics that comes from remaining patient with the moments before and after so-called revolution, even as it also looks for the utopian uprising and outburst. Public Feelings is about rethinking activisms in ways that attend to its emotional registers, including the frustrations that come from trying to keep activism and scholarship together.

Feminism as Affective Turn

The affective turn also doesn't seem particularly new to me because the Public Feelings project represents the outcome of many years of engagement with the shifting fortunes of the feminist mantra that "the personal is the political" as it has shaped theoretical and political practice and their relation to everyday life. Many of our members are part of a generation that was schooled in the feminist theory of the 1980s, which emerged in universities that were no longer connected to a strong movement-based feminism and hence was more focused on specifically academic questions and institutional change. We were taught to be suspicious of essentialisms, including those associated with affect, such as the idea that women are naturally more emotional than men or that emotional expression is inevitably liberatory. Feelings were nevertheless at the heart of this theoretically informed scholarship, including projects on emotional genres, such as the gothic, the sentimental, the sensational, and the melodramatic, and sophisticated accounts of the history of emotions, the relation between private and public spheres, and the construction of interiority, subjectivity, embodiment, and intimate life.[19] To put it in shorthand, the feminism of Virginia Woolf and "a room of one's own" was joined by the feminism of Harriet Beecher Stowe and domestic economy; feminists turned their attention from Mary Wollstonecraft and the political treatise to Jane Austen and a more covert politics of drawing-room manners and the intimate public sphere documented in the novel. Rather than feeling drawn to search for and recover neglected feminist heroines, my generation of feminist scholars emphasized the social power of popular and denigrated cultural genres ranging from the conduct book to the novel. Influenced by poststructuralist theory, especially Foucault, and focusing on gender more than on women, we emphasized that the social power of women's genres, which frequently trafficked in powerful emotional experiences both in the text and for their readers, was not always feminist and could be attached to consolidating and sustaining middle-class power and promoting imperialist, nationalist, and racist agendas.

An important agenda for Public Feelings, then, has been what Lauren Berlant calls the "unfinished business of sentimentality," which can refer not only to the persistence of sentimental culture itself but also to the way that feminist critiques of sentimentality have not yet fully been taken up in the public sphere.[20] For example, the models of sentimental representation that pervade eighteenth- and nineteenth-century discourses of abolition are relevant for understanding contemporary human rights discourses that still traffic in the generation of affect through representations that aim to touch their audiences.[21] While abolition is sometimes acknowledged to be an early discourse of human rights, the history of human rights is frequently told as though it begins with the Universal Declaration as a response to the Second World War. Moreover, the popular origins of this highly sanctioned form of emotional politics need to be more fully acknowledged so as to better explain its tensions and failures. In contexts ranging from the testimony of truth and reconciliation commissions, to Amnesty International reports, to documentary films that explore human rights abuses, liberal models by which the representation of suffering is presumed to have a salutary effect on an audience that is removed culturally and geographically (but connected by representation and global economies) are pervasive. There are many different variations on these strategies, but they rarely include a critical perspective on the presumed transparency of representation that is commonly found in feminist scholarship on affect. In continuing to explore the connections between emotion and politics that have been a long-standing concern for feminism, Public Feelings seeks to craft new forms of feminist intellectual politics that are still lacking in the public sphere.[22]

Feminist cultural critique has also been careful to scrutinize overly simplistic models of gender identity and the way that the privileges of class, race, or other categories complicate personalist stories of oppression and require that they be carefully situated. Alongside such critiques, the personal voice has persisted as an important part of feminist scholarship, enabled, if not also encouraged, by theory's demand that intellectual claims be grounded in necessarily partial and local positionalities. The Public Feelings project builds on these lessons and strategies in an effort to bring emotional sensibilities to bear on intellectual projects and to continue to think about how these projects can further political ones as well. As we have learned to think both more modestly and more widely about what counts as politics so that it includes, for example, cultural activism, academic institutions, and everyday and domestic life, it has become important to take seriously the institutions where we live (as opposed to always feeling like politics is somewhere else out there) and to include institutional life in our approaches to intellectual problems. At this point, theory and affect are not polarized or at odds with one another, and Public Feelings operates from the conviction that affective investment can be a starting point for theoretical insight and that theoretical insight does not deaden or flatten affective experience or investment.[23]

One origin for the Public Feelings group was reflection on feminist futures catalyzed by the impending twentieth anniversary of the controversial Scholar and Feminist conference on Sexuality in 1982 at Barnard College.[24] It seems appropriate that Public Feelings would emerge out of a return to a divisive and emotional moment in feminist sexual politics, one fraught with the question of whether dichotomies between pleasure and danger can be strictly maintained. The presumption that sex-positivity does not necessarily mean nice sex and that the queer messiness of sexuality has important political implications remains an important legacy. This history is an important starting point for thinking about the politics of affect within the longer history of feminism (including the relation between first-wave feminisms and women's genres) and its deep-seated wish, as manifest in practices of consciousness-raising, that emotional expression lead to good politics. The sex wars of the 1980s have also been formative for Public Feelings because they are such a powerful example of political conflict, which has been especially vexing for feminist ideals of sisterhood. Academic feminism in the 1980s was forged from tensions around sexuality, race, and essentialism, and my ongoing fascination with the negative feelings of political dispute has led me to a reparative perspective that embraces conflict rather than separating out right from wrong, whether generational, racial, sexual, or theoretical. Some thirty years after the publication of formative books such as *The Madwoman in the Attic* and *Women and Madness*, both of which I might once have critiqued for romanticizing the madwoman, it is interesting to find myself writing a book about depression that begins from my own (female) experience to imagine how mental health might be reconstructed (and not just for women but for everyone).[25] As part of the project of Public Feelings, this book rethinks the 1980s critique in order to establish a new rapprochement with legacies of 1970s feminism such as consciousness-raising, personal narrative, and craft.

Keywords: A Note on Method

In the methodological spirit of cultural studies, Public Feelings takes up *depression* as a keyword in order to describe the affective dimensions of ordinary life in the present moment. Such an investigation emerges from important traditions of describing *how capitalism feels,* but it also puts pressure on those left-progressive projects not to rush to meta-commentary. This project has been present in the rethinking of modernity by Walter Benjamin, George Simmel, and others that focuses on the felt sensations of the lived environment, especially the city; the British cultural studies work of Raymond Williams and Stuart Hall that understands culture as a "way of life" and "a structure of feeling" and has flexible models for understanding how everyday experience is a manifestation of social life; the anthropology and sociology of Kathleen Stewart, Michael Taussig, Nadia Seremetakis, and Avery Gordon that focuses on sensation, tactility, and feelings.[26] In this tradition of thinking, accounts of sensory experience are important for understanding the present (and its histories), and they resist what have sometimes been overly reductive models within Marxist theory for analyzing the mechanisms of social change. Moreover, the focus on sensation and feeling as the register of historical experience gives rise to new forms of documentation and writing, whether in the aphorisms and spiritual materialism of Benjamin, the modular writing of Taussig, the creative nonfiction of Stewart, or the turn to fictional forms of thinking in Gordon. Their varied writing practices often turn the ordinary into the scene of surprise, and they slow down so as to be able to immerse themselves in detail and to appreciate the way that magic and mystery sit alongside the banal and the routine.

The documentation of everyday life is not just an end in itself, however. The richer accounts of the ordinary sought by the Public Feelings projects are also new ways of providing the more systemic accounts of power that have been central to cultural studies. Depression, or alternative accounts of what gets called depression, is thus a way to describe neoliberalism and globalization, or the current state of political economy, in affective terms. Lisa Duggan suggests that neoliberal economic and social policy is characterized by the shrinking of the public sphere and that affective life is forced to bear an increasing burden as the state divests itself of responsibility for social welfare and affective life is confined to a privatized family.[27] Depression can be seen as a category that manages and medicalizes the affects associated with keeping up with corporate culture and the market economy, or with being completely neglected by it. Alain Ehrenberg suggests that the discourse of depression emerges in response to the demand that the self become a sovereign individual defined by the ability to create distinctive projects and agendas; those who fail to measure up to this demand through lack of will, energy, or imagination are pathologized as depressed.[28] The neoliberal management of racial conflicts and differences through policies of multiculturalism and diversity cultivates certain affects of polite recognition at the expense of really examining the explosiveness of racialized histories. What gets called depression in the domestic sphere is one affective register of these social problems and one that often keeps people silent, weary, and too numb to really notice the sources of their unhappiness (or in a state of low-level chronic grief—or depression of another kind—if they do).

Looking at neoliberalism from the vantage point of everyday affective life offers, however, an alternative approach to master narratives about global conditions that are currently circulating in cultural studies. Talk of permanent war, states of exception, and new security states, important and useful as it might be, frequently operates at such a high level of abstraction that it fails to address the lived experience of these systemic transformations.[29] Although it shares some of the same impulses that lead to these large conceptual categories—a desire to track the histories of the present so as to provide critical insight about current conditions and help in planning for the future—the Public Feelings project aims to find new ways of articulating the relation between the macro and the micro and new forms of description that are more textured, more localized, and also less predictably forgone in their conclusions about our dire situation. My emphasis on depression as ordinary represents an effort to describe the present through attention to the felt experience of everyday life, including moments that might seem utterly banal in comparison with the moments of shock or ordinary extraordinariness that can be found in modernists such as Benjamin and Woolf, both of whom are important theorists and writers of the ordinary.

One mark of this difference in approach is the way that Public Feelings works with the tradition of the keyword, significantly popularized by Raymond Williams as a way of making Marxist concepts more readily accessible for cultural analysis.[30] Part of a tradition of Marxist thinking that has aimed to refine models of capitalism by developing critical categories that can account for the present, terms such as *postmodernism* and *postcolonialism* have been updated or replaced by terms such as *globalization, transnationalism,* and *diaspora,* and more recently *neoliberalism.* The notion of the keyword has been central to the work of Public Feelings, but we have often replaced definitions of the Zeitgeist or traditional theoretical categories such as *ideology* and *culture* with terms such as *rest, impasse,* and *sentimentality* that might not seem as wide-ranging in their explanatory power but which nonetheless provide entry points into social and cultural analysis.[31] Williams's suggestive notion of a structure of feeling (generative in part because of its sketchiness) opens the way for affective terms, such as *depression,* to become keywords, nodes of speculation that offer new ways to think about contemporary culture.

Public Feelings generates an expanded set of keywords in part because, in addition to its Marxist lineages, the project is also influenced by queer and feminist work that keeps categories of gender and sexuality central to investigations of the war front and governmentality and hence looks to sometimes unexpected sites of analysis in order to see their effects. Depression is another manifestation of forms of biopower that produce life and death not only by targeting populations for overt destruction, whether through incarceration, war, or poverty, but also more insidiously by making people feel small, worthless, hopeless. It is another form of the "slow death" that Berlant attributes to the seemingly epidemic spread of obesity, but one that takes the form not of bodies expanding to the point of breakdown, but of an even less visible form of violence that takes the form of minds and lives gradually shrinking into despair and hopelessness.[32] New conceptual categories and new modes of description are necessary to capture these feelings.

This project's inquiry into depression, then, is also about new ways of doing cultural studies that move past the work of critique or the exposure of social constructions. Although I explore the history of depression as a cultural discourse and the pervasive and widespread contemporary representation of it as a medical disease that can be treated pharmacologically, this book is not primarily a critique of that discourse. Instead, I seek to use depression as an entry point into a different kind of cultural studies, one with an interest in how we might track affective life in all its complexity and in what kinds of representations might do justice to its social meanings.

In investigating the productive possibilities of depression, this book aims to be patient with the moods and temporalities of depression, not moving too quickly to recuperate them or put them to good use. It might instead be important to let depression linger, to explore the feeling of remaining or resting in sadness without insisting that it be transformed or reconceived. But through an engagement with depression, this book also finds its way to forms of hope, creativity, and even spirituality that are intimately connected with experiences of despair, hopelessness, and being stuck. Under the rubric and inspiration of Public Feelings, it hopes to spend some time with the word *depression* in order to generate new forms of cultural studies and new public discourses about feelings.

KEYWORD DEPRESSION

I'd like to be able to write about depression in a way that simultaneously captures how it feels and provides an analysis of why and how its feelings are produced by social forces. I'm interested in how, for many of us (an "us" that includes a range of social positions and identities in need of specification), everyday life produces feelings of despair and anxiety, sometimes extreme, sometimes throbbing along at a low level, and hence barely discernible from *just the way things are*, feelings that get internalized and named, for better or for worse, as depression. It is customary, within our therapeutic culture, to attribute these feelings to bad things that happened to us when we were children, to primal scenes that have not yet been fully remembered or articulated or worked through. It's also common to explain them as the result of a biochemical disorder, a genetic mishap for which we shouldn't blame ourselves. I tend to see such master narratives as problematic displacements that cast a social problem as a personal problem in one case and as a medical problem in the other, but moving to an even larger master narrative of depression as socially produced often provides little specific illumination and even less comfort because it's an analysis that frequently admits of no solution. Saying that capitalism (or colonialism or racism) is the problem does not help me get up in the morning.

Thus I've been looking for forms of testimony that can mediate between the personal and the social, that can explain why we live in a culture whose violence takes the form of systematically making us feel bad. Ideally, I'd like those forms of testimony to offer some clues about how to survive those conditions and even to change them, but I'd also settle for a compelling description, one that doesn't reduce lived experience to a list of symptoms and one that provides a forum for feelings that, despite a widespread therapeutic culture, still haven't gone public enough. It's a task that calls for performative writing, and I'm not sure I know what that would look like or, even if I did, whether I'm up to the task of producing it. Some years ago I began this project with the following statement, a rant about the inadequacies of both pharmaceutical cures and the available public discourse, including memoirs, that cast depression as either utterly mysterious or a manageable, if chronic, medical problem.[33] It's a call to memoir that I'm still trying to answer.

Depression Manifesto

This is my version of a Prozac memoir, bad connotations included. But I want to write it precisely because I don't believe in Prozac. No, I think it's a scam, even if that makes me one of those quacks, like the people who don't believe that the HIV virus causes AIDS. Discussions about the biochemical causes of depression might be plausible, but I find them trivial. I want to know what environmental, social, and familial factors trigger those biological responses—that's where things get interesting. A drug that masks the symptoms of a response to a fucked-up world or a fucked-up life doesn't tell me anything. I want to hear about the people like me who've decided not to take drugs.

But in addition to writing a polemic against drugs, I also want to write about depression because my own experiences of it have been so unexpected and so intense, the sensations so invisible and yet so spectacular, that I feel compelled to honor them with description. I want to know how it was that not just my mind but my body experienced such excruciatingly bad feelings. But also such excruciatingly *ordinary* bad feelings insofar as during the most extreme bouts I was overwhelmed by a sense of how easy it was to get there—the slide into numbness was brought on by such common events as moving, breaking up with someone, trying to finish a book, starting a new job. Huge life transitions, yes, but also ones that, in my culture at least, are an inevitable part of growing up, of learning to take care of oneself, of facing the fear of being alone. I want to say something about that state that satisfies me in a way that all those bestsellers don't because they make depression seem so clinical, so extreme, so pathological, so alien. Why do these accounts not call my name? What name am I trying to call?

I think I can only know why I want to talk about depression by describing it. *What* before *why*. My own experience is the antidote to all of those other descriptions I've read, whether in theory, or pop psychology, or memoirs. Have I read anything that I liked? That moved me? That seemed true enough to haunt me? No. Then I'll have to make it up myself.

Over the course of a number of years, I wrote, although often with a sense of secrecy and writerly inadequacy. My desire to write a depression memoir has been fraught with ambivalence because of the problematic place of memoir within therapeutic culture, where it has a tendency to circulate in sensationalizing and personalizing ways that don't lend themselves to the social and political analysis that I'm looking for. Equally controversial is memoir's place in academia, where its developing status as a forum for new kinds of criticism has also been met with skepticism about its scholarly value. At the same time, memoir has allowed me to circumvent the resistance I've often encountered to a critique of antidepressants, which some people take very personally—I can simply speak for myself by offering my own case history. Although for the sake of manifesto or emotional outburst it might seem otherwise, I'm not against pharmaceuticals for those who find they work. I myself don't find medical explanations of depression's causes satisfying, but I do understand that many people find them helpful either for themselves or for family members because it relieves them of debilitating forms of responsibility and self-blame. I do, though, want to complicate biology as the endpoint for both explanations and solutions, causes and effects.

The book that grew out of this initial writing and ongoing experiment with process combines memoir and criticism in order to explore what each genre can offer to public discourse about depression. I found that neither on its own was satisfactory. Although the critical essay, the genre with which I have the most familiarity and skill, had much to offer, it also felt like it had some limits. If I wrote about depression in the third person without saying anything about my personal experience of it, it felt like a key source of my thinking was missing. Memoir became one of my research methods, a starting point and crucible for exploring my ideas about depression, an opportunity to figure out what kind of case history might have the richness and nuance I was looking for by actually creating one, and a way of presenting my understanding of depression as emerging from my ongoing daily experience.

At the same time, I couldn't accomplish everything I wanted to do in the genre of the memoir. There were too many other things I wanted to say, too much context that could not have been incorporated without breaking the frame of the memoir itself. Some readers suggested that I might want to combine the two in order to represent them as mutually constitutive. As attractive as that idea was, I ultimately decided to let the memoir stand alone in order to reflect its status as the first phase of my thinking and because it ended up telling a story that I wanted readers to have access to as a single coherent piece of writing. The end result, then, is a diptych, a narrative that uses two different strategies for writing about depression, with the aim of reflecting on which forms of writing and public discourse are best suited to that task.

On Being Stuck

The first part of this book, and the starting point for my subsequent thinking about depression, is a memoir about the place where I live on a daily basis, academia, where the pressure to succeed and the desire to find space for creative thinking bump up against the harsh conditions of a ruthlessly competitive job market, the shrinking power of the humanities, and the corporatization of the university. For those who are fortunate enough to imagine that their careers and other life projects can be meaningfully shaped by their own desires, depression in the form of thwarted ambition can be the frequent fallout of the dreams that are bred by capitalist culture—the pressure to be a successful professional, to have a meaningful job, to juggle the conflicting demands of work and leisure, or to have a "personal life" in the form of a sense of self that lies outside the circuits of capital. Although academics often like to imagine that they are crafting alternatives to the socially sanctioned versions of these goals, that aspiration also creates its own set of pressures.

I turned to memoir in order to track what it's like to move through the day, focusing in particular on the crucial years in which I was writing a dissertation, starting a job, and then finishing a book for tenure. My episodic narrative tells the story of how academia seemed to be killing me, a statement that seems very melodramatic given the privileged nature of my professional status and the specialized task of writing a dissertation or book, the stakes of which are often ultimately only personal. But to feel that your work doesn't matter is to feel dead inside, a condition that is normalized for so many. Academia breeds particular forms of panic and anxiety leading to what gets called depression—the fear that you have nothing to say, or that you can't say what you want to say, or that you have something to say but it's not important enough or smart enough. In this particular enclave of the professional managerial class, there is an epidemic of anxiety-induced depression that is widely acknowledged informally but not always shared publicly or seen as worthy of investigation. In its own way, this book adds to a body of work on the current state of the academy, especially the humanities, where ongoing versions of the culture wars are one site of struggle in efforts to preserve forms of creative living and thinking in a market culture. It contributes to discussions of the role of the corporate university in neoliberal policies that shape (so-called) private and affective life.[34] In this context, depression takes the shape of an anxiety to be managed, a failure of productivity that is then addressed by a lucrative pharmaceutical industry and a set of accompanying discourses that encourage particular ways of thinking about the self and its failures.

For this local account of life in academia that is not just individual but available for systemic analysis, one of my target audiences is graduate students and untenured and adjunct faculty, especially those in the humanities, whose relation to these conditions is often a very palpable sense of fear, anxiety, and, very frequently, diagnoses of depression. Why is a position of relative privilege, the pursuit of creative thinking and teaching, lived as though it were impossible? What would make it easier to live with these sometimes impossible conditions? Calling it impossible might seem presumptuous, but I'm willing to take that risk.

Academics too often struggle with long-term projects such as dissertations and books while squeezed on the one hand by an intensely competitive job market and meritocratic promotion and reward system and driven on the other by a commitment to social justice that often leaves us feeling like we're never doing enough to make a difference. I see this fear creep up on graduate students all the time, perfectly capable people who fall apart in the process of writing a first chapter or who wallow in partial dissertation drafts unable to put it all together. This form of nonproductivity may seem very specialized and almost phantasmatic in nature—how could people be so incapacitated by the relatively nonurgent task of doing some cultural readings? But my aim is to take seriously the forms of unhappiness and hopelessness produced even by these relatively privileged and specialized projects and ambitions. The forms of productivity demanded by the academic sphere of the professional managerial class can tell us something more general about corporate cultures that demand deliverables and measurable outcomes and that say you are only as good as what you produce. (In this context, it can be especially hard to justify creative or individualized intellectual work, and teaching or administration may feel more concrete than pursuing creative thought.) What would it mean to make thinking easier? Or to make its difficulties and impasses more acceptable? What is going on when you can't write?

One of the most important turning points in my depression memoir is the moment of a major conceptual breakthrough in completing my first book, *Mixed Feelings*, about the politics of affect in the Victorian sensation novel. (See below, "The Inspiration," 67–68.) While writing my introduction, I got stuck, torn between my desire to find evidence of feminist subversion in these lurid stories of women's bigamy and adultery but schooled in Foucauldian paradigms that emphasized the containment and management of resistance. Although conceptual blockage can come in many forms, I don't think it's accidental that what had me caught was the sense that my Foucauldian reading of the management of affect in the sensation novel allowed for no escape.[35] My friend Lora Romero's essay on *Uncle Tom's Cabin*, which ingeniously suggested that Foucault could be used in ways that didn't lead to this impasse, provided the opening I was looking for and encouraged me to find a way of reading the sensation novel that was more open-ended and flexible, or what we have come to call "reparative."[36] I needed an intellectual framework that allowed me to believe in the possibility of sensationalism as productive, even as I also needed to insist on critique. Had I been able to see in 1984, when I first discovered and wrote on *Lady Audley's Secret*, then an obscure Dover Press publication, that the sensation novel would be important enough to become Penguin and World's Classics editions and the subject of multiple scholarly works, I might have approached my work differently. How can we make room for crazy thoughts to become intellectual projects and communities and movements?

While there is an especially neat convergence here between the content of my intellectual impasse and the experience of it—both were about hopelessness—connecting depression to hopelessness or frustration also suggests that it has solutions, however difficult they may be to conceptualize or achieve. Indeed, I was delighted when I discovered that *impasse* was one of the keywords being explored by Feel Tank Chicago, and their thinking has encouraged me to take impasse seriously as a concept and an experience. I've benefited from being able to think alongside elaborations such as the following by Berlant: "An impasse is a holding station that doesn't hold but opens out into anxiety, that dog-paddling around a space whose contours remain obscure. An impasse is decompositional—in the unbound temporality of the lag one hopes to have been experiencing all along (otherwise it's the *end*), it marks a delay."[37] For Berlant, an object of knowledge becomes a (productive) impasse when it slows us down, preventing easy recourse to critique or prescription for action and instead inviting us to see it as "a singular place that's a cluster of noncoherent but proximate attachments that can only be approached awkwardly, described around, shifted" (434–35).

With its spatial connotations of being at a "dead end" or "no exit," impasse captures the notion of depression as a state of being "stuck," of not being able to figure out what to do or why to do it.[38] The material dimensions of being stuck or at an impasse are important to its more conceptual meanings and suggest the phenomenological and sensory dimensions of depression, which can literally shut down or inhibit movement.[39] As a theoretical concept, impasse imports its spatial or literal sense into conceptual and social circumstances; it suggests that things will not move forward due to circumstance—not that they can't, but that the world is not designed to make it happen or there has been a failure of imagination. As a political category, impasse can be used to describe moments when disagreements and schisms occur within a group or when it is impossible to imagine how to get to a better future—conditions, for example, of political depression or left melancholy. It can describe intellectual blockages, such as those produced by forms of critique that get stuck in the formulaic repetition of the failure of cultural texts to be progressive. It can also describe the experience of everyday life when we don't know what to do. And, in ways that will be relevant to the discussions ahead, it is related to the category of spiritual crisis as well, those moments when a system of belief or belonging loses meaning and faith is in question. Public Feelings approaches the impasse as a state of both stuckness and potential, maintaining a hopefulness about the possibility that slowing down or not moving forward might not be a sign of failure and might instead be worth exploring. Impasse is an important category for Public Feelings because it wants to work with and connect blockages created by critique, by desperate political circumstances, and by an everyday life that doesn't change.

If depression is conceived of as blockage or impasse or being stuck, then its cure might lie in forms of flexibility or creativity more so than in pills or a different genetic structure. *Creativity* is thus another keyword for this project. Defined in relation to notions of blockage or impasse, creativity can be thought of as a form of movement, movement that maneuvers the mind inside or around an impasse, even if that movement sometimes seems backward or like a form of retreat. Spatialized in this way, creativity can describe forms of agency that take the form of literal movement and are thus more e-motional or sensational or tactile. Indeed, my memoir focuses on the body at rest, unable to get out of bed, for example, as well as many efforts to keep it moving, whether through exercise, such as yoga or swimming, or through ordinary daily activities ranging from washing the dishes to sitting at a desk. This notion of creativity as movement can also benefit from queer phenomenologies, as well as queer ways of thinking about temporalities that move backward and sideways rather than just forward.[40] Creativity encompasses different ways of being able to move: to solve problems, have ideas, be joyful about the present, make things. Conceived of in this way, it is embedded in everyday life, not something that belongs only to artists or to transcendent forms of experience.

Although academics frequently try to justify the significance of their work by appeal to scientific notions of progress or contributions to society, one of the most important aspects of the humanities may be the way they provide room for creativity. Sedgwick has notably defined queerness in relation to creativity, suggesting the powerfully non-normative implications of focusing on creative thought that doesn't have an immediate outcome.

> Millions of people today struggle to carve out—barely, at great cost to themselves—the time, permission, and resources, "after work" or instead of decently-paying work, for creativity and thought that will not be in the service of corporate profit, nor structured by its rhythms. Many, many more are scarred by the prohibitive difficulty of doing so. No two people, no two groups would make the same use of these resources, furthermore, so that no one can really pretend to be utilizing them "for" another. I see that some find enraging the spectacle of people for whom such possibilities are, to a degree, built into the structure of our regular paid labor. Another way to understand that spectacle, though, would be as one remaining form of insistence that it is not inevitable—it is not a simple fact of nature—for the facilities of creativity and thought to represent rare or exorbitant *privilege*. Their economy should not and need not be one of scarcity.[41]

In making this statement, Sedgwick neatly bypasses the way progressive or left cultural studies often tries to justify itself by appealing to political and social justice. As important as such work is, and indeed my own career is steeped in it, the experience of "impasse" has to be acknowledged—it occurs at moments when the social relevance of what we're doing and thinking is not clear. At such moments, a commitment to creativity, or to pursuing one's own ways of thinking and being, can be salutary; it is certainly the impulse that enabled me to imagine that writing a memoir could be a useful part of my academic projects, even without the laminated or flamboyant style that Sedgwick describes as one of the pleasures of writing for her (although imagining that self-narration might be meaningful even when not justified by style is its own form of flaunting).

My goal in exploring the relation between depression and academic careers is thus to create more space for creative thought, for whatever it is that provides more pleasure or happiness, even if its immediate professional or social gains are not obvious. More space for "creativity" also means a higher tolerance for "impasse," which is sometimes the only route to new thinking and to the creation of stronger, more resilient communities that can do work in the world. I have found my work with various Public Feelings groups sustaining because they have been able to make me feel that work that didn't make sense actually did. If we can come to know each other through our depression, then perhaps we can use it to make forms of sociability that not only move us forward past our moments of impasse but understand impasse itself to be a state that has productive potential.[42]

Writing Depression

This book is divided into two halves, the first of which consists of the memoir that provided the seed for this project—an episodic account of the troubled path to finishing my dissertation and writing my first book. The critical essay that forms the second half of the book consists of three chapters, although it should ideally be read as one extended piece of writing that aspires to the form of the essay as a public genre for speculative thinking, rather than the scholarly book divided into chapters that stand alone as individual cases. This combination of memoir and essay constitutes my version of what Jill Dolan has called "critical memoir" and is inspired by the desire to craft new forms of writing and knowledge that come from affective experience, ordinary life, and alternative archives and that don't necessarily follow the usual methods of cultural critique.[43] Across its different sections, including the memoir, the book seeks to craft—and it's no accident that crafting is one of its topics—a cultural analysis that can adequately represent depression as a historical category, a felt experience, and a point of entry into discussions not only about theory and contemporary culture but about how to live.

I came to writing memoir because of my interest in its power as a public feelings genre, one that is both immensely popular and a vehicle for alternative testimonial and scholarship. As my "Depression Manifesto" proclaims, I was also dissatisfied with more popular mainstream depression memoirs—such as William Styron's *Darkness Visible*, Elizabeth Wurtzel's *Prozac Nation*, Lauren Slater's *Prozac Diary*, and Andrew Solomon's *The Noonday Demon*—all of which largely, if ambivalently, endorse pharmaceutical treatment, but I decided that rather than critique memoir it would be more useful to engage in writing it as a form of research method. *The Depression Journals* has been a formative crucible for the more scholarly essay, not only by inspiring its intellectual questions, but also by revealing the emotional investments that guide it. The title not only riffs on other memoir titles such as *Prozac Diary* but also indicates the writing's status as a form of notebook or experimental inquiry rather than a fully fledged piece of literature or scholarship. In the brief reflections that follow it, I discuss what I learned from the project, including the writing process itself, and explain how it serves as a resource—a "feel tank," to borrow from the Chicago collective—for the critical essay that more explicitly articulates a Public Feelings approach to depression.

In the extended essay of the book's second half, chapter 1 grapples with the failure of cultural studies to make a significant intervention against the overwhelming predominance of the medical model within the huge body of popular writing on depression. It is easy for scholars in the humanities to feel that arguments about the cultural construction of feelings have been overlooked, but rather than fully indulge that resentment, I have been motivated by a desire to develop forms of scholarship and writing that offer alternatives to critique and new ways to describe feelings—or the intersections of mind and body that encompass not just more cognitive forms of emotion but the embodied senses.

Chapter 1 also looks to the longer history of the category of depression and its conceptual relatives, especially melancholy, in search of resources for alternative understandings to the medical model and finds them in the early Christian category of *acedia*, a form of spiritual despair that resembles depression. The concept of acedia as sin or visitation by a demon is dismissed by medical models as either moralizing or superstitious when compared with contemporary medical notions that simultaneously relieve one of responsibility (it's just genes or chemicals) and provide agency (you can fix it by taking a pill). By contrast, I explore acedia's value as a model for thinking about depression as a spiritual problem and for elucidating distinctions between left melancholy and political depression that turn on whether the presence of feeling in political movements is suspect or welcome.

Chapter 2 sets aside the medical model in order to pursue the speculative hypothesis that the cause of depression is not biochemical imbalances but the long-term effects of racism and colonialism. Its point of departure is the histories of genocide, slavery, and exclusion and oppression of immigrants that seep into our daily lives of segregation, often as invisible forces that structure comfort and privilege for some and lack of resources for others, inequities whose connections to the past frequently remain obscure. These are depressing conditions, indeed, ones that make depression seem not so much a medical or biochemical dysfunction as a very rational response to global conditions.

Thinking about depression in relation to racism (as well as desperation and hopelessness about changing it) requires a different set of archives, ones that don't necessarily explicitly mention depression and are not on the radar screen of most popular literature on the subject, which so frequently and invisibly presumes a white middle-class subject. Chapter 2 devotes extended attention to books by two scholars of the African diaspora—Saidiya Hartman's *Lose Your Mother* and Jacqui Alexander's *Pedagogies of Crossing*—that articulate the scholarly impasses, including writer's block and political depression, created by the absent archive of slavery and the long-term effects of racism. The chapter suggests how histories of geographic and political dispossession can usefully illuminate what gets called depression, and how indigenous notions of sovereignty and what Alexander calls "radical self-possession," or decolonization that includes not just the mind but the senses and feelings, enable a psychogeographical understanding of depression. This premise serves as a framework for reading two memoirs that are more explicitly about depression—Sharon O'Brien's *The Family Silver* and Jeffery Smith's *When the Roots Reach for Water*—in which the vulnerabilities of class aspiration, including those of academia, can be productively read in terms of histories of displacement in the Americas.

While chapter 1 looks to alternative histories and chapter 2 looks to alternative cultural geographies in order to generate new archives for depression besides those provided by medical science, the third and final chapter moves closer to the intellectual home of Public Feelings in queer and feminist archives of the ordinary and the domestic, or the intimacies of so-called private life. It emerges from now quite established feminist scholarship on the politics of feeling that has explored sensational modes and genres such as sentimentality and melodrama in order to explain the relations between the private and the public, the psychic and the social, and lived experience and social systems. It begins with the premise that depression is ordinary, building on my previous work on both trauma and sensationalism, which has kept me intrigued by the relation between that which seems notable, catastrophic, or the visible sign of trouble and moments or experiences that are less remarkable and less distinct as events.

In order to explore practices of living that both accommodate depression and alleviate it, the chapter draws on the contemporary queer culture that accompanied and shaped my thinking by making me feel better. The archive of feelings that helps me make the turn from depression to the reparative work of daily living, and what I call the utopia of everyday habit, includes Kiki and Herb's cabaret performance of maternal melodrama and Gregg Bordowitz's exploration of ongoing AIDS depression and ordinary life in the autodocumentary video *Habit*, as well as an extended meditation on the queer and feminist resurgence of interest in crafting. Drawing on ideas about utopia among fellow travelers in queer studies, the chapter links spiritual practice and creative practice by describing both as forms of felt or embodied response to getting blocked or stuck in activism and academia.

Cumulatively the book envisions depression as a form of being stuck, both literal and metaphorical, that requires new ways of living or, more concretely, moving. It seeks to be a form of reparative scholarly work that can help facilitate that path. It challenges medical and scientific methods as the only way to know depression and aims to craft ways of writing about depression that differ even from much scholarship in the humanities that relies on conventional forms of research. Its unconventional archive thus includes, in addition to personal narrative, the spiritual and religious traditions of the first chapter, the indigenous traditions and everyday experiences of racism of the second, and the queer cultures that are part of my daily life. I hope to reinvigorate forms of humanities writing that are based in creative and speculative thinking and feeling. The brief epilogue reiterates this methodological desire through the insights of a diverse group of writers—Lynda Barry, David Foster Wallace, Audre Lorde, and Eileen Myles. More than any pill or theory, their words have moved me forward not only by inspiring my thinking but, quite literally, by making it possible to get up in the morning.

Part I

THE DEPRESSION JOURNALS

(A Memoir)

Going Down (1986–1989)

THE SPRAINED ANKLE

It's hard to say exactly when my troubles began because the pervasive and relentless anxiety that settled in during the fall I went on the job market was difficult to pinpoint or describe. Sometimes, though, there were more obvious signs.

Like my sprained ankle, which was no accident. I was on my way home from a protest, part of ongoing campus activism for divestment from South Africa. The previous spring there had been daily sit-ins and a shantytown in the middle of campus, and although the intensity had dwindled somewhat, students were now demonstrating on the central quad by sitting inside of big refrigerator boxes that represented shanties. On this particular day, the campus police decided to clear them out, dragging people away with extreme force by pinning them in headlocks and subduing them with a device inserted in their nostrils. I was outraged. Although some protestors went off to the police station to provide support, I ended up heading home by myself. I was so busy applying for jobs that I had been unable to participate actively in this latest wave of protests. I felt distant from the events and regretful about not being more involved.

As I headed down the hill from campus, my mind was spinning. I was fretting about the scene I had just witnessed but also obsessing about job letters and a troubled romance. When I stepped off the curb at an intersection, my ankle buckled beneath me. I fell to the ground and, immediately feeling embarrassed and self-conscious, I picked myself up as quickly as I could and continued to walk the remaining blocks home. My main concern was to avoid a spectacle, and I tried to keep my limp as slight as possible. Once home, my attention was focused on getting ready to go to a party at a friend's house, where I could get more news about the demonstration and its aftermath.

A couple of hours and a few drinks later, having been filled in on events at the police station and having shared my indignation about police brutality, I suddenly realized there was a problem with my ankle. I was standing while talking to people and increasingly couldn't put any weight on my foot. I didn't feel any sensation of pain; I just couldn't stand up anymore. Before I had a chance to investigate further, I realized I felt faint. I managed to sit down before I actually fell over, but I was very close to blacking out. When I finally removed my boot, I discovered that my ankle was swollen to twice its usual size. The visual evidence forced me actually to feel the pain and to realize that I could no longer walk. An x-ray the following day showed no serious damage, but I had to use crutches for the next two weeks and walk with a cane for quite some time afterward.

Although it was very inconvenient, the most disturbing aspect of the whole episode was the fact that I had been so able to ignore the initial pain. By ignoring it, I had made it worse. I was able to recognize this as a warning sign—a notice about my inability to pay attention to the sensations of being in my own body—but I didn't really have any idea what it would mean to live differently.

It was also a sign of the upended nature of my life that a significant injury meant very little in comparison with the ongoing anxiety of being on the job market. I couldn't feel physical pain because I was so busy feeling other kinds of pain, which often took the form of feeling nothing at all. Everything blurred together in an amorphous sense of dread. I didn't notice autumn coming on or any other details of Ithaca's beautiful landscape of gorges and lakes. I couldn't focus on anything other than the pressure of deadlines that seemed unending.

Being on the job market is one of academia's major rites of passage. Huge uncertainties about the future—Is my intellectual work any good? Will I get a job? Where will I be living? Is this really what I want to do?—coalesce around an endless array of tiny tasks and decisions about everything from which font to use on a cv to how to describe one's dissertation, which represents years of work, in a single paragraph that will capture the attention of an unknown reader. I agonized for most of September over that one paragraph, and I spent the next month writing one letter after another, crafting endless small revisions in order to fit each different job description.

I spent one horrible week completing the last application, for short-term appointments at Yale that weren't even tenure-track positions but that required a five-page dissertation prospectus. Everything else I had just done suddenly seemed so much easier because it had been more about packaging than substance. With a longer description, I felt I could no longer hide—this time I had to tell the real truth about my dissertation and face up to the weaknesses in my conception. I cried, I revised, I spent every waking hour possible in front of the computer. And when that was over, I had to get my writing sample ready. I had spent the entire summer trying and failing to revise a chapter and now had to settle for sending out the same old paper I'd written the year before rather than a real dissertation excerpt. I couldn't even figure out how to cut it to writing-sample length.

I've now seen many people made crazy by the job market, but at the time I couldn't understand what was going on and why the pressure seemed so relentless. I had dealt with crises before, and the rest of my life was also currently in a state of major upheaval, but this felt very different. The abstract concept of being on the job market and the lived experience of daily anxiety didn't match up. *Depression* is too blank and unhelpful a term to explain what I was living, and the catch-all term *anxiety* that I often use here is also a vague and feeble substitute. The sprained ankle, however partial and tangential to the real problem, tells the story.

THE DISSERTATION DEFENSE

Although academic jobs in English are notoriously scarce, there was a mini-boom in the mid-1980s. I had over a dozen interviews, four campus visits, and three job offers, and ultimately accepted a job at the University of Texas in Austin. The external recognition lifted my spirits and focused my attention. I not only survived the interviews and campus visits, I also really enjoyed them. Buoyed by my success, I made good progress on my dissertation in the spring.

During the summer, though, the clock started running out, and the deadline for my dissertation defense loomed ominously on the horizon. I handed in a rough draft of the whole dissertation sometime in June, and after that, I got completely stuck. I couldn't make revisions on the chapters that were already drafted, and I still had an introduction, a conclusion, and a chapter to write.

I was living alone in an apartment perched halfway down the hill that separates the Cornell campus from the town of Ithaca. I loved the space—it was on the top floor of an old building, and the rooms were asymmetrically shaped by sloping ceilings. Since there were no windows at eye level, only one tiny window at ground level and skylights up above, it felt sequestered from the outside world. Up a twisting flight of stairs there was a windowed cupola with a spectacular view of the lake and the hills beyond. It was the perfect setting within which to play out the fantasy of having a room of one's own, and I had felt liberated by the combination of seclusion and expansive view. Eventually, though, the apartment became the prison in which the standstill drama of writer's block was played out. In an effort to move my mind, I moved my desk out of the tiny office space and into the roomier dining area of the kitchen. The desk's metal geometry, the white walls, the window high up by the ceiling, the closet under the eaves—I gazed at these familiar spots with a blank mind that contained only the details of what the room looked like rather than ideas for writing.

Sometimes my heart started pounding so fast that I had to stop working. I would leave my desk to lie on the living room floor, hoping that the brief respite would allow my beating heart to still itself. Everything seemed so quiet and ordinary; why was I so terrified?

Breathing as slowly and consciously as possible seemed to help. I didn't know much about yoga or meditation at that point, but I had an intuitive sense that changing my breathing was important. I didn't know that some people would call these panic attacks, but I went to the medical center and got my first ever prescription for Xanax. The pills offered little solace—they sometimes dulled the edge of the panic, but they didn't make me any more productive. Far more helpful was my friend Z, who knew the patient art of caretaking and had the skill it requires to keep company with people in trouble. She would bring me food, spend the night, proofread, say encouraging things.

All my efforts to write came to nothing. The only thing I really did in those final weeks was get scared while watching with envy as my other graduating peers experienced the closure of the defense. I set my defense date as late as possible in the hope that with more time a breakthrough would arrive, but to no avail. The fatal deadline came, and although I had eked out some form of introduction and even a brief conclusion, my Wilkie Collins chapter remained stubbornly unfinished. At the last moment, I scrapped a number of its pages because they weren't leading to any kind of conclusion. Much to my disappointment, I handed in the final version of the dissertation with a meager fifteen-page chapter that ended in midargument.

I can honestly say that I don't think I've ever attended a defense that was worse than mine. It wasn't that I performed badly in response to my committee's questions or that they criticized me; if anything, it was an exceedingly gentle affair because my chair knew that I was upset and protected me from any aggressive questioning. But as we discussed my work, I couldn't feel any sense of connection to it, couldn't claim it as my own to defend or celebrate.

THE FAIRY TALE

My dissertation reminded me of one of my favorite fairy tales from a beautifully illustrated volume I cherished as a child, one of the first books I was able to read on my own. In Hans Christian Andersen's story "The Wild Swans," a young girl is sent away by her stepmother, who also turns her eleven brothers into swans. In search of her brothers, the girl discovers them when the swans turn back into men at night. A woman comes to her in a dream to tell her that she can free her brothers from the spell by using nettles to make coats that will turn them back into men, but only if she remains silent during the entire process. She works in secret all night long, gathering the nettles that prick her fingers, spinning them into thread, and then knitting the coats. Running out of time, she is unable to complete the sleeve of the last coat, and one of her brothers has to live with a wing instead of an arm. So too with my ugly, scraggly, unfinished dissertation.

In *The Golden Book of Fairy Tales'* lavish illustrations by the French artist Adrienne Ségur, the blonde maiden delicately holds a strand from the spindle of woven nettles in the fingers of her white hand, watched over by a bird perched on her shoulder. One of her swan brothers sits in her lap, his humanity symbolized by his jeweled crown and the single tear he sheds, which is matched by the tear that rolls down her pale cheek. Although heartbroken and silent, the girl has the company of the animals with whom she can communicate in ways other than words.

As problematic as the image of the mute and pale white maiden might be from my adult feminist perspective, she was an icon of the melodrama of silent suffering that was part of my dissertation and the process of writing it. The story of lonely labor and unarticulated feelings was also a poignant reminder for me of the terror of being unable to make a deadline despite working as hard as you can. But the girl also represented the creative and reparative impulses of witch-craft, of being able to spin the pain of stinging prickles into something that, even if unfinished, could be powerful enough to transform swans into brothers.

Sometimes I tell this story to my own students, and I remind them that it's possible to live with a wing in place of an arm.

THE NEW JOB

It seems obvious now that starting a job and moving to a completely new place would be difficult. I grew up in Canada, and even though I'd crossed the border more than ten years earlier to go to college in Portland, I had always lived within striking distance of it. Now I was headed to the other border, a place that was off the map for most people I knew, who often indulged in stereotypes about the South and rednecks. I was too ambivalent about academia to be prepared for a real job or invested in the professional status that came with it.

The pop psychology lists that put moving and new jobs right up there with death and divorce provide some warning. But no one prepared me for the form that the stress would take, especially the relentless physical symptoms. Going on the job market, finishing my dissertation, and moving were all dis-crete events, with a beginning, middle, and end. Now I was experiencing a daily life of dread stretching endlessly into the future with no respite from anxiety.

Especially disturbing was the impossibility of physical relaxation. An unend-ing series of mornings in which no matter how much I had slept, I did not feel rested. Nap times in which I would lie in bed aching with an amorphous set of pains—a mid-back ache that would not go away, persistent headaches, a furi-ously beating heart. Downtime, especially at the end of teaching days when I could give myself a break, was filled with fear, or tears, or a dull blankness that made no dent in the relentless pace of obligations and things to worry about. There was no rhythm of ups and downs, of challenges ventured and accomplished—just a dull and steady invasion of sensations without respite.

To describe anxiety as a psychological state or as subject to mental persuasion doesn't capture it. In my experience, it was a feeling deeply embedded in different parts of my body. Like physical pain, it kept me fixated on the immediate present, unable to think about other things. But it was also dull enough and invisible enough—no blood, no wounds—that I could live with it. I was confused about what to do because I no longer knew how to avoid it or how to imagine it ending.

CORPUS CHRISTI

One moment of relief lifted the seamless web of anxiety and allowed me to get outside of myself for long enough to remember that things could be different. A friend came to Texas for Thanksgiving. His parents lived in Corpus Christi, where he had grown up, and he invited me to visit him there and to go to their cottage in Port Aransas on the Gulf Coast beach.

That this friend from Ithaca also had Texas history made it seem as though the two worlds could coexist, that I had not just been shipped off to a place that was not on my personal or historical map. I was welcomed into the comfort of his upper-middle-class family life. His parents were pleasant, his brother was an interesting enigma, and, even in my dazed state, I could apply myself to one of my favorite pastimes: meeting other people's families.

The November light on the beaches of Port Aransas was beautiful, reflecting off of pastel-colored buildings, the flamingoes in the marshes, my friend's 1970s sports car. I took photos—classic American road trip images with the car and the landscape beyond as backdrop. We stayed up late talking, cozy in sleeping bags on couches. I was having fun.

And that was a miracle. Not only was the respite from the physical symptoms of stress welcome, but the knowledge that it was possible brought me additional conceptual relief. I could have something good happen to me in Texas, something that was new, not just a reminder of past comforts. Most recommendations for relieving anxiety are like this. Perhaps you can't avoid it all the time, but if you can have one moment of relief—doing exercise, watching a movie, getting a massage—it serves as a reminder that such a feeling is possible. The visceral experience of pleasure is a more powerful antidote than any memory, and I was getting desperate because most of the daily forms of respite that had served in the past were no longer working. This trip not only brought useful flashbacks, but it was definitely happening in a present that included my scary job in a strange state.

Corpus Christi. Body of Christ. Transubstantiation and resurrection in the ocean like the wine that is the blood, on the beach like the wafer that is the body. This was the Gulf Coast, the third coast, not like the Atlantic and the Pacific that link the U.S. and Canada. This was the water that links the U.S. to Mexico, so close by and so much a part of this unknown Southwest Texas, and to the Caribbean Islands beyond. A different version of the Americas. We walked on one of the piers late at night where people were still fishing, catching strange fish like none I know. There were huge jellyfish, like floating brains, everywhere. It's a different world but one that I could be interested in getting to know. I could be a tourist on vacation here, charmed by all that is not like home. That's a familiar feeling. And a pleasurable one. Corpus Christi, a place of Catholicism, and hence of ritual. I began to learn how to let the ocean rescue me.

MELODRAMA

After my first year of teaching in Texas, I returned to Ithaca for the summer. Although I was fortunate to have Z's house as a sanctuary, I felt some shame about how it was an escape from the demands of my real life into a cocoon of past comforts. The rhythms of summer in Ithaca were familiar—lunches and dinners with my many friends still in grad school there, swimming in the lakes and pools in the beautiful summer weather that compensates for the harsh winters, and the constant backdrop of relentless writing anxiety.

My task for the summer was to revise one of the chapters of my dissertation as a publishable article, part of the long march toward a book manuscript. I was thinking about maternal melodrama for my chapter about the popular Victorian sensation novel *East Lynne*, in which a married woman abandons her husband and children to run off with another man and then returns in disguise (after being disfigured by a railway accident that kills her illegitimate child!) to work as her children's governess. I wanted to bring the sensation novel into conversation with exciting new work on melodrama by feminist film theorists, who were making a case for the value of films like *Stella Dallas*, *Now, Voyager*, and *Imitation of Life* that had seemed like trashy women's culture. But to no avail—I read and reread, I took notes, and I started writing, but I'm not sure I produced any usable prose, and even if I had, I would probably have scrapped it later. In previous years, Z's apartment had been a magical space for taking myself seriously as a writer and an artist. Now—shuttling between the desk in her bedroom, the couch in the living room, and the big chair that lived by the kitchen window that summer—I would sit and sit, lost in contemplation with nothing to show for it.

But not quite nothing. I read two books that summer that had a lasting impact: Sarah Schulman's *After Dolores* and Toni Morrison's *Beloved*. Although I didn't make the connection at the time, both books were good choices for someone thinking about melodrama and women's popular genres, since *After Dolores* is a queer feminist adaptation of noir and *Beloved* is in deep dialogue with nineteenth-century slave narrative and sentimental fiction. Speeding through *After Dolores*, something I rarely got to do anymore, reminded me that reading could be a pleasure. And I was gripped by *Beloved*, which twisted the story of a mother separated from her children far beyond anything that classic maternal melodrama ever imagined. I later became friends with Sarah, whose work on lesbian culture and AIDS activism was a major inspiration for my own. *Beloved* remains a crucial touchstone for how to circumvent conventional forms of documentary sentimentality in cultures of public feeling.

I can see now that I did get something done and that my brain was functioning, despite my sense of aimlessness and futility. It's an important lesson, and I often tell students and colleagues not to expect to do anything in the first summer after finishing their dissertation and starting a new job. It's important to have the experience of not being required to do anything after meeting those demands. The mind will take care of itself without needing to be forced. I've had to teach myself not to work when I can't, that there's no need to work from the blank mental state that anxiety produces.

The other great irony of that apparently useless summer is that in the end it resulted in an article publication and a book contract. In desperation, I resorted to repackaging what I already had, sending out my unrevised Collins chapter and my unrevised dissertation to an editor who had inquired about my project.

By the end of the fall, *Novel* had accepted my article without requiring any revisions and Rutgers had given me a book contract. But as in a melodrama, this miraculous happy ending seemed like a matter of fate, and I could not, at least not yet, find in this success any formula for avoiding anxiety and despair.

THE ECLIPSE OF THE MOON

The article and the book contract were followed by a postdoctoral fellowship for the upcoming year in Connecticut, where I would have the added benefit of proximity to New York. But as soon as I actually got there in the middle of the summer, I started to feel a sense of dread that was confusing because all outward signs suggested I should be happy. Those can be the most dangerous moments: when there seems to be no apparent reason for anxiety, the irrationality of it becomes its own source of fear and can very quickly escalate. Although I appeared to be a successful junior faculty member with all the conditions in place for finishing her book, I was actually about to crash harder than I ever had before.

The summer vacation that wasn't one became an ominous warning sign. Ever since moving to Austin, I had been yearning to visit British Columbia, where I was born and raised. I was so consumed during graduate school that I didn't feel I could make the time, so my trip to see my family at the end of the summer was the first in some years. Although I was mostly too distracted by creeping fear to enjoy it, the most comfortable days were spent with my grandmother in Campbell River, a small pulp mill town on northern Vancouver Island known to tourists for its salmon fishing. My grandparents' house, whose address for a long time was simply "Above Tide," sits alongside the rapid river that just a short distance downstream meets the gentle ocean waters of the Discovery Passage, which separates Vancouver Island from the jagged British Columbia coastline. The landscape of river, ocean, driftwood beaches, and dark and quiet evergreen forests was a powerful presence in my childhood years.

My grandparents moved there in the 1930s, shortly after getting married, and raised four children in the house by the river. My grandfather, Roderick Haig-Brown, wrote books, novels, and essays about fishing and nature that established his reputation in British Columbia as a regional writer, and also served as the town magistrate. My grandmother, Ann, was the high school librarian and a leader in the Catholic church and the community. Their house was a hub of cultural and creative activity, with interesting visitors constantly congregating in the book-lined study that my grandfather built himself. It was also just *home* to me, the scene of many childhood trips and days spent swimming in the cold and rushing river, eating fruit from the trees in the orchards, riding horses, and listening to the adults talking.

My grandfather died in 1976, the year I went to college, and the energy of the house moved to the kitchen, where my grandmother, accompanied by the constant sounds of classical music and CBC radio, read or worked in her office alcove with the pink electric typewriter. The routine on this visit to the house was soothingly familiar. Grandmother cooked for me, talked to me, gave me her full attention when I wanted it, left me alone when I didn't. I could, as I had so often done there in the past, spend the entire day reading. I made my usual rounds of Grandfather's study (still left as it was when he died) to think about what the familiar books meant to me now and spent a good deal of time reading books by Raymond Williams in preparation for an article I was supposed to write (and never did). Wandering outside, I made a pilgrimage to important sites across the twenty acres—the apple trees in the orchard, the plum trees in the field on the other side of the garden, the entrance to the river by the fallen tree and the dam of rocks just downstream, the sprawling lawn, the barn, the secret hiding spot under a tree along the river.

We didn't go much of anywhere, except for one night when there was an eclipse of the moon and we went downtown to the wharf to look at the moon being slowly obscured as it rose above the islands across the waters of Discovery Passage. Grandmother was game to explore further so we drove up the hill above downtown to see if we could find a view of the eclipse from a higher vantage point. By the time we came home, the moon was beginning to re-emerge from behind the sun. In order to see it one last time, we went up to the second floor of the house. Going upstairs was hard for Grandmother because her knees were bad, but she did it anyway, and we looked out the windows of the room that I often slept in as a child. The moon was there, hovering above the evergreen hedges that separate the sprawling lawn and garden from the wilder fields beyond and lighting up the familiar landscape of so many childhood pleasures.

I thought of that moment many times over the next year, when Grandmother tried to help with my despair. She made her presence felt by sending letters with her special style of advice, a combination of love and intellectual passion condensed into aphoristic prose. She sent me a book of poems with some leaves from a tree outside the house pressed inside the front cover. It was a vivid reminder of her ability to balance the intellectual and the material, the worldly and the domestic. We shared books and ideas, but her garden was something completely unimaginable to me even as I dimly sensed that this literal form of being grounded in the local was a good way to make an attachment to being in the world.

As it turns out, my instinct to go home was a good one despite my distracted condition. It was my last visit with Grandmother—I returned less than a year later for her funeral.

THE FIRST DEPRESSION

Campbell River was not just the scene of happy visits to my grandparents. It was also the place where my family came apart. One summer day when I was nine, my mother was hanging out the laundry to dry in the yard of our new house—the house I loved because I finally had my own room—and she told me that my father had a *mental illness* called *manic-depression*. This explained why he'd been acting so—well, *crazy*—that summer, going out all the time and planning big projects, the most spectacular of which was running for political office. He managed to get himself nominated as the Liberal Party candidate in the provincial elections. The party was so weak in the province that there was very little chance he would win, but just being a candidate gave him a sense of status and visibility. He liked being written about in the local newspaper, meeting with important people, planning a big campaign party (at which my sister and I were going to be go-go dancers until my mother nixed that plan), and seeing his name writ large on the campaign posters.

But after he lost the election, he was crushed. On Christmas day, my sister and I opened up our presents with my mother while he stayed in bed. That was the year we had managed to find all of our presents in a closet before Christmas, so we weren't surprised about any of them, but we didn't care. I loved my new Casey doll—Barbie's mod friend with the pageboy hair and the single earring. In the pictures taken at my grandparents' house, where we went to dinner later that day, my sister and I, wearing the matching red velvet dresses with lace trim that an aunt made for us, look untroubled by my father's absence.

In that next year, my father lost everything. My mother left without warning, and my sister and I were sent to live with an aunt and uncle in Vancouver. He was hospitalized, his law practice was closed down, and he had to sell the house. When he became manic again in the fall, my aunt and uncle were worried that my sister and I were in danger with him, and we were again abruptly moved, this time to Toronto to rejoin my mother. In 1967, the year of the summer of love and of the Canadian centennial, my father lost it all, like a doomed scenario from one of the tragic Joan Baez folk songs I was listening to then, in which terrible violence happens all the time and people wither and die from sorrow.

Twenty-odd years later, I wondered if my experience was anything like my father's. Once, a good friend, someone who could really get in close to the bone, asked if I was afraid that I would become my father, and suddenly, rather than just shrugging off the question, I did feel genuinely afraid. Contemplating the repetition across the generations, I sometimes fell into a superstitious fatalism. I noticed, for example, that I turned thirty-three in 1990, the same age at which my father rose high and fell hard. Was it something that happened in one's Christological year?

Most of the time, though, the hereditary explanations just didn't *feel* true—if depression were passed down, I was more inclined to think of it as the cumulative effect of long histories, not as a flaw in the gene pool. The connections would have to be made the hard way, by unpacking memories and telling stories, rather than by accepting a diagnosis as fate. I was convinced that my father's story was not just a medical one. The child of Croatian immigrants, he was only three when his father, who worked in the copper mines of Anyox and Princeton, died, and his mother struggled to raise three young children on her own in one of Vancouver's poorest neighborhoods. He was the son who was targeted for upward mobility—who went to university and to law school and married the daughter of a respected writer and magistrate. When things didn't seem to be quite working out with the corporate law job and the two children in the house in a suburban neighborhood, they moved to the small town on Vancouver Island where things would be calmer. They could be close to my mother's parents, and a family friend in real estate could help him establish a private law practice by sending easy business his way. When that plan didn't work out, he must have felt pretty desperate, but he amped it up long enough to put his political dream into action. When that dream too failed, he was devastated.

Sometimes I did have the feeling that I was doomed, destined for an insanity like the hereditary madness in a Victorian novel, or more likely just a deeply ingrained sadness from proximity to suffering. Sometimes it was just fear that I was stuck with the more mundane problem of a family that was in trouble. But if my family history explains my depression, this is only one strand of a complex story. Moreover, the explanation was not the cure. If I didn't want to repeat my father's story or be blocked in the way that he was, I would have to learn other ways of living. It might be an inheritance, but it was not a destiny.

Swimming (1989–1990)

THE ALARM CLOCK

During my fellowship year, my sense of time became very distorted, and I lost the ability to inhabit the normal rhythms of the day. Hours could go by while I attempted to focus on a task. If I didn't absolutely have to do something, it was very easy to get stuck in a moment with nothing prompting me to move on, least of all any internal sense of desire or motivation. I'm amazed that I got anything done at all, but it seems my sense of shame about failure or irresponsibility was so strong that I could push past the inertia to complete the absolutely obligatory tasks like teaching and attending seminars.

Getting out of bed in the morning was especially hard. I know it's commonplace for people to say they were so depressed they couldn't get out of bed in the morning, so much so that excessive sleeping has become one of the official clinical symptoms of depression, but the lived experience has many nuances not captured by colloquial expressions and abstract diagnoses. I would wake up, but I would be unable to make the next move, as though I were literally paralyzed and the only physical difference between being awake and being asleep was that my eyes were open. My state of immobility seemed aimless and unmotivated, not something I could change in any way. I couldn't even really recognize what possessed me as dread or anxiety.

I would lie in bed thinking but unable to get up, often covered in a layer of sweat that would soak the sheets. It was not the sweat of heat but something else, a kind of animal fear exuding through my pores and leaving a sticky film on my body. During that fellowship year, the bed in my furnished rental apartment never became comfortable. I was sleeping on odds and ends of sheets that had been left there; the faded pastel polyester was worn and pilled and felt bad against my skin. (Eventually, I learned to bring my own bedding when I move, a simple but effective technique for making my body feel at home.)

It was an impossible struggle with the alarm clock—its buzz no longer had any urgency or meaning. No matter what time I set it for I could not make myself get up. During that fellowship year, I usually didn't have to be anywhere early, so it didn't really matter. But on the days when I did have an obligation—such as the morning discussion sessions that followed the weekly lectures—I would somehow drag myself out of bed at the last possible moment that still allowed me to make it on time. I wouldn't be able to give myself the half hour or hour it took to get ready—instead, the threat of not being present would somehow impose itself on my consciousness and force me out of bed with just enough time to throw on some clothes (another decision-making dilemma) and make it to the session.

One weekend I was trying to make it to a Lesbian and Gay Studies Conference at Yale. I could not retain the schedule in my head or plan for the necessary departure time to make it to the opening session. Eventually the desire to get there was strong enough to pull me out of bed and I drove to New Haven at some random hour. Despite my mental haze, I was present for a conference that became historic, the third in a series between 1987 and 1991 that marked the arrival of queer studies. Douglas Crimp delivered "Mourning and Militancy," Ray Navarro presented his AIDS activist videos, Eve Sedgwick made Foucault queer for the first time in my experience, and Judith Butler, having just published *Gender Trouble*, talked about the difficulties of "performing lesbian." The rooms and halls were pulsing with energy—ACT UP activists mingled with academics, and everybody looked sexy and cool; long before the mainstream media reported on it, lesbian chic had already arrived. Even though I was barely present emotionally, I could feel it enough to be able to save the experience for later use.

THE GROCERY STORE

Shopping for groceries, one of those ordinary routines of self-maintenance that often lie beneath notice, became another impossible task. I was living in a college town with no major grocery store and almost no restaurants, so I had to change the comfortable middle-class pattern I had developed in Austin of eating out a lot and shopping on an almost daily basis at the friendly health food store in my neighborhood. (In fact, it was the first Whole Foods, which, for those who can afford it, aims to transform grocery shopping from the invisible drudgery that can induce depression into an aesthetic experience.) Instead I had an almost half-hour drive to a large chain supermarket. Over the course of the year, I developed a weekly shopping list, reminiscent of my childhood years, when Saturday grocery shopping was the necessary ritual for a family with a working mother.

This new routine was a challenge to my current lack of domestic habit and discipline. The combination of my inability to focus, a large chain store with florescent lighting, and average people going about their everyday business was grim. On the one hand, my task was fairly circumscribed: buy groceries. On the other, the difficulty of doing even that became a painful sign of my incapacity. Other people could stroll the aisles and get on with this routine activity—looking functional and in some cases even cheerful. But I found it extremely challenging to figure out what to buy in those aisles full of too many things to choose from. I would pause in front of the bread and become lost in thought for minutes at a time. In fact, sometimes shopping gave me an excuse to space out—under cover of having to choose a brand, I could let the minutes pass.

Whereas some ordinary activities—hanging out with friends, going to the dentist, exercising—could be comforting, others, like shopping or getting up in the morning, were excruciating, providing a mocking reminder that I was incapable of even the simplest task. I think the difference is one of agency—

some everyday activities require very little effort because you have to follow institutional structures or someone else's agenda (which can also make them really boring). Others, even relatively minor tasks, require a degree of agency that, however minimal, is still beyond the reach of a severely depressed person. Consumerism is the arena of agency and desire held out by a culture that forecloses other options—you're in the store, and you can ask yourself *What do I want? What's my pleasure?* If the answer that comes back resoundingly is *I don't know*, or worse yet, *Nothing*, and you thus seem to have stepped beyond even capitalism's seductions, what is to become of you?

And yet to the extent that I *was* able to accomplish this everyday chore, I did find some small comfort. I never returned empty-handed even if I had no idea what to buy and selected objects arbitrarily by miming the motions of a shopper. Somehow I did have food, even if, when I got home to my sparsely appointed kitchen, the dishes were the odd assortment that accumulates with multiple tenants, and the cheap pots and pans were stained and dented. Just as I have had to learn how to make my bed, so too have I had to learn how to feed myself.

THE THANK-YOU NOTE

There were many occasions on which I would attempt to write postcards and find myself unable to compose a single sentence. Sometimes I would get off to a promising start but fail to complete even the simplest message. The most extreme case of this writer's block in the realm of everyday correspondence was the thank-you note I tried to write to a new friend after visiting her for the weekend. She had invited me to an art opening, and, having until then only met with her at conferences, I was looking forward to spending time with her under more leisurely circumstances. Before I could leave, though, I had to grade a batch of papers. I had had them for a while but had been unable to finish them because I was having such difficulty focusing, and they absolutely could not be further delayed. I sat down the evening before I was leaving and had to stay up all night in order to finish what would, under more normal circumstances, have taken a few hours. Each paper took close to an hour, and because I was incapable of following the logic of the arguments, I had to craft comments not in relation to the prose but out of some reservoir of stock phrases. Like an amnesiac, I would try to reconstruct what it was that professors wrote on papers. I never got any faster, but somehow, far into the night, I made it to the end of the batch. The loss of sleep didn't really matter because there was no real distinction for me anymore between being rested or not.

When I got back from my visit, I wanted to write my friend a thank-you note, particularly because I was grateful to have been able to forge a new relationship even in my state of complete lethargy. I started writing on university letterhead—the half sheets that are good for a short note. I was hoping to fill perhaps a single sheet. Instead, I was unable to progress beyond a few words before I could write no more. It was as if I were trying to trick myself into composing something by beginning a sentence but then would be unable to think of anything to say. Sometimes I would cross out a word hoping that the apparent decisiveness of deciding against a phrase would lead me to what I did want to say. Hours later, I had a pile of sheets—starting anew was also a way of trying to jump-start my brain. Each one had no more than a sentence—sometimes they were exactly the same. I was more and more disturbed by the compulsive product of my inability to write, but I couldn't throw away the evidence. Instead I put the sheets into a manila envelope and stored them in the top drawer of my desk for the rest of the year, where they served as testimony to the discrepancy between my ability to make the trip and my inability to conduct the more solitary activities that preceded and followed it. I still have the envelope somewhere. And every once in a while I come across unmailed postcards from that year, often with an address and a date, an image carefully chosen to fit the recipient, and one or two lines that break off in the middle of a sentence.

THE DENTIST

That fall I finally went to the dentist for the first time in five years. I was ashamed to admit to myself that even having dental insurance since getting my job had not prompted me to go; somehow I just couldn't seem to organize myself to figure out how the insurance worked or to find a dentist, much less make the appointments and go. One of my back molars had chipped two years previously, but I was too busy with more pressing concerns like finishing my dissertation and moving to take care of it. I was good at ignoring pain, but finally the regular and intense toothaches got to be too much.

It turned out to be my first root canal. What followed was a seemingly endless series of visits to the dentist, Dr. B. He was effusively warm, a reassuringly friendly presence in the midst of my ongoing and relentless mental distress, beside which dental pain seemed inconsequential. He valued education and our shared professional status, and while he worked, he would dispense bits of wisdom about life, advice I found curiously attractive because of his constant cheerfulness. I wondered what struggles he might have faced in becoming a successful black middle-class professional in a small town in Connecticut.

In addition to his enthusiasm about my life, Dr. B was also very enthusiastic about the future of my mouth. My teeth were very worn down from a lifetime of jaw clenching, that now much-publicized sign of stress that turns your dentist into your psychoanalyst (and sells another bite guard). The root canal involved multiple sessions of drilling, poking, and crown fitting, and my many hours in the dental chair that year were an experience of welcome submission. I was too bereft of agency to do more than simply show up for the appointments and let the doctor do as he deemed necessary. I would focus my gaze on his blue overhead light or beyond it to the holes of the acoustic tile in the ceiling and go blank. Afterward I would return to work with my jaw completely numb, unable really to feel the difference between the frozen and unfrozen states, but with a sense that I was taking care of business.

Dental care is something of a metaphor for the state of other affairs in my life. Taking care of the tooth disasters involves an act of faith that when something is wrong it can be fixed and that it's possible to move on. A replacement crown and a dental implant later, though, Tooth 18's persistent presence in my dental life has been a reminder that I will continue to pay for my inability to take care of myself. Health maintenance has become for me a sign of self-love, although it also gives rise to some nagging questions about class. Regular dental care seems to be part of the secret life of middle-class domesticity that passes for normal—one of those things that no one talks about but everyone is supposed to do (and if you don't have the money to go to the dentist you keep your mouth shut). Brushing and flossing every day seems to be the invisible foundation for all other good habits and daily rituals, but it's a routine that continues to elude me.

THERAPISTS

The dentist was ultimately of more use to me than the therapists. The bland wisdom of the advice columns—"Seek professional help"—is a cruel prescription for the depressed, for whom exercising good judgment about such a major relationship is a lot to expect. I had a number of comically pathetic encounters during my year in Connecticut. I began by perusing the list of doctors who were members of my HMO plan's network. I didn't have to be referred by a primary care physician so I could make my own choice, but I had no idea how to pick. It felt ultimately just as random a process as being assigned to someone arbitrarily.

The visit to therapist number 1 began with an adventure in navigation on a rainy day. Along with losing a sense of time, I had lost my normally very keen powers of spatial orientation. I couldn't seem to retain the relation between maps or directions and actual movement. After numerous mistakes finding my way there, I finally just made a guess and parked. The therapist's office was in her house, which was messy and dark, and she smoked while we talked, which I found disconcerting.

I think I picked her because she said she didn't charge for the first session. A good thing too because, even in my hazy state, I knew I wouldn't be going back. Her one attempt at helpful advice was to observe that I was being "too hard on myself." We talked about the women's rights march in Washington, which was coming up that weekend—she was going and asked if I would be too. Getting that together seemed unimaginable, and I felt a little wistful about the things normal people could do. She worried about my getting back to my car in the rain and escorted me there under her umbrella. It seemed quite possible that she was depressed too.

Therapist number 2, my next arbitrary pick on the list, had one of those well-decorated offices whose bourgeois comforts are supposed to be soothing. The furniture was poofy and floral, and the walls were painted a calming and chic shade of green and decorated with attractive prints. She seemed more like a businesswoman or real estate agent than a therapist, and I had no faith in her ability to dispense anything other than clichés. I was so thoroughly mute with despair that I could barely articulate my situation in the session. Her one contribution was to recommend medication and send me on to a psychiatrist.

He was the absentminded-professor type. His office was sparse, tasteful, and bookish, in a house shared with other shrinks within walking distance from the campus. It was rather like going to a professor's office and thus seemed reassuringly familiar. The great thing about pill doctors is that they don't ask many questions—they just dispense the pharmaceuticals. I got a Prozac prescription after one visit and returned about a month later for a brief follow-up. That was it. This guy was so absentminded that he never billed me and never contacted me to check in when I failed to make a return appointment. It was the very beginning of the Prozac era and I didn't know I was part of a rapidly growing population of users; the explosion of news stories and books was just starting, and I hadn't really heard much about this new drug other than the name. I had a six-month prescription for Prozac, and I was on my own.

SWIMMING

Sometimes saving the day is all it really takes to save a life. If you can hold the despair at bay for just a little bit longer, there's a chance that something will come along to change things. Swimming has saved my life, or at least saved the day, on numerous occasions. When you're depressed, and all you want to do is sit still or curl up in a ball in bed and never get up, putting the body in motion is a major struggle and a major accomplishment. Exercise is recommended as a cure for depression because it produces endorphins, but I think it also works for the simple reason that it keeps you moving and hence strikes a blow against inertia. When the brain is vacant, or shut down, or endlessly fearful, there's something reassuring about showing signs of physical life.

My friend Z got me in the habit of swimming again. She came from California, where she had trained to swim in the outdoor waters of the East Bay, and she was wise in the ways of the body. We had met taking ballet classes together, which became an important escape from the life of the mind. She taught me about caretaking, about how talking about the problem or trying to figure it out isn't the only way to make someone feel better. She would feed me, bring me coffee and orange juice in bed, keep me company in silence. And she would take me to the pool.

Even now, after a long day of futile attempts to write, I can, if nothing else, go swimming. I swim in order to think. At the bottom of the pool, I see the twists and turns of an intellectual problem; the black lines of the lanes against aqua blue are a path to inspiration. The rhythm of breathing and the ease of the strokes keep my body flowing, and, with it, my mind. With the breathing, panic subsides somewhat and it's possible to think again. By the end of the swim, I usually have some glimmer of an idea about how to tackle whatever writing problem I arrived with.

When I returned to Austin after the summer of reading about melodrama, I made it through the hot hot days and the writing anxiety by swimming in the late afternoon at Barton Springs, the miraculous spring-fed outdoor pool, and then going home to write some more. Later, in the even darker years, I would swim in indoor pools in the winter, prompted by a therapist's advice to get physical exercise. It's a bit of a hassle, getting undressed and dressed, dealing with wet hair, and being immersed in so much chlorine. I would often sit in the dressing room or by the side of the pool for a long time, wondering what act of will would propel me to get into my bathing suit or into the water.

Once I was actually in the water, though, it was pretty automatic. After years of childhood swimming lessons and training to be a lifeguard, I'm very comfortable in the water. Swimming is just an extension of breathing. I can keep moving without really thinking about it or exerting a lot of effort. Moving lets me off the hook a little bit. I can space out and let my mind continue with its obsessions because my body is carrying on, and carrying on without me. Exercise becomes an opportunity for sanctioned dissociation, and swimming is such a graceful way of moving that it seems okay to let my brain do whatever it wants. I'm sealed off from the rest of the world in the womb-like space of the pool. There's no need to respond to others or to communicate—it's like being in those sensory-deprivation chambers that are supposed to make you calm. Of all my stories of the depressed body, the ones about swimming are the happiest.

THE VIRGIN

The healing powers of water made sense, but it came as a surprise when ritual began to work its magic in my life. When I started living alone in graduate school, I made my first altar. It was an arrangement of rocks from the Alberta Rockies near where my mother lives. Sheared off in flat geometric squares and triangles, the mountain rocks looked like abstract sculpture. But their visual appeal was less important than their value as a sign of connection to family and to a Canadian landscape, an early version of what I would later call an archive of feelings. Altars were a way of making home with objects that didn't have to be expensive or beautiful, only emotionally meaningful.

Then came hints of voodoo: a friend took a piece from the tomb of Marie Laveau, and this sacrilege brought so much bad luck that she rode the bus all the way from Ithaca back to New Orleans in order to return it. I was mysteriously drawn to Maya Deren's films about Haiti, but also, of all things, *Angel Heart*, a Hollywood film set in New Orleans with a Gothic voodoo theme. Spooked by the film, I started wearing the crucifix I had inherited from my Croatian grandmother. Madonna had made it fashionable so it didn't necessarily mean much, but eventually I started to take the crucifix quite seriously as a fetish object. Its intimations of Catholicism also reminded me of my other grandmother, a hugely devout, if unorthodox, Catholic, whose involvement in the little church across the road from her house added to Campbell River's mystical power in my imagination. Although I was raised Catholic, I hadn't been a regular churchgoer since childhood, and like many secular academics, I became a vehement atheist as a teenager.

My move to Texas brought me my first Virgen of Guadalupe—not the traditional image itself but a painting by my friend John, who rendered her in rudimentary shapes and bold colors that gave her an expressionist power. The moment I saw the rough unstretched canvas on the wall at his boyfriend Skip's apartment I was mesmerized, even though I had no knowledge of what the image meant. Eventually I was schooled, by writers and artists like Gloria Anzaldúa, Sandra Cisneros, Ana Castillo, Yolanda Lopez, Esther Hernandez, Alma Lopez, and my friend Kay Turner, in the ways of the Virgen as a symbol of not just traditional Catholicism but Mexican independence, Chicana feminisms, and mestiza and indigenous identities. But she also functioned at a more intuitive level for me, as a sign of how it might be possible to find a place in the borderlands of Texas. Although I felt self-conscious about being yet another white girl appropriating other cultures—both Tejano and indigenous—I desperately needed the emotional solace the Virgen provided and I considered her appearance in my life to be a version of a miracle. I inherited John's Virgen after he and Skip died, and she has remained on my bedroom wall ever since.

Given my increasingly intense encounters with Catholicism, it's not entirely surprising that religion managed to weave itself into my movement from deep despair to manic enthusiasm. One of the most spectacular moments was my encounter with the Russian Orthodox Church on East Second Street in New York City. I had been staying away from the city, largely because of a bad breakup, but in the spring, as the medication began to take effect, I started making visits again. Unable to sleep one night, I went out at about 6 A.M. and while pacing the streets, I came upon the church. It was a Sunday morning, and I decided to return later for mass.

I stood at the back, something of an interloper, captivated by the foreign language and the rituals that were both familiar and unfamiliar in this small, intimate church. At a certain point in the liturgy, people began to line up to kiss the icon of the Virgin. I boldly stood in line, understanding, as I never had about Holy Communion, why it might be useful to engage in such rituals.

I was stopped, though, by a church member who asked me how I crossed myself. When I showed her, she told me I couldn't stand in line because I had done it backward and revealed myself to be Roman, not Orthodox, Catholic. Disappointed, I retreated to my corner. As the mass continued, I found myself quietly weeping, wrought up by the combination of ritual and rejection. The weeping was not really attached to any feeling or situation, and it was accompanied by a sense of sweet and gentle relief, as though something inside me had been opened and released and my personal sadness was not mine alone. As if to acknowledge the sacredness of my experience, someone from the church offered me wine and bread from communion—the first I'd ever taken in my life.

By this point, after taking Prozac for a month or so, I was what the doctors would call manic, a term I use with some caution because of its clinical resonances, but with an interest in giving it some more vernacular meanings. Part of the reason I couldn't sleep, I'm sure, is that the drugs running through my body affected me like time-release speed or cocaine and were keeping me awake. The drugs also made me bold enough to walk into the church as a total stranger and not feel like an intruder. However drug-induced, it was a magical moment in which the church, and the Orthodox tradition of ritual and icons, provided sanctuary.

THE EASTER ALTAR

In the midst of my manic sensibility, Easter suddenly came alive. I was presenting my new book chapter about sensationalism in Marx's *Capital*, the major goal of my fellowship year, on an Easter Monday, and in the crazy intense burst of final writing the week before, I started making an altar on the table of my office. In addition to incorporating religious candles and images, I piled onto it pictures of family and friends, letters and mementos, and other objects that had special meanings for me, and I bought an Easter lily as a centerpiece. [Note: The photographs reproduced in this section were all part of that altar.] The impulse driving me to do this seemed inexplicable but not to be ignored—possibly a sign from elsewhere but also an instinctive gesture. The altar stood as my material inspiration, the embodiment of the mysterious links between the chapter, my ability finally to write it—a miracle after so many months of despair—and my emotional life.

I had been talking about the new writing to anyone who would listen, finally busting through my often painfully silent presence at this humanities think tank to participate in the collective conversation. I was planning to present a multimedia lecture that included slides, music, and text. In an amazing act of self-display, I transferred my altar from my office to the lecture hall. It expressed my genuine passion for this chapter on Marx's *Capital*, which would be the capstone to my book on Victorian sensation novels. I was sure of my argument and of my readiness to go public with it in a way that I had never been before.

Was it the Prozac talking? Quite probably. It was shortly after this triumphant event—for the evening went very well, at least in my estimation, which counts for something given my despair the semester before—that friends started to caution me about my erratic and uncontrolled behavior. Although the dramatic effects of Prozac ultimately proved unsustainable, I think it released some powers, whether manic or magic, that were already there to be tapped and that have ultimately offered far more solace than the drugs.

I have continued to make altars that render material my emotional states and my hopes and dreams. And I have continued to write in a much freer way, although I would still have another season of deep despair ahead of me before my book was done. On that particular Easter weekend, I felt that I, too, had been reborn. On Good Friday, I called my grandmother to send her greetings and share the good news of my writing breakthrough. It was my last conversation with her before her death a month and half later and, since we hardly ever spoke on the phone, I thank the drugs for making me so urgent about making the connection.

My religious enthusiasms ran more to ritual and popular devotion and a pagan and Marian Catholicism than to Jesus and the organized church, but in that spring season, I did make links between Jesus' resurrection and my own. It was still my Christological year, and I took seriously the notion that I had had to die, to be laid low by suffering, in order to come through to the other side. Subsequent Easters are now always marked by the memory of transformation into a different self that I hold out as an ongoing possibility for myself and for others. But it's not an instantaneous conversion, resurrection, or cure. It's the result of the slow and painstaking accumulation of new ways of living.

GRANDMOTHER'S FUNERAL

When I got the call that Grandmother had died, I knew I had to get to Campbell River as soon as possible. Two days later I was on a plane to Seattle, and by nightfall—very late on a June night in that northern latitude—I was making my way up the driveway to my grandparents' familiar house. The distance between what seemed like separate worlds—school and home, work and family, East and West Coasts, U.S. and Canada—miraculously disappeared. I had rented a car for the trip to Vancouver Island, and as I made my way north through Vancouver and across the Lion's Gate Bridge, I saw the mountains unveiled on the other side of the Burrard Inlet, and I was filled with a sense of how profoundly beautiful this part of the world is. "God's country," I whispered to myself in an odd moment of reverence. "Why did I ever leave?"

A year earlier I had traveled this same route, plagued by anxiety and despair, unable to appreciate the beauty except in some form of painful nostalgia. Now I was having the feeling of homecoming I had sought then—except that Grandmother was no longer here.

It was a remarkable family reunion. I had just missed one of even more lavish proportions for Grandmother's birthday the month before, but it didn't matter because so many important people assembled anew: my mother, sister, and nephews, every single aunt and uncle, as well as their kids, and people I knew from childhood came from all over Vancouver Island and BC. My best friend from high school in Toronto, who had loved visiting my grandparents with me one summer and eventually settled in Victoria, came up. Alongside the business of planning the funeral, the family partied and played and talked, just like at any other gathering.

Even the funeral arrangements produced much hilarity—determined to go for a reasonably priced coffin, the aunts and uncles also negotiated to have it returned to us for reuse once they realized that the undertaker would do his own recycling by cremating the body without the coffin. The family was having its own version of a return with a difference, replaying the memory of Grandfather's funeral, a very perfunctory and quick one without any real rituals for open grieving. Although I had been in college not far away, no one even encouraged me to attend. This time the body would come back to the house the night before the funeral and then be carried through the meadow, on the same path walked by my aunts for their weddings, to the Catholic church on the other side of the road, built on land donated by Grandmother and Grandfather. The church was about to move to a bigger building on the hill in town, and this would in all likelihood be the last funeral held in the modest wood-frame building.

I had never seen an open coffin. It seemed right for her to be there in the book-lined study where my grandfather had done his writing and where we all gathered on so many evenings over the years. As the solemn undertakers brought in the coffin, we laughed and joked. The kids milled around in fascinated curiosity. Others decided they couldn't handle seeing the body. For me, she was there, present. I had been so sad to have missed the moment of her death, but this was a way of getting to make a final visit. And she was presiding over this family gathering—the house and her body went a long way toward making up for the absence of her activity and voice and mind. The candle that she kept by her bedside to be lit when Grandfather returned was next to her. We stayed up for an all-night vigil.

Still quite manic, I made the most of the opportunity to socialize with the family. I was able to keep pace with my uncle, the great talker of the bunch, with whom I had a long session in the middle of the night during the vigil. I played with my younger cousins and nephews in the familiar activities of summer visits: croquet on the lawn, water games with the sprinklers, the walk across the bridge to the Ideal grocery, swimming at Elk Falls. I'm older than all of my cousins by many years, and I loved that some of them were now old enough to be peers and to talk about family history and dynamics. The extended family network could mute the sometimes more vexed connections with my immediate family.

In the midst of all these overlapping relationships and layers of history, I felt powerful love—both my love for them and theirs for me. I could also feel very poignantly how much I had lost by living so far away and visiting so infrequently. Overwhelmed by that loss the summer before, I now felt capable of picking up where I'd left off, being part of the big extended family. Even mania didn't seem out of place here among all the talking—it just allowed me to go with the flow.

I was so wrought up that the details of the funeral itself are rather fuzzy. But I know I got up and told the story of watching the eclipse of the moon with Grandmother the year before. Even though it caused me to ramble some, a manic boldness carried me forward, and I'm glad that I made a public statement about the importance of my family and my history. Amid the hilarity and the sense of closeness was also a real and palpable grief about Grandmother's death. I could feel it enough to weep effortlessly, connected anew to that sense of the sacred that had been so powerful all spring.

It was the beginning of a new sense of attachment; if I made the effort to visit regularly, I could feel a part of this world. It was not gone forever. It would be a long time before I made it back to Campbell River itself, but I knew that even with Grandmother gone it would still be necessary to make the trip.

THE *VILLAGE VOICE*

In that spring of mania, I made it into the *Village Voice* twice. I was lunching with a friend at Jerry's, a Soho restaurant that was a casual hangout spot not only for me and my friends but for many of the neighborhood's more stellar residents, and we realized that Sandra Bernhard was in the booth behind us. As we were leaving, I was seized with the need to approach her, so I walked back to her table, where, as it turns out, she was being interviewed. I had just been reading the latest issue of *Vanity Fair* with Madonna featured on the cover as part of a glamorous pictorial spread by Steven Meisel, and I was disappointed that in the accompanying story she was so coy about the rumors that she and Sandra were having an affair. As politely as I could, I interrupted the conversation to ask if she could please ask Madonna to talk more honestly about their friendship.

In response to my request, Sandra was noncommittal, explaining that she wasn't really in touch with her famous friend. My m.o. with celebrity encounters is to make a snappy point and a hasty exit in order to minimize the imposition, so I left it at that. But I was satisfied that I had had my moment and that I would have a good anecdote.

A friend who shared my Madonna and Bernhard fandom in this peak year for celebrity lesbian chic dryly announced my appearance in the story as though it were not even really a surprise. It turns out that Sandra was being interviewed by Michael Musto, the *Voice*'s queer gossip columnist, whom I unfortunately didn't recognize. I had showed up when Musto was in the midst of pressing her on her reluctance to be a dyke icon. This was the beginning of Sandra's resistance to having to be a celebrity lesbian and her often acerbic response to anyone daring to suggest that she should be. It was also later revealed that her relationship with Madonna had soured by then.

In retrospect, I find it rather amazing that she wasn't openly rude to me. I caught her by surprise with my somewhat unusual entrée and a self-confidence that could not be easily refused. Musto referred to me in his column as a "très serious woman" and used my intervention to raise the issue of lesbian visibility with Sandra. I was delighted to have been of help to him, however unwittingly, and it confirmed my sense that my social vision as a manic person was not entirely off target.

Alas, my second appearance in the *Voice*, only a short time later, was somewhat less flattering. I had attended a Dia Foundation conference about critical fiction, and, disturbed by what seemed like the overly chic version of multiculturalism on display, I framed a question to the writers on one of the panels, including Michelle Cliff and Arturo Islas, about how they understood their place in New York, in Soho, at Dia, gathered there to be put on display for the art world. Much to my surprise, even now, some people in the audience hissed. I didn't understand then that it can be hard to make a successful critical intervention unless you carry a great deal of authority. I was bold enough to feel suddenly entitled within a world where I had doubted my place. The force of breaking through a sense of limitation and fear was extremely violent, and the resulting energy was received as aggression directed at others rather than an invitation to discussion.

I was very disturbed by the vehemence of the response, though, and I wonder what made the question so threatening to people. Part of it was the demon Prozac, which made me think my ideas were right and necessary. The next day some total stranger, not unsympathetically, asked me if I was a Marxist—as though my question was an expression of political orthodoxy. And I received some vindication from Jessica Hagedorn, who on another panel said that she thought the "Canadian woman" (one of the ways I had situated myself in relation to the New York art world's ambitions to multiculturalism) had made perfect sense.

A couple of weeks later, another friend called, also with a wry tone, to say "You're in the *Village Voice* again." The "Serious Woman" turned into the "Canadian Stalinist" in Stacey D'Erasmo's report on the conference, and she had used me as a kind of alter ego to articulate her own ambivalence about the proceedings. That my intervention was so notable that it constituted an event to be reported on was nonetheless a surprise to me both then and now.

These two events, and especially the flamboyant stories and names attached to them, stand as signs of the power of mania, including my own. Even as those of an unknown person, my thoughts were worthy of public attention, and I had the power to generate media coverage. I think these stories revealed an important truth and allowed me to see both then and now that I was significant. Although it's not the only way to do so, Prozac can get rid of the fear and the self-consciousness that keep people from being their biggest selves. I have become committed to getting there without drugs, but I do think those drug-enhanced moments were instructive of how big an impact I could have in the world. My mania cut straight to the heart of the matter, and I remain grateful for its vision.

ACTING UP

Was it mania or was it just another coming-out story? That spring and summer were marked by the intersection of my own history with a very fertile moment in queer culture—indeed even calling it "queer" was a breakthrough. The activist groups ACT UP and Queer Nation and the artist collectives associated with them, such as DIVA-TV and GANG, the lesbian club nights Girl Bar and Clit Club, cultural events such as the New Festival, Madonna fandom, and more—there was a lot of action both cultural and political, and my mood was undoubtedly boosted by the collective energy at bars, meetings, and demonstrations. Gay Pride 1990 I marched with ACT UP, wearing a bright pink Jackie O–style vintage dress. Before the march even started I got separated from the friend who was with me, but I didn't care because I was surrounded by thousands of queers. At numerous points along the way, we laid ourselves down on Fifth Avenue as part of an AIDS activist die-in. It was the year of the "I Hate Straights" manifesto, a document that inaugurated the group Queer Nation and spawned considerable controversy about queer politics. I ran into old friends and lovers on lower Fifth Avenue, making contact with moments in my past while striding into the future. After resting some in the evening, I set out for a night of partying— failing to meet up with friends at the Palladium, I found myself very very late at an event hosted by Girl Bar in a space on First Avenue whose name at the time was Cave Canem. In the basement, there are the remnants of a bathhouse, and on this night the tiled bath that was usually a lounge area was filled with water. Naked women were dancing in it, and leather dykes had taken over the dance floor nearby. It was a marvelous spectacle—the sign of a new era. I've seen many like it since then but this one remains a highlight in my experience of an ever-evolving lesbian nightlife and club culture.

I never felt alone because I was surrounded by community in lesbian spaces. I might be more self-conscious now—we're not all instant friends just because we're lesbians—but I don't think that's necessarily a more enlightened attitude. Girl Bar got dumped from the First Avenue space, as so often happens with lesbian nights, but next landed at the Pyramid, where I went almost every week that summer. At the end of the summer, Clit Club began; I had to leave town just before the debut event, but I was there for the cultural crucible out of which it emerged.

Coming out in the nightclubs is a familiar story, one that in my case had begun at Ithaca's Common Ground. Access to dancing and nightlife gives you access to a collective community and an experience of the body that is erotic even if you're not having sex. It's also a great outlet for the pent-up energy that some would call mania.

In 1990, AIDS activist culture gave rise to new queer club cultures. I went to Queer Nation meetings and joined discussions that were frequently contentious, finally fearless about speaking out in those huge meetings in the community center. Although the most glamorous girls seemed to be elsewhere, I went to ACT UP's women's caucus meetings in order to meet people and work on projects. I went to a party somewhere over in the far East Village sponsored by the visual collective GANG to celebrate their cap emblazoned with word "DYKE," one of many projects aimed at lesbian visibility. I presented DIVA-TV's videos *Target City Hall* and *Stop the Church* at the Marxist Literary Group meetings. My involvement in New York's activism during the limited period of a summer was somewhat peripheral, but the year before, in another burst of energy, I had been very involved with Austin's ACT UP group. Queer activism gave me a culture that shaped me as much as having sex with girls.

It was also a summer about being in New York City, where queer cultures have always overlapped with bohemian ones. I was living right in the middle of everything on MacDougal Street. I wrote by day and played by night, spending the afternoons going to galleries and window-shopping as respite from writing. Some twenty years later, it's a routine I still adore. Although queer activism has encountered challenges in sustaining an agenda other than gay marriage, and queer culture's capital and visibility often leave the most interesting people on the fringes, I'm still here, and still in love with both New York and lesbianism. My desire was literally in the right place during that manic summer—I had a sense that I could do anything, including becoming part of a queer cultural life in New York City.

The Return (1990–1991)

THE DEADLINE

At the end of the emotional whirlpool of my fellowship year and my manic summer in New York City, I had to return to Austin to resume my teaching job. Within the month, I plunged back into a state of despair that seemed as bad as the one the year before. My descent might be explained by the fact that upon realizing that Prozac was speeding me up too much, I stopped taking it, tapering off slowly but unmonitored by a doctor. But I was also no more settled in Austin than I'd ever been, and after having been gone for over a year, I had to build my community there all over again. My closest colleague had left for another job, and what meaningful connections I did have seemed fragile.

My looming book deadline should also not be underestimated as a cause for what felt like both heightened anxiety and a state of frozen arrest, the two extremes of panic. I called my editor when I got back to Texas and we agreed that I would turn in the manuscript by October 15. I wrote the date on a Post-it and stuck it on the refrigerator to remind me that things might change after that. Oddly enough, my inability to think worked to my advantage. Unable to discern whether or not the book was done, I simply did what I could and sent the manuscript off by the deadline.

Within about a month, I got back a reader's report asking for some minimal clarifications, and, at the editor's request, I wrote a response. The result was a final book contract, one of the most important milestones in an academic career, and certainly cause for celebration—especially when it comes in your fourth year of teaching and hence well in advance of the review for tenure. But I couldn't feel it; the good news made no impact on an unrelenting sense of dread that now had no particular end in sight. If I was back where I had been a year ago, how was I going to find a way out? Whatever relief had come in the spring was meaningless now that I was returned to a daily routine in which every task was flattened to the same degree of overwhelming difficulty. I went through the motions—I even went to the next Gay and Lesbian Studies Conference at Harvard, which was bigger and even more glamorous than the previous one, and I gave the paper on Madonna, race, and voguing that I'd been so excited about when I wrote the proposal in the summer—but I couldn't feel anything.

THE SECOND DEPRESSION

I have a theory that depression is much worse the second time around because it's so disappointing to have it return. Suddenly, whatever respite you had, whether manic or peaceful or just mercifully uneventful, seems meaningless because it can all be snatched away so emphatically. After you've been through it once before, the feelings of dread, despair, and hopelessness settle in all too rapidly because they're now attached not only to future prospects but to the state of being depressed, which, as you know all too well, can stretch on and on indefinitely and now looks very probably to be a fact of life, an endless cycle. As soon as the shadow of anxiety begins to fall over you, you start to panic, and the panic brings you down fast—it wakes you bolt upright in the morning, makes you sweat, leaves you unable to think about anything else. You're caught in the downward spiral of feeling bad about feeling bad. Whatever you thought you might have learned about staying out of this trouble has clearly proven inadequate, so now what are you going to do? And if you come up with a plan (doubtful, but let's try to imagine for a moment that it might be possible), how are you even going to begin to execute it when depression's stealth destroys your agency?

FISH DINNER

That fall my friend John was sick with various AIDS-related illnesses. He was at home but he was in bed all the time and his boyfriend Skip was taking care of him. I was feeling so bad that I couldn't really do anything to help them, but I gradually fell into a pattern of going over there about once a week to have dinner and spend the evening. Skip liked to orchestrate people, and they often objected to his controlling behavior, but in my state of depression-induced passivity, I didn't care—and he liked the fact that I was totally malleable. He would often make fish for dinner, I think because it was something John could eat. He'd sauté very thin ruby trout filets quickly in some butter, and serve them with potatoes and green vegetables. We'd watch TV or chat, and John would get out of bed to smoke cigarettes by the kitchen door. He and Skip would sometimes squabble, and I would listen mutely.

I felt bad about not being able to participate more actively—I never cooked, I never brought anything over, and I never had ideas about how to make things better for John. But those nights remain memorable because they felt comfortable and gave me something to do. We were company for each other, which was its own kind of gift. All I had to do was be there—there was no additional pressure to entertain or to say the right thing—it was company in its most basic form, the presence of another person. In addition to the comfort of their lack of demands, I received the vision of Johnny's struggle with both life and death. Eventually he really didn't care to be fighting anymore—as the fall wore on, he lost more and more energy and enthusiasm, although he remained sweet and patient. He couldn't eat; he couldn't get comfortable; he had no real prospects of getting any better. It was Skip's will that kept him going—his careful way of keeping the bedroom supplied with tuberoses, buying new music, and arranging visits and activities.

I coasted vicariously in the slipstream of that determination, taking advantage of the energy directed at keeping a dying man alive. Inwardly, I felt that I was less alive than they were. Their crisis had a tangible shape that seemed to give them a power and agency that I lacked. I felt goaded and shamed by the thought that depression seemed worse than dying. But it also provided a perverse shred of hope because I knew this wasn't really true, in which case the sense of despair that made it seem so might be vanquished.

YOGA

I started doing yoga at a class at the Y. It met twice a week, taught by a big soft-spoken woman with a nurturing manner. The atmosphere was very unpretentious—lots of different kinds of people, many of them not very experienced in bodywork, were crowded into a big cinder-block room. The new yoga boom had just barely begun, and the glamorous studios full of beautiful people had not yet arrived in Austin.

I gave myself over to the experience; during that ninety-minute class, twice a week, I didn't need to think about anything else except following instructions. The positions were easy, taking me back to the memory of the many dance classes I had taken over the years, as well as some yoga I had learned as a teenager in the 1970s, when it was also being popularized. Sometimes we worked in partners, but mostly I could just be inside my body—a concept I had been inclined to dismiss as a cliché but was now coming to understand. Going to class became a ritual, and I would return home ready to work again, feeling completely different inside.

Bodywork was crucial to my well-being but I had let it drop when I came to Texas. I grew up taking dance classes of all kinds, starting with ballet when I was five or six, and although I had some less active periods in high school and college, during graduate school I was taking classes almost every day. My secret world of dance classes offered an alternative to the intellectual work of reading books and talking and writing papers. I loved the daily routines of working each part of the body, stretching, repeating exercises, and learning little pieces of choreography that moved me through space in new ways.

In Austin, I had too little time and felt too old in the dance classes I tried, where I was shocked to discover that I was so tense I couldn't do the exercises without fearing I would hurt myself. Movement that had once been an intuitive process that required no thought now became a struggle. Yoga was much kinder—it didn't induce the self-deprecating perfectionism that dance can foster, and yet it also felt connected to that lifetime of bodily experience. It legitimated my earlier history as a dancer as a quest for embodied knowledge, not a frivolous or damaging pursuit of an idealized femininity. Like swimming, it has now become a permanent fixture in my life and one of my most important tools for using my body to tend to mind and spirit.

THE MEMORIAL

I was making my way through even the smallest daily obligations with tremendous difficulty, and yet somehow I had agreed to take on the task of organizing my friend Johnny's memorial service when he died. How could I say no to this request? It was an honor to be asked, and after spending so much time with him and Skip that winter, I knew it was a responsibility I couldn't refuse. And saying no would have required more agency than I had. In that particular time of AIDS, people were planning their memorials in advance, and although Johnny wasn't very specific about details, he had an intuitive vision and his one major request was that the event be based on the four elements. As usual, Skip was orchestrating behind the scenes, and at his urging, I organized a meeting at my house, relying on my artist friends to come up with the ideas, while I patiently listened and took notes.

Johnny died at home later that week. Skip laid his naked body out under a sheet in the living room, which he emptied of everything else, as though crafting a stage set or a performance installation. Johnny's open eyes were covered with coins, and the smell of rosemary branches, which surrounded his body, filled the air. As he had been in life, Johnny was beautiful, but now heartbreakingly so as he lay there still. People gathered throughout the day to create yet another of the queer rituals prompted by AIDS.

The memorial a week later came together as a group effort for which I felt myself to be merely a passive conduit. We gathered in a beautiful spot by the river, just below the nature center where Skip had helped design and plant the gardens. It was a chilly afternoon but the sun was bright. In the first of many collaborations to come, my friend Kay was my fellow emcee, standing alongside me. She led the way, devising a structure that incorporated each of the elements—we poured water, we picked up earth, we lit candles that combined fire and air. The rituals appealed to me, and I could tell that we were making something beautiful happen.

It got dark, and people were cold, but Kay and I pressed on, standing in the middle of the big circle. We invited people to tell stories, a memorial ritual that has become familiar to me over the years but was new then. I told the story of how I fell in love with Johnny's painting of the Virgen of Guadalupe before I even really knew what it meant and how it made it possible for me to understand that Texas could be home. Despite my sense of incapacity, it was a watershed moment for me in learning how to speak from the heart and to do so in the form of public testimony. The power of death and mourning managed to transcend the weight of my hopelessness in a way that life could not.

THE INSPIRATION

Some people might say that I was finally able to finish my book because I tried antidepressants again. In the winter, during the last phase of writing, I started to take imipramine, a first-generation antidepressant that was supposed to relieve anxiety without the manic effects Prozac had for me. The drugs no doubt played some role in my transformation back from the land of the walking dead, but I remain convinced that the change had much more to do with solving a serious intellectual block that had plagued the writing of the introduction and the conception for the book as a whole. In the end, it was my new colleague Lora Romero who made the difference and became one of my best friends in the process. (I name her because this section also serves as a memorial to Lora, who died by suicide in 1997 after her own struggle with depression.)

I talked to her about my introduction, and she offered to read my draft. She gave me great feedback and also lent me a copy of her article about *Uncle Tom's Cabin* to read. It was an incredibly lucid discussion of the implications of Foucault for reading domesticity in Stowe, which was analogous in lots of ways to sensation in the Victorian novel. In a brilliant conceptual move, she pointed out that Foucauldian readers who argued that there was no escaping power through resistance simply reproduced the punishment model that Foucault was displacing with the notion of discipline. Thus, she argued, domesticity could be a mode of resistance even if also a mode of power and domination. Reading this argument had a miraculous effect on my thinking for the introduction, for it meant that I could still keep my Foucauldian critique and introduce the possibility of sensationalism as a progressive force. I felt enabled by her elegant theoretical move in a way that replicated the argument itself, which was about the tension between feeling blocked and feeling enabled. I realized this impasse had been bothering me throughout, and suddenly I could see my way clear to what needed to be said in the introduction about the productive uses of sensational representation. I wasn't stupid; I had just been stuck on a difficult problem that I had now resolved.

I've never written with such passion or conviction. The skimpy introduction that I kept cutting in despair every time I had to turn in a manuscript now expanded to a robust size that seemed to have a natural structure. I had things I needed to say and I wasn't vague about how to articulate them. I was absolutely sure in a way I had never been at any point in the long process of writing the dissertation or the book. I even found a way to include a discussion of contemporary feminism and the AIDS crisis as part of my argument about the positive potential of sensationalism and emotional expression. This was the heart of the book coming through. There really was a solution to my problem, and it made my despair seem like it had an understandable cause. I am convinced that depression is like this—that there are real and possible solutions for the problems that ail us. There is nothing wrong with our biology or our intelligence; sometimes we are just stuck.

RETURN TO THE RIVER

After my Grandmother died, it was eight years before I went back to Campbell River again. In the interim, the house had been taken over by the British Columbia provincial government and was being run as a bed and breakfast and an education center for the environmental issues that my grandfather had promoted through his writing. Although it's a bit odd to see my family's house turned into a heritage property, it has meant that it is maintained as it was when my grandparents lived there and thus remains remarkably similar to the house I knew as a child.

I wondered if I was perhaps setting too much store in a place by cutting short precious time with relatives to visit. But the house and the land around it have been one constant in my otherwise geographically dispersed life. Returning there, I think about Proust and the bodily sensations of emotional memory, all the more so because Grandmother's three-volume Pléaide edition, which now sits on my bookshelves in Austin, was among the books on the shelves in the study that fascinated me as a child. One summer, I read Proust while lying on the lawn, putting her French edition alongside my English translation.

On my first morning, I went down to the river to what used to be our little beach by the apple orchard upstream from the lawn in front of the house and past the rocky outcropping we call the dam. It was so overgrown that it was almost unrecognizable, all the more so because in the fall the river is much higher than its more familiar summer level. The fallen tree we used to climb on over the river was gone; the sand for making miniature houses on the rocks was underwater; the paths and fences in the fields had been rearranged; the wooden boat that had been a parade float we made to represent our school, Discovery Passage, was finally almost completely disintegrated after thirty years. (One of my grandfather's books was about Captain Vancouver's famous voyage through the waters that separate Vancouver Island from the mainland, and we were thrilled to bring the boat to his house when my sister miraculously won it in a raffle.) Despite the changes, everything was still deeply familiar and evocative of the past.

On one of my nights there, I spent time in the study by myself. It's a beloved space, a dream version of a writer's studio with the desk in the corner facing onto a large picture window with a view of the river, and the fireplace and large wooden coffee table (that he built himself) around which people could gather. But, unless there were a lot of other people staying in the house, we didn't go in there much after Grandfather died. There were many years in which the life of the house was largely in the kitchen, where Grandmother read, worked, and entertained. But being alone with the books that line every wall of the study is just as powerful as being there with lots of people, and the memory of it as a social center keeps it alive and full.

Every corner of the bedrooms upstairs was also charged with memories. The green and violet room at the front of the house, where as children we slept in the twin beds that belonged to my mother and her sister. The smaller middle room that was my uncle's, where my grandmother and I watched the eclipse. And the blue guest room overlooking the river, where my sister and I stayed when we were old enough to visit on our own during the summers. The yellow down comforters were gone, but it still felt the same lying in bed listening to the sound of the river below.

The November days were rainy and dark. I'd forgotten how short the days can get this far north, and I raced against an encroaching sunset to make my outings. The constant rain was not really an obstacle, though, because it is so much a part of the landscape. The wetness added to the appeal of both ocean and river—the seaweed and driftwood of Miracle Beach and the evergreens, waterfalls, and clay walls on the path at Elk Falls. Even though the land is vulnerable, encroached upon by industry and development, it remains not just beautiful but palpably sacred. Even white people sense the need to respect nature in this place, where it's hard not to notice the indigenous presence.

My grandfather's first book, *Silver*, was about the life cycle of a salmon, and he also wrote a book called *Return to the River* about the migration of the Chinook between river and sea. After his death, friends and colleagues formed the Kingfisher Creek Society to reconnect a stream on his land to the river so that salmon could reach it to spawn. The creek provides a beautiful model for sustainable development and community involvement with a natural microcosm. A combination of English country gentleman in the tradition of Izaak Walton and William Wordsworth and progressive New World settler, my grandfather believed that environmental politics could develop from familiarity with one local stream or piece of land. As I toured the new creek with the caretaker from the house, I realized I'd never been in the area up behind the barn where the land had been cleared—even after so many years there were new places to be discovered. We saw several adult coho dead or dying. They were spotted with white and looked old and bedraggled. Slowly one flapped its tail, not really moving, having made its way home. In this era when so many salmon are unable to return to freshwater because of dams and contamination, it is a miraculous sight.

I, too, looked for home on the river. When I had returned almost a decade earlier, I was making a pilgrimage, seeking some form of enlightenment or grounding to stave off despair. I wanted to be able to fall back on a family intimacy that seemed to elude me. This time I wasn't really expecting it, and I was surprised by the new relationships with my much younger cousins, now becoming adults.

I sometimes jokingly call Campbell River "my ancestral home" to acknowledge the grandparents who provided a sense of stability and identity as well as the power and beauty of the land, even though I know it's not really their land to own or mine to inherit. Not so long ago this was indigenous land whose history long precedes my grandparents' arrival, and, although it's not the same thing as being returned, it's appropriate that it has now been given over to public use. This land that made me has a complicated history. It's also the scene of despair, the place where my father cracked up and that I left very abruptly, moving three times in a single year before landing far away in the flat and alien Great Lakes landscape of Toronto. I don't want to naturalize or romanticize home, especially since I consider dislocation to have been a productive force in shaping me. I have found other ways of being at home or in the body besides "going home," especially because I know there is not always a home to return to.

But I sometimes feel the need to touch the land of my childhood in order to remember myself to myself. I'm not recalling a lost paradise; I'm acknowledging the troubled history that led to my departure as part of figuring out what it means to go back. My own history of dislocation connects to the histories of immigration and displacement that affected my father as much as any biochemical imbalance. In this place, too, the settler colonialism (including that of my grandparents) that displaced the indigenous people is not hard to see because it has touched down so recently. I can also feel the ongoing presence of the Kwakwaka'wakw people who live in houses and reserve lands on the road between my grandparents' house and town and who were part of my community as a child. The skepticism about origins that I've learned in academia, especially from queer diaspora studies, is matched by my awareness of indigenous thinking about making a connection with the land. My "ancestral home" is the site of many histories, both happy and sad, both my own and those belonging to others.

MY HEART WAS IN THE RIGHT PLACE

I was not wrong to go back to the landscape of my childhood. It wasn't a futile or misguided quest because, even at my darkest and craziest moments, my intuition was quite literally headed in the right direction. The phrase that keeps coming to mind is "my heart was in the right place." Although it's a clichéd way to describe good but misplaced intentions, it also captures the way that you can sometimes be doing the right thing even when your efforts are feeble or bumbling. If the dead metaphor is further revivified, it's a phrase that presumes that feelings have a corporeal location (however incorrectly named as the heart) and thus can be in the right (or wrong) place. It thus articulates my efforts to transform a psychic quest into a physical or geographic one in search of some location or landscape that would provide an answer.

Naïve though it might be, the phrase also expresses an attunement to knowledge that doesn't come from the mind. I've risked sentimentality and the vulnerability of self-exposure here in the face of both theoretical critiques of naïve feeling and aesthetic critiques of bad ways of writing it. I can't help being drawn to, for example, another well-worn metaphor—that of the salmon returning to the river. After all, I come by that image honestly, since my grandfather wrote books, as well as a poem, about "river-born fugitives." In borrowing an image that is central to the indigenous cultures of the Pacific Northwest, was he appropriating Native cultures or acknowledging them? Does the salmon's return to the river offer too easy an image of resolution or undercut it, since the fish makes the stubborn journey upstream not just to reproduce but to die? My habits of mind make me incessantly question the insights of feeling and intuition. I continue to unpack phrases like "my heart was in the right place" and "return to the river" just as I hold on to the images I've also collected in order to mull over feelings attached to them—the swan with an arm instead of a wing, an altar of mountain rocks, a Texas painting of the Virgen of Guadalupe, a little girl looking at a salmon.

As is often the case with photographs that have sentimental value, I have no memory of the moment recorded in the picture of me and my Dad on the lawn in Campbell River, but I've grown attached to it over the years. The girl encircled in her father's protective embrace could be an image of lost or longed for intimacy, a counterpart to the image of himself being held by his mother that Roland Barthes uses for his theories about feeling photography. But there's something so odd about the presence of the fish that is as big as the little girl, who recoils slightly even at the same time as she is inspecting it with curiosity. And the photograph's sentimental value lies as much in the place as the people—it was taken on the lawn in Campbell River against a backdrop of the same hedges and trees separating lawn and field, the domestic and the wild, that were the scene of the eclipse I watched with my grandmother. I like the blown-out white space of the sky, which gives the photograph a ghostly quality and adds to its power as a paper image, not a document of an actual moment or place.

When I'm swimming laps in the pool, I'm just moving back and forth without thinking about where I'm headed. I've been trying to give up worrying about whether I'm having too much feeling or too little, the right kind of feelings or the wrong ones, so that I can just follow where they lead. In crafting a life that moves with and through despair like swimming laps in a pool, I am still learning to trust the knowledge that comes from salmon, river, tree, and heart.

Reflections

Memoir as Public Feelings Research Method

MIXED FEELINGS (AGAIN)

As enabling as the process of writing it has been, I've had mixed feelings about the decision to publish "The Depression Journals," and my uneasiness has taken a number of predictable forms: that the writing is not good enough, that even if the writing process was useful the product need not be published, that telling this story makes me embarrassingly vulnerable, that sharing my experience (including my ambivalence) constitutes an unseemly flaunting. Given how frequently memoir is disparaged as easy or self-indulgent, I've been surprised (in yet another example of the value of practice for theory) by how difficult it is go public.

It is also with some chagrin that I have watched myself fall into the familiar pattern of trying to evaluate memoir and its accompanying politics of feeling. While there is much in its history and success to be critiqued, I have to keep reminding myself not to make blanket claims about the genre, especially since it circulates in so many different forums, from mainstream to progressive. To dismiss or champion memoir in some monolithic way seems misguided given its multiple possibilities and especially its ability to stage interventions within particular public discourses.[1]

Although up until the last drafts of the book, I was not sure if "The Depression Journals" would remain, the vitality of memoir within minoritarian cultures (which constitute a very different point of reference than the memoirs debated in the mainstream public sphere) remained a significant counterweight to my fear of exposure.[2] Memoir has been an undeniable force in queer subcultures, where it has been an entry point into the literary public sphere for working-class writers, the backbone of solo performance, and a mainstay for small presses.[3] The AIDS memoir, which has been crucial in depathologizing the HIV survivor, offers a queer take on personal narratives about illness and disability that can provide alternatives to medical discourse by giving agency to the patient.[4] Oral history's populist inclinations have also been a generative inspiration for me, as is testimony's role in trauma histories, including debates about the inadequate or sketchy archive of slavery and about whether the subaltern can speak.[5]

Moreover, especially important in my case is the example of a highly regarded generation of feminists that includes Nancy Miller, Marianne Hirsch, Jane Tompkins, Jane Gallop, Cathy Davidson, and Eve Sedgwick, among many others, who have forged new critical paths using their own experiences as the foundation for scholarly projects.[6] Although academics versed in theory have frequently critiqued memoir, theoretical critique has also inspired an outpouring of academic memoir. Exemplifying deconstructive principles, academic memoir can expose the material conditions and subject positions that underlie intellectual production. It has been a forum for scholars whose careers and scholarship have been shaped by identity politics to make visible their institutional projects and their efforts to establish new fields of inquiry. Indeed, given how widespread the use of memoir is among this generation of feminists, it's surprising that debate continues about its value as a critical mode.[7]

Although the turn to memoir by feminist academics was a significant catalyst, much of "The Depression Journals" was also written under the influence of the early 1990s zine culture associated with the riotgrrrl movement and spoken word forums like Sister Spit, which sparked a return to confessional forms of feminism that I had been taught to view with suspicion while in graduate school in the 1980s.[8] Although somewhat late to the trend, I thoroughly enjoyed making two issues of a zine called *Topical Treatments* with my girlfriend Gretchen Phillips in 1996 and 1997. In the wake of the ease and pleasure of writing short pieces about shopping, fashion, art, and lesbian culture, I started writing the first sections of "The Depression Journals" without any real sense of what their future might be. I returned to them after I finished *An Archive of Feelings*, continuing to write more episodes and pondering their potential as a public essay, and eventually they found their way into this book's project, the initial goal of which was to write an extended critical essay, not a memoir.

Reflecting on that point of origin now, I am struck by the extent to which both the writing and the publication of "The Depression Journals" constitute an ongoing response to the complex legacies of 1970s feminisms. It took a younger generation of feminists who refused to be intimidated by the critiques of confessional discourse that I had internalized when I was their age to bolster my return to the promise of the personal as the political. Although schooled to be wary of the confessional (indeed, *Mixed Feelings*, the book whose writing is the subject of my memoir, is all about that ambivalence), I maintained an attachment to the culture of consciousness-raising and an investment in how the expression of emotion can have collective and public impact.

WRITING AS CREATIVE PRACTICE

The thematic emphasis of "The Depression Journals" on transformative daily habit as an antidote to depression was exemplified by the process of writing it. Writing personal narrative was an experiment in trying a new practice, one that reflected my interest in the ordinary by integrating writing into daily life. Not only was I hoping to access a more personal voice that would then feed into my scholarly projects, but the growing intensity of my workload in the years following tenure, which turned out to offer far less freedom than I'd been led to expect, made me desperate for time to write. Inspired by the short forms of the zine, I wrote in little spurts of forty-five minutes during periods when I didn't have time to do more sustained forms of writing. I was resisting the protracted temporality of academic scholarship, where interruptions for teaching, meetings, and the rest of life mean that books often take ten years to finish and can stall out along the way.

The short pieces of the finished product also reflect a resistance to the scholarly injunction to analyze and connect in order to make a coherent whole. The segments in the memoir are thus semi-autonomous and differ from the more continuous form of the academic essay, with its careful transitions. Most of the pieces were generated by using specific objects, images, or locations as prompts, inspired by the process-based approach to writing promoted by Nathalie Goldberg, Anne Lamott, and others, who often draw on Buddhism and other spiritual traditions in their emphasis on writing as attention to a material present.[9] My writing has also been informed by the practice of solo performance artists such as Deb Margolin, Carmelita Tropicana, Holly Hughes, the Five Lesbian Brothers, and Sharon Bridgforth, all of whom have led workshops I have had the good fortune to attend.[10] Many of these artists use writing prompts and forms of automatic writing that have their origins in surrealism and other modernist practices that seek to circumvent the conscious mind in order to generate material from the places of feeling, including the body.

Although such practices and communities often operate outside the academy or in locations where art is segregated from scholarship, there are significant crossovers. I was, for example, also inspired along the way by Michael Taussig's account of modular writing—short pieces that can be pulled apart and stuck together in different ways.[11] Taussig's writing style and structure draw from Benjamin and other modernists who experimented with montage and forms of writerly logic that are not linear. (Even though I eventually decided that my short sections fit best together chronologically, I did not write them that way.)

My style is ultimately very spare. It was suggested to me at one point that this might be the hypotactic style of a depressive who doesn't have much to say. I also wondered if I was a bad writer who lacked the finesse of the queer aesthetes or aspiring poets and novelists who become literary critics. But given that one aim of this project was to legitimate process-based writing whose rough edges might enable fresh thinking to emerge, I felt in the end that I should accept my style as it is.

Literary polish is thus ultimately less important than making a case for the value of writing that is open-ended and process-based. This way of working can be particularly useful for those whose usual idioms and practices are scholarly because such writing can make speculative and personal claims rather than requiring the validation of research. It produces what Audre Lorde describes as forms of truth that are felt rather than proven by evidence, the result of "disciplined attention to the true meaning of 'it feels right to me.'"[12] Process-based writing also enables forms of creativity that transform mental labor into manual labor; as long as the pen keeps moving across the page (or the fingers keep moving on the keyboard), thinking is happening.[13] This way of working can provide an important pushback against the tremendous pressure to acquire "discipline" in academia, nowhere stronger than in the internalized voices that tell us we are stupid or that keep us from daring to dream in bigger ways about our ideas. For these reasons, writing in the genre of memoir has not only rescued me from being stuck, blocked, or "depressed" (and not by preventing it but by making it possible to move through it), it has also been enabling for my life as a scholar.

MEMOIR AS RESEARCH METHOD

As both a writing process and a laboratory for ideas, "The Depression Journals" became a resource for the essay that follows. I came to think of my practice of memoir as a research method, as a way of addressing debates about memoir in both academia and the public sphere and about the medical model of depression that dominates the expansive subgenre of depression memoirs. While I could have written a critical essay that analyzed the genre, the results seemed rather predictable (a combination of critique and endorsement that would be another variant on Sedgwick's "kinda subversive, kinda hegemonic").[14] Although the book includes some discussion of the huge subgenre of depression memoirs, my turn to practice exemplifies the activist principle of presenting criticism in the form of a productive or alternative suggestion. It seemed more interesting to enter the fray about memoir by actually writing one, in the reparative spirit of figuring out what memoir can do for public discourse rather than being exclusively concerned with critiquing where it fails.

"The Depression Journals" was initially prompted, as so many memoirs are, by the desire to tell a story that didn't seem to be represented despite the proliferation of depression discourse in the public sphere. It picks up where the mainstream Prozac memoirs leave off, giving me a chance to tell a story whose focus is not primarily medication and its effects. It's not that drugs are not present—I did take antidepressants during the two years that are chronicled—but they are not central to the story I wanted to tell. Those partial to a medical model might read my account as the story of how Prozac failed me, especially when administered without adequate supervision, and how the right medication set me on the path to a cure. (In the interest of full disclosure, I gradually weaned myself off imipramine after a year and have not taken antidepressants since.) But although the drugs may have played a significant role, I'm more interested in the changes I had to make to sustain their effects. For that reason, I also don't pursue in detail my early family history; although my father's manic-depression is crucial, I wanted to address its impact on the present, including my own strongly held convictions about the social causes of mental illness.

Instead the story is about daily life and about how anxiety and what gets called depression are ordinary feelings embedded in ordinary circumstances. I wanted to capture how depression feels—the everyday sensations that don't immediately connect to any larger diagnosis or explanatory framework, whether medical or social. The first section in particular focuses on the everyday life of depression, its minutiae and often boring effects. The temporality is ongoing, perhaps excruciatingly relentless, but also dull and chronic. In order to get at the felt experience of depression without using clinical labels, I tried as much as possible to avoid terms such as *depression* and *anxiety*, although the instances in which I didn't succeed in eliminating them are also telling about the challenges of finding vocabulary. Careful readers will note the presence of alternative terms such as the somewhat antiquated *despair*, a relative of early Christian *acedia*, which is taken up in the essay that follows, and *dread*, a word that has special meaning for me because it is used with some frequency by George Eliot and analyzed by Neil Hertz (in *George Eliot's Pulse*), both of whom were central to my dissertation. Another keyword is *respite*, which I use to describe moments of relief from despair aptly captured by the word's legal origins in the delay of a prison sentence. "The Depression Journals" implicitly argues for terminology and definitions that emerge from the practice of writing, which adds emotional and personal meanings to historical and scientific ones. Another value of memoir is that it avoids demographic generalizations in favor of detailed case histories, although the case history is a genre whose relation to scientific method is complex, since it can be used to complement statistical evidence (and clinical terms) as much as to displace or challenge them. Moreover, my version of the case history resists its tendencies toward the melodramatic and the sensational by seeking to represent feelings as ordinary or flat.[15]

"The Depression Journals" is also about the ordinary practices that helped me survive feelings of despair and even transform them or combat them. It provides some suggestions for daily living, but in the form of a story rather than the formulaic self-help genre, with its lists of things to do or generalizations from case histories. The daily routines of self-care and of moving the body—swimming, yoga, dinner with

friends, visits to the dentist, or just getting out of bed in the morning—
are modest forms of transformation, but my experience, and writing
about it, taught me that they are nonetheless meaningful. In its sometimes banal attention to detail, my writing chronicles a relation to self
and to the world that is established through the physicality of both
body and home as forms of sensory environment. Habit—the development of everyday routines, practices, and connections—became an important concept in the essay that follows but first made itself known in
my own bodily practices. The forms of "self-help" embedded in habits
are ordinary, not the stuff of heroic or instantaneous transformation,
and they can't simply be named in the abstract but instead must be integrated through the ongoing activity that forms a life story. But they are
also what constitutes hope and the antidote to despair and political depression.

As an account of depression as political, then, "The Depression Journals" doesn't suggest collectivity and political action as an alternative
"cure" in any simple way. (It also doesn't say much about love and romance because I wanted to focus on collective attachments rather than
the happy ending of the couple form. But love and attachment, especially in their queer forms, are fundamental to my story and should be
understood as necessary for transformation even if they can't always
ensure it.) It certainly chronicles the powerful influence of an explo-
sive moment in queer activism, one galvanized by the urgency of death
and mourning. But it also shows the interplay between militancy and
mourning that I later tracked in my work with AIDS activists. The memoir tries to be honest about the ways that activism can sometimes stall
out in the routines of daily life, rather than offering revolution as a
prescription for change. It depicts transformation as a slow and painstaking process, open-ended and marked by struggle, not by magic bullet
solutions or happy endings, even the happy ending of social justice that
many political critiques of therapeutic culture recommend. It suggests
that when asking big questions about what gives meaning to our lives,
or how art or politics can promote social justice or save the planet, ordinary routines can be a resource. The revolution and utopia are made
there, not in giant transformations or rescues.

The memoir also functions as a research method because it reveals
the places where feeling and lived experience collide with academic
training and critique. I have a feeling that this conflict is one of the

causes of political depression among academics and activists, and writing personal narrative encourages the hunches, intuitions, and feelings that intellectual analysis can restrict with a taboo-like force. For example, the role of ritual and the sacred, so frequently disparaged in academia, in my transformation ultimately led to my exploration of the "sacred everyday" of home and habit in the critical essay. Its somewhat inchoate or incipient appearance in "The Depression Journals" provided the basis for new forms of thinking and new concepts.

"The Depression Journals" also rubs up against critiques of "nostalgia for lost origins" within the fields of migration and diaspora studies. Schooled to question concepts of home and nation, I was surprised to discover the force within the narrative of the images of rivers and oceans and the trips to British Columbia. The psychogeography of going "home"—not just to the places named Campbell River, Vancouver Island, British Columbia, and Canada but to the distinctive landscape of that region—entails touching on or feeling (or, equally significantly, *not* feeling) longer histories of genocide and displacement. Although the presence of indigenous and migration histories in "The Depression Journals" is oblique, the critical essay that follows, including an extended chapter on depression, racism, and indigenous spiritualities, affords an opportunity to bring those histories more explicitly into view as a way of addressing the disjunctions between my white middle-class background and those histories. The obscurity of the connections between our own despair and the collective despair that is present in the places where we live adds to our confusion and (political) depression.

My narrative seemed to be telling me that a connection to where you are from, especially if it's been denied to you, is crucial; if anything, naturalization covers over the hard process of making home somewhere on the planet. One value of memoir, although it is not exclusive to it, is to track the life of the sensate being in the world, including its material attachments to environment and geography and to see *how capitalism feels* or *how diaspora feels* without screening out nostalgia or sentiment or melancholy. Rather than worry that I shouldn't feel attached to my grandparents' land or the Vancouver Island psychogeographies that shaped me, I wanted to explore the nature of that attachment, which includes histories of separation and loss, both my own and those of colonization. While, from the perspective of diaspora theory, the desire to find home might be as naïve or problematic as recommending drugs to cure depression, the persistence of that impulse on a daily basis is important for the politics of feeling, as is the question of how to claim an emotional attachment to home and land without inciting violent nationalisms or separatisms. It is in the spirit of Public Feelings not to tell people what to feel or to judge how they feel, but instead to find better ways to describe the complexity of what they are feeling.

Personal narrative can be a forum for the places where ordinary feelings and abstract thinking don't line up. The impasses of depression and writer's block can live in those interstices, and alternative forms of writing can spring them loose as foundations for innovative thought. The value of bodily and creative practice and of politics, ritual, and home is sometimes merely an incipient insight in "The Depression Journals" because the knowledge they represent was embedded within experiences of anxiety, inertia, and despair. Unbeknownst to me, I was sometimes healing myself by just waiting and doing nothing, or through what seemed like ordinary or insignificant activities—going swimming, doing yoga, getting a cat, visiting a sick friend. Writing about them became a first step toward trying to unpack that fledgling knowledge, often through descriptions of bodily states and sensations rather than reflections on their meanings. The essay that follows picks up on these insights, providing the more sustained analysis that builds on them, but I wanted to include the memoir as a record of the process by which I got there.

[handwritten margin note: fledging knowledge about recovery]

Part II

A PUBLIC FEELINGS PROJECT

(A Speculative Essay)

Writing Depression

Acedia, History, and Medical Models

Describing the desert monk who "begins to forget the object of his profession, which is nothing but meditation and contemplation of the divine purity which excels in all things, and which can only be gained by silence and continually remaining in the cell, and by meditation," the fourth-century Christian John Cassian considers how the rigors and isolation of the ascetic life can lead to spiritual crisis.[1] In *De Institutis Coenobiorum*, a set of guidelines for collective monastic life, Cassian outlines the "faults" or "bad thoughts" (which will eventually serve as the foundation for conceptions of the seven deadly sins) that can impede the ascetic. One of these is *acedia*, or "carelessness," an antecedent to later conceptions of sloth, which is also described as "weariness or distress of heart" (*taedium sive anxietatem cordis*, I).[2]

Although it is a form of spiritual crisis, acedia has significant physical manifestations, which Cassian describes in vivid detail: "When this has taken possession of some unhappy soul, it produces dislike of the place [*horrorem loci*], disgust with the cell [*fastidium cellae*], and disdain [*aspernationem*] and contempt [*contemptum*] of the brethren who dwell with him or at a little distance, as if they were careless [*negligentium*] or unspiritual [*minus spiritalium*]. It also makes the man lazy and sluggish [*desidem et inertem*] about all manner of work which has to be done within the enclosure of his dormitory" (II). Acedia gives rise to varied and even contradictory responses that complicate its popular representation as sluggish inertia. As might be expected, it produces the carelessness and desire to do nothing or to "sink into slumber" (III) that is the literal version of the more spiritual "soul that sleeps" [*dormitat anima*] (IV) also mentioned by Cassian. But acedia is characterized not just by lack of affect but by intense feelings—disgust (*horrerum*), dislike (*fastidium*), and disdain (*aspernationem*)—that lead to a powerful urge toward movement or flight, which can be so strong that the solitary "fancies he will never be well while he stays in that place unless he leaves his cell (in which he is sure to die if he stops in it any longer) and takes himself off from thence as quickly as possible" (II). Manifesting the restlessness and desperation that suggest why acedia has been called the "noonday demon," the monk suffering from this affliction "often goes out of his cell, and frequently gazes up at the sun, as if it was too slow in setting, and so a kind of unreasonable confusion of mind takes possession of him like some foul darkness, and makes him idle and useless for every spiritual work, so that he imagines no cure for so terrible an attack can be found in anything except visiting some one of the brethren, or in the solace of sleep alone" (II). The longing to escape is not just spatial but temporal; the monk's desire for the sun to move more quickly in the sky, for the day to be over and for the relief of sleep to arrive, reveals an impatience with things as they are and a desire to be not only in a different place but a different time. Activity and inactivity—restlessness and sleep—are not opposed but are both forms of escape for body and mind, and the monk can be distracted from the solitary contemplation of God as much by doing good deeds for others as by "staying uselessly [*infructuose*] and with no profit [*sine ullo profectu*] in his cell" (II). Drawn out from the monastery to become "restless and a wanderer," the "mind of an idler" is "little by little ensnared by dangerous occupations, so that, just as if it were bound up in the coils of a serpent, it can never disentangle itself again and return to the perfection of its former profession" (VI). The image of the serpent adds to representations of acedia and other "bad thoughts" as demons or external beings who can tempt the ascetic away from the spiritual path toward more worldly concerns.

The affliction that strikes fourth-century monks in the desert who want to forsake the contemplative life in favor of either sleeping or running away might seem an unlikely candidate for a model of contemporary depression. But the category I've come to think of as "spiritual despair" is strangely resonant with the experiences of both activists, whose political disappointments can lead to "a loss of faith" in collective ideals and goals, and academics, who often question the solitary life of intellectual work and seek the distractions or more concrete and meaningful activities of the "real world." When represented as a form of temptation or sin, acedia can seem alien to modern secular sensibilities, but read more carefully in its original context, Cassian's acedia also strikes a familiar note for those who do yoga or meditation to calm the mind or free it from distracting thoughts. This chapter begins with acedia in order to defamiliarize the medical model of depression and its accompanying histories, and it considers how the historical resources offered by accounts of spiritual crisis such as acedia can contribute to alternative models of depression.

I first encountered the concept of acedia in Andrew Solomon's *The Noonday Demon*, one of the most respected of recent popular books on depression because of its compelling mix of scholarly erudition and personal narrative and its balanced and wide-ranging overview of debates about treatment for depression. Yet despite Solomon's attention to historical antecedents for modern notions of depression, he falls into a routine dismissal of acedia as an aberration from the "dark ages," when depression was stigmatized as a sin. In doing so, he follows contemporary medical paradigms, which are suspicious of the wildly unscientific, and even superstitious, representation of acedia as a visitation by demons.

But what if we don't see acedia's connection to religion, and even sin and demonic possession, as a liability? Solomon's disparagement of acedia strikes an odd note when read through the lens of queer medievalists such as Carolyn Dinshaw, who question the use of negative stereotypes about the premodern to underwrite constructions of modern culture as enlightened or civilized. As part of this critique of conventional historical narratives, Dinshaw embraces forms of transference and affective connection that link past and present.[3] I take inspiration from her in pursuing the possibility that the writings of an early Christian on monastic life might be relevant for understanding contemporary depression, not necessarily because acedia and depression are the same, but because their unexpected juxtaposition produces insights about contemporary practices of contemplation and action that unsettle received wisdom about depression as a medical condition.

Within histories of depression and even melancholy, acedia often functions for contemporary readers as the sign of a distant, alien, or false conception of depression; although sometimes attractively exotic, it mostly carries negative connotations. Emerging from early Christian conceptions of the deadly sins, the term itself is hard to translate and thus remains quite literally foreign, perhaps better left in its transliterated Latin form as *acedia* (which became *accidie* in medieval English usage), because when translated as "sloth," it too easily slides into notions of laziness that deplete it of its spiritual meanings and its origins in a specific kind of monastic experience. In its original Greek, $\alpha\chi\eta\delta\iota\alpha$ means "without care" or "carelessness," but Cassian also describes it in Latin as *taedium sive anxietatem cordis*, which is variously (and sometimes loosely) translated as "weariness or distress of the heart," "the anguish of the troubled heart," or even "spiritual dryness."[4] Its usage can be traced to the desert fathers, the fourth-century Christian ascetics who lived in solitary retreat in the deserts near Alexandria in Egypt, as well as developing collective forms of life in the monastery. Although also written about by one of the first and most prominent ascetics, Evagrius Ponticus, a key figure in the representation of acedia and the other sins is John Cassian (ca. 360–435), the author of two important texts on monastic life, *De Institutis Coenobiorum* (about 425) and *Collationes Patrum* (426–28). Written some twenty years or more after he had left Egypt and was living in France, where he founded two monasteries, Cassian's texts were widely circulated in medieval Europe, where their specific origins in monastic life eventually served as a source for subsequent writers and thinkers to refine and comment more generally on the system of the deadly sins. Cassian's model of eight faults was later replaced by Gregory's system of seven sins; an important development in the history of acedia was its conflation with *tristitia* (sadness), which linked it with the category of melancholy.[5] Within later medieval writings, as it became known as sloth or *otiositas* (idleness), acedia was represented as an experience less specific to the monastic life and the solitary contemplative's wavering devotion to God and, by referring more generally to a failure to follow one's spiritual obligations, thus came to mean laziness.[6]

Cassian's representation of a state that resembles contemporary depression as a sin, holding the monk responsible for his failure to keep to his spiritual mission, earns the ridicule of more recent thinkers, such as Solomon, who in their eagerness to destigmatize depression are understandably reluctant to see the depressed person cast as a sinner.[7] For many popular writers on depression, the medieval framework of sin stands as the opposite (in a psychically charged way) of the lifting of the burden of agency and responsibility that comes with medical diagnosis. New scholarship in medieval studies that questions the familiar construction of the period as the "Dark Ages," as well as in early modern studies that is less inclined to celebrate the Renaissance, suggests that acedia warrants closer attention. If aversion to the medieval period as primitive, benighted, or premodern underwrites models of science, then acedia is indeed relevant to the search for alternatives to a medical model of depression.

Although somewhat orthogonal to the concept of "melancholy" and indeed the subject of debate about how and whether the two terms are related (such as in the merging of acedia and *tristitia* into the single sin of despair), acedia is also intriguing because it disrupts progressive or continuist histories of melancholy, which has been another important antecedent for contemporary models of depression. In addition to being played off against medical models of depression, acedia often serves as a negative figure in positive constructions of melancholy by Renaissance, Romantic, and even psychoanalytic writers. In these contexts, melancholy is a secular category distinct from acedia's connections with the sacred. Renaissance and Romantic views of melancholy as a source of creativity lend themselves to a familiar narrative of Western culture, which privileges those periods as the sign of enlightenment and scientific progress. In *Saturn and Melancholy*, their famous study of melancholy genius, for example, Klibansky, Panofsky, and Saxl pass relatively quickly over medieval acedia because they see it as too negative and too religious, belonging to a period during which the insights of Aristotle in *Problemata* 30, one of the key touchstones for Renaissance theories of melancholy, were overlooked.[8] ("One may say that the Italian Renaissance of the fifteenth century was the first age that grasped the full significance of the Problem [Aristotle's *Problemata* XXX]," 42.) The Renaissance construction of melancholy as creative is accompanied by its secularization, and the construction of the deadly sins as a backward and superstitious set of beliefs accompanies the desire to separate melancholy from a term like *acedia* that is embedded in a religious context. Even alteritist models that embrace melancholy's negativity tend to be secular, and one potential value of turning to acedia rather than melancholy to historicize depression and political feelings is to explore whether its sacred and religious dimensions can be useful rather than a liability.

One sign that the dichotomy between an antiquated medieval acedia and modern medical depression is not as firm as we might think is the return of the repressed in the form of the concept of the noonday demon that pervades the discourse of depression and provides the title for Solomon's book. Stemming from its biblical source in Psalms 91:6, the term *noonday demon* aptly describes the desert monks' horror at finding not darkness but light to be their oppressive enemy. Even as Solomon seeks rational and scientific explanations for his depression, he, like others who invoke this metaphor, ultimately reaches for more ancient and poetic modes to describe his condition. This striking paradox suggests that histories of depression can be told in many different ways and that the resources of history might be at least as generative as new pills and medical diagnoses.

WRITING DEPRESSION

This book began from a simple premise: that depression should be viewed as a social and cultural phenomenon, not a biological or medical one. Within cultural studies, this statement is absolutely unobjectionable, so much so that a book that makes this argument might seem utterly predictable. It would no doubt proceed via a historical or genealogical inquiry in order to show how the category of depression changes over time and is constructed in relation to shifting social and ideological demands. But this is not that book. Instead the very banality of that premise is part of my subject here. As valuable as the historical critique of medical discourse can be, it is not my ultimate goal, in part because it has been done (and done well) by others but, more importantly, because what is taken for granted in cultural studies is not the commonsense view elsewhere, and that disconnect is my real interest. Within medical and scientific circles that construct depression as a treatable disease, the premise that depression is social and cultural can seem not so much suspect as irrelevant, especially in the context of the practical urgencies of treatment and new pharmacological discoveries. Within the popular imaginary, the medical model also holds powerful sway, especially the rhetoric that depression, pervasive though it might be, is manageable because it is a disease that can be detected, diagnosed, and treated. Although significantly bolstered by powerful economic and institutional interests, this commonsense understanding has widespread popular appeal particularly because a medical model based on biology relieves people of individual blame or responsibility and makes for a tangible set of solutions that contrast with the over-whelming, diffuse, and messy tendencies of social or cultural analysis.

At stake here are not just different understandings of depression but questions of [cultural authority.] Who are depression's public intellectu-als? Is it the doctors and scientists? Ordinary people who are experi-encing depression? The historians and humanists who can tell us about the cultural and social record? Artists whose attention to form and genre might create new ways of representing depression? Monks in the desert? Depression is an interdisciplinary phenomenon not only in the academy but in popular culture, where doctors, journalists, patients, and self-help experts weigh in through a variety of genres and media, including talk shows, memoirs, advice books, journalism, and middle-brow historical and medical surveys. Like many academics, I am moti-vated by a desire to see cultural studies approaches play a more promi-nent role in public discourse and to [provide an alternative to scientific expertise as the primary authority on depression.] But my archive— which includes not only early Christian monks but indigenous spiritu-alities, political burnout, and queer subcultures—is far outside the orbit of medical science.

cultural authority

alternative story of — power of social sciences

Yet medical science remains the central point of reference for many discussions, even critical ones. Beginning a discussion of depression with an account of acedia, for example, differs sharply from the fre-quent use of statistics as a starting point for underscoring the serious-ness of depression as a problem, even when it's viewed as a socially con-structed problem rather than a real one. Whether popular or academic, and whether medical or cultural in orientation, a remarkable number of studies use as a touchstone statistics about the rising rates of diagno-sis and pharmaceutical treatment that make depression a global public health epidemic. Andrew Solomon offers the following enumeration, for example:

> According to recent research, about 3 percent of Americans—some 19 mil-lion—suffer from chronic depression. More than 2 million of those are children. . . . Depression as described in DSM-IV [*Diagnostic and Statistical Manual of Mental Disorders*] is the leading cause of disability in the United States and abroad for persons over the age of five. Worldwide, including the developing world, depression accounts for more of the disease burden, as calculated by premature death plus healthy life-years lost to disability,

than anything else but heart disease. Depression claims more years than war, cancer, and AIDS put together. Other illnesses, from alcoholism to heart disease, mask depression when it causes them; if one takes that into consideration, depression may be the biggest killer on earth.[9]

Although he also notes that "it is a mistake to confuse numbers with truth," Solomon lets the "figures tell an alarming story" of depression's pervasive reach (25). Such statistics are often attached to accounts of the need for medical treatment. Along with offering statistics on depression as a leading cause of disability worldwide, for example, the World Health Organization's (WHO) website notes that it can be "reliably diagnosed and treated with primary care" that consists of "antidepressant medications and brief, structured forms of psychotherapy."[10] Even for those who aim to tackle depression in more qualitative ways or to critique the medical model, statistics provide incontrovertible evidence of an unprecedented problem.[11]

Although popular books about depression are easy to critique, their formidable cultural power is nonetheless compelling, and I have been unable to ignore them when pondering what it would mean to write about depression differently. They offer instructive models for why other nonmedical approaches and topics fall off the radar in the mainstream media—historical critique is too cranky; acedia is irrelevant; new age therapies have an air of quackery. Sustained by persistent debates about the pros and cons of drugs (and the implications for conventional psychotherapy), books about depression have become a mainstay of public discourse. Solomon's *The Noonday Demon*, where I first encountered the concept of acedia, is only one of an ongoing flood of books that have emerged since the marketing of the new generation of SSRI (selective serotonin reuptake inhibitor) antidepressants in the late 1980s. One of the best known, Peter Kramer's *Listening to Prozac* (1993), responded to the Prozac revolution by considering whether antidepressants could be used cosmetically to change personality and created a public discourse around pharmaceutical treatment that is as much a part of the culture of depression as the medical science itself. Combining medical and scientific research with the case history (which gives depression a human face), popular medical books on depression are often very compelling rhetorically; they are rigorous but accessible, seemingly balanced in their consideration of both cultural and scientific theories, and affectively sympathetic.[12] Like Solomon, the authors often use their own case histories to provide the forms of expertise that come from patients. (Kay Redfield Jamison's *An Unquiet Mind*, although about manic-depression, is probably the most well known of this genre in which the doctor's professional authority is bolstered by a first-person account of her experience as a patient.)[13] There are some glimpses of what Public Feelings would call "political depression," as when Solomon, perhaps because he is a writer, not a doctor, suggests that a culture of disconnection is largely responsible for the current high incidence of depression and that love and community would be the antidote. But even when, as Solomon does, these writers combine both scientific and cultural understandings and both personal narrative and scholarly research, in order to present a "balanced" or pluralistic view, they ultimately operate within the framework of a medical model of depression as a disease.

Indeed, with its many firsthand accounts, the work generated by medical experts is strongly connected to the other crucial genre of popular discourse about depression, the memoir. Although memoir might seem to offer an alternative to medical expertise, it frequently confirms it since its equally vast proliferation has also been catalyzed by the antidepressant revolution and, like many subgenres of memoir, can be quite homogeneous in its vision. Published in 2001, Solomon's *Noonday Demon* builds on a steady stream of titles spawned by the marketing of Prozac in the late 1980s, of which some of the most popular and most significant include William Styron's *Darkness Visible* (1990), in which the famous writer demonstrates how depression can strike even those who appear to be successful and productive; Elizabeth Wurtzel's *Prozac Nation* (1994), in which the infamously whiny twenty-something describes the woes of her generation in terms of depression; and Lauren Slater's *Prozac Diary* (1998), in which the psychologist turned writer applies her considerable skill as a memoirist to the dramatic effects of Prozac on her life.[14]

These memoirs and others like them are largely structured around some version of a drugs-saved-my-life narrative and hence consolidate a medical model. As a writer suddenly felled by depression at the peak of his career, Styron captures the feel of depression as something that cuts him off from normal relations and work, but he presents it as a largely mysterious visitation, and the process by which drugs and therapy alleviate it remains vague. Drawing on Styron's stature as a writer, this approach renders depression poetically powerful but ultimately opaque, and it has limited value for cultural explanations for depression. Wurtzel and Slater are both among the first generation of people to be treated by Prozac in the late 1980s and thus grew up with psychic distress that seemed utterly untreatable. Wurtzel shares all the lurid details of her emotionally chaotic childhood, adolescence, and college years, and Prozac comes in to save the day in her conclusion. Slater starts with Prozac, structuring her narrative as a detailed account of how it transformed her personality, a version of a conversion narrative in which she takes stock of the sick person she left behind and grieves, and the world she comes into after medication. Written more recently, Solomon's book reflects both the wider range of antidepressants now available and increasing doubts about their efficiency. He adopts the balanced view that drugs must be combined with other approaches to depression but also that "to take medication as part of the battle is to battle fiercely, and to refuse it would be as ludicrously self-destructive as entering a modern war on horseback."[15]

In addition to being marketable because they link their stories to public debate about pharmaceuticals, these books are also produced by and for a very privileged demographic; their authors are not just white and middle class but have the cultural capital that comes with an Ivy League education and access to publishing networks based in New York, as well as, in Slater's case, the authority of being a medical professional or expert, and they often presume a readership with the same profile. They are also written in the idiom of professional creative writing, with the eye for detail encouraged by MFA programs and venues such as *The New Yorker* (where the essay that became Solomon's book was first published). The results are well-polished documents that have none of the rough edges and messiness of the queer writing and performance art that have been my touchstones for memoir. The medical literature often gets its start in publications such as *The New Yorker* as well, which, along with other middlebrow intellectual publications such as the *New York Times Magazine*, *Atlantic*, and *Harper's*, serves as the place where science and humanities meet in order to produce popular accounts of research questions.[16] The relations between medical research and memoir, and between case history and literature, are fluid; the case history, for example, spans the spectrum from the scientific to the creative (and is thus an important genre for this project because it suggests the possibility of combining them).[17] All of these books about depression are part of a larger category of writing about science that is central to its operation and epistemological and cultural power.

If writing is integral to scientific thinking, though, it can also produce something other than the medical or scientific model of depression. Furthermore, depression might be capable of producing other kinds of writing and knowledge besides science.

HISTORY AS CRITIQUE OF THE MEDICAL MODEL

> History can be therapy too. And reading a book in which you understand how a doctor came to say to you "You have a biochemical imbalance and here's the drug for it" could be as therapeutic as exercise, as therapy, and as taking Prozac. — Gary Greenberg, interview

In a radio interview with Gary Greenberg about his new book, *Manufacturing Depression*, Leonard Lopate persistently presses Greenberg about whether his argument that it may not be helpful to view depression as a biochemical problem means people shouldn't take drugs. Greenberg carefully skirts the question by explaining that although antidepressants may be effective for some people, we don't really know how they work, and that his real point is that it makes a difference whether or not we believe depression is a disease. It's not surprising that Greenberg has a tough time presenting the nuances of his historical critique of the medicalization of depression given how accounts of depression as a medical disease often lack even the simplest version of the historical understanding so central to cultural studies. Instead, in popular and scientific discussions of both current medical advances and ancient medicine, a common starting point is the notion that depression is universal—that people have always suffered from what we would call "depression," regardless of what it was named in its time.

Typical of such universalizing histories are statements like this: "People have experienced symptoms of depression throughout human history, even though depression was not recognized as a disease. Accounts from Greece and Egypt four thousand years old describe people suffering from symptoms that would now be labeled as depression."[18]

Even Andrew Solomon, who allows that "the climbing rates of depression are without question the consequence of modernity," begins with this premise:

> It appears that depression has been around as long as man has been capable of self-conscious thought. It may be that depression existed even before that time, that monkeys and rats and perhaps octopi were suffering the disease before those first humanoids found their way into their caves. Certainly the symptomatology of our time is more or less indistinguishable from what was described by Hippocrates some twenty-five hundred years ago. Neither depression nor skin cancer is a creation of the twenty-first century.[19]

Such statements about the history of depression contrast with Greenberg's more historical argument: "I started to look at where did this idea of depression come from. And I was surprised actually to discover that there is a very traceable history of how the idea was assembled. Starting in about the middle 19th century with the development of magic bullet medicine, the idea that you could find a drug, target a molecular target, and kill the disease. Starting there and working right up until the present day, unhappiness was increasingly put into the category of the kinds of suffering that could be treated that way." Greenberg's historical explanation emerges when Lopate, in his dogged pursuit of scientific answers, tries to pinpoint Greenberg about his "scientific method," asking, "What kind of research are you basing your arguments on?" Greenberg emphatically responds, "Historical. My research is entirely historical."

This answer never really registers with Lopate, who continues to focus on medical research. Greenberg is able to answer his questions with considerable authority as someone who has not only practiced psychotherapy for twenty-five years, but has himself been diagnosed with depression. At the heart of Greenberg's book is his experience of participating in a clinical trial to test the effects of fish oil on depression, in which to his surprise he was diagnosed with major rather than minor depression. Over the course of the study, measurements of Greenberg's condition (based on his own responses to survey questions) showed he was improving, but he ultimately discovered that he had been receiving the placebo. With this incontrovertible evidence—from both doctor and patient—that the science of treating depression is very sketchy, Greenberg has a very compelling story, precisely the kind of story that plays well in the public sphere. (Before its publication as a book, his account of his participation in the clinical trial was a cover story in *Harper's*, yet another case in which the medical debate about depression remains a media mainstay.)[20]

Although their arguments are often confined to the more specialized audiences served by university presses, cultural historians offer support for Greenberg's historical account of the medical model of depression. For both medical and cultural historians, the story of the triumph of a medical model that favors biochemical explanations and treatments over explorations of psychic history and talk therapy often revolves around two crucial developments: the history of psychopharmacology after the Second World War and the creation of *The Diagnostic and Statistical Manual of Mental Disorders* (DSM), first published in 1952, which gave clinical psychology a more respectable foundation in scientific methodology.

Even in more narrowly medical histories that focus exclusively on pharmacology and endorse the idea of a paradigm shift or definitive scientific progress and revolution, the random and multiple ways in which drugs often developed for one purpose were discovered to be effective for the treatment of mood disorders is a tangled story with many strands. One version of the history of psychopharmacology begins with the almost accidental discovery in France in 1951 and 1952 that chlorpromazine, a drug initially developed during the testing of antihistamines (then also relatively new) for use in anesthesia, also had an effect on moods. David Healy, himself a psychopharmacologist and one of the field's most prominent historians, gives this event watershed status in his narrative, calling it "one of the seminal events of human history," as important as Freud's change of mind about the reality of sexual abuse.[21] Edward Shorter writes that "chlorpromazine initiated a revolution in psychiatry, comparable to the introduction of penicillin in general medicine."[22] In Healy's rendition, the story has a lot of drama, including the fight over who should get credit for the discovery: Henri Laborit, who used the drug for anesthesia but suspected it might have other uses, or Jean Delay and Pierre Deniker, the French psychologists who presided over the studies that more overtly used the drug for mental patients in the Hôpital Saint-Anne in Paris. Similar stories are told about other drugs: iproniazid, the first of the MAOI (monoamine oxidase inhibitor) antidepressants, was initially used as a treatment for tuberculosis patients and was discovered to have an effect on their moods. Imipramine, credited as the first antidepressant, developed out of research on antihistamines and was initially used as a treatment for schizophrenia.[23] Reserpine, another drug that was discovered to have applications for treatment of mental illness, was used in studies with Rockland State Hospital mental patients by Nathan Kline, one of the important American psychopharmacologists, who found signs of improvement in patients who were deemed completely untreatable.[24] These discoveries catalyzed numerous research projects by scientists interested in establishing the biological basis of mood disorders, and hence their possible treatment with drugs, and in challenging psychoanalytic models and treatments.

Despite this emphasis on watershed moments, the story of each individual drug is actually part of a more complex cumulative process whereby researchers began to explore pharmaceuticals, however crude in their effects initially, as an alternative to psychotherapy as a treatment for mental illness. As might be expected, the cultural historians widen their focus to show how the putatively "purer" science of testing the effects of drugs is tangled up with the culture and business of scientific research, which includes not only contests over intellectual property and the ethics of human subject research but also funding for potentially lucrative commodities. Jackie Orr, for example, describes how the creation of the Psychopharmacology Research Center within the National Institute for Mental Health (itself relatively recently established in 1949) and its substantial funding in the 1950s paved the way for the establishment of medical and pharmaceutical models, as did significant conferences on pharmacology that brought key players together.[25] Jonathan Metzl suggests that the model of pharmacological revolution should be resisted since it splits biological psychiatry too emphatically from the psychoanalysis that it replaced.[26] Indeed, the model of revolution suggests a singular change in what is a complex phenomenon even at the medical level.

If Prozac and its precursors constitute a revolution, cultural historians suggest that it is a revolution in marketing, not a revolution in science, as the push to solve psychological problems with pharmaceuticals opens up a lucrative market. Accounts of depression by cultural historians who historicize the present by insistently returning to the

1950s provide a reminder that other stories are part of the history of depression. Thus the full history of pharmacology entails not only multiple histories of science and medicine but their connection to broader histories of research funding and politics, as well as social and cultural histories that might not initially seem relevant, such as Metzl's account of how the marketing of drugs reinforces traditional gender roles and Orr's discussion of the relation between panic and the rise of cybernetics and the cold war.

The same is true for studies of the DSM, which complement the history of pharmacology since the invention of a diagnosis has been central to selling drugs and is also deeply embedded in institutional and economic politics.[27] The story of the DSM, which in multiple important editions since its first edition in 1952 has attempted to put psychiatry in the domain of science by categorizing mental illnesses, is another intricate one that involves groups of psychiatrists, prominently led by Robert Spitzer, overseeing its production and promoting their vision of a scientific psychiatry through well-organized efforts to marshal often questionable data.[28] As with pharmacology, there are important economic and political aspects to the story of psychiatric science, since the health insurance industry depends on diagnoses of conditions such as low-grade anxiety (dysthymia) and depression for those seeking access to treatment, including talk therapy. With its convenient checklist of symptoms that can be used to diagnose major depressive disorder— depressed mood; diminished interest; change in weight or appetite; psychomotor retardation or agitation; insomnia or hyperinsomnia; fatigue or loss of energy; feelings of worthlessness or guilt; lack of concentration or indecisiveness; recurrent thoughts of death or suicidal ideation—the DSM projects a tone of medical authority.[29]

Critiques of the medical model, therefore, often hone in on the DSM as the place where claims to science break down, as well as where interesting cultural stories can be told. But although the DSM might be on questionable scientific grounds, it is a powerful cultural and social institution with multiple effects. Depression is only one of many "diseases" such as trauma (and homosexuality) to have undergone significant revision and contestation over the years. The DSM-III of 1980 was particularly important in this process of revision, firmly consolidating the disease model of mental illness and creating an ambitious system of classifications, one that remains current, for the diagnosis of depression and other disorders. The use of diagnoses such as PTSD (posttraumatic stress disorder) in the military or GID (gender identity disorder) for transgender people in order to provide access to treatment has revealed that the medicalization enabled by the DSM cannot easily be either dismissed or celebrated.[30] Medical categories and diagnoses thus constitute an important cultural formation that shapes contemporary experience and merits careful cultural and historical analysis.

The social construction of depression is a theoretical premise that is only the beginning of a complex story, however, and medical histories of all kinds suggest that it is by no means obvious how to write the history of depression when its focus is widened to include culture. Even narrow medical histories of pharmacology provide a broader context for the Prozac or antidepressant revolution of the 1990s, by situating it in relation to earlier pharmacological discoveries going back to the 1950s. In a move reminiscent of research in the history of sexuality, where the narrative of the Stonewall riots in 1969 as a watershed moment that inaugurates the contemporary gay liberation movement has been complicated by being grounded in earlier periods and new histories of the 1950s and 1960s that show those decades to be a time of transition and double meanings — both repressive and productive, conservative and liberatory — the history of depression and pharmacology has fuzzy origins and involves multiple stories.[31]

Leonard Lopate's befuddled reaction to Gary Greenberg's use of history to critique medicine suggests why cultural studies faces an uphill battle to make even the most banal historical argument or cultural theory of depression intelligible in the public sphere, much less to affect scientific research and clinical practice. There is, though, a growing popular backlash against the Prozac revolution, as predicted by Jonathan Metzl in his study of the waxing and waning of the craze for "wonder drugs" such as Miltown in the 1950s and Valium in the 1960s. Prozac and other SSRIs now seem to be subject to more cautious estimates after the wild enthusiasm that accompanied their marketing in the late 1980s and early 1990s, which was facilitated by publicity from the popular science of books such as Kramer's *Listening to Prozac*. But the debate still essentially maintains itself in medical terms: Is depression a disease or not? Can it be cured by drugs? In *Against Depression*, for example, Kramer follows up on *Listening to Prozac* with a reiteration of the importance of conceptualizing depression as a (treatable) medical disease, faulting as romanticizing claims that it might be culturally useful or connected to creativity. (This seems to be something of a straw argument, though, since Renaissance and Romantic notions of melancholy that connect depression to creativity aren't the only alternative to the disease model, nor does rejecting the medical model automatically mean that one is somehow "for" rather than "against" depression.)

In response to arguments such as Kramer's, Greenberg's book joins a cluster of others that have appeared in recent years, including Charles Barber's *Comfortably Numb*, Allan V. Horwitz and Jerome C. Wakefield's *The Loss of Sadness*, Dan Blazer's *The Age of Melancholy*, and Irving Kirsch's *The Emperor's New Drugs*, all of which use scientific expertise itself to question both the proliferation of depression as a diagnosis and the use of pharmaceuticals to treat it.[32] From the field of clinical psychiatry, Horwitz and Wakefield suggest, for example, that the distinction between "normal sorrow" and "depressive disorder" is compromised by the DSM because of its focus on symptoms at the expense of context.[33] These books have received considerable critical attention in reviews and other media, keeping alive the medical debate about depression, since even when they critique the medical paradigm they remain embedded in it.[34] Like the previous decade's more enthusiastic books about antidepressants, they are all written by medical experts, and in the case of both Greenberg and Barber, by experts who have also been patients. Yet even as they point in the direction of what Public Feelings would call "political depression," like the first generation of SSRI literature, they generally stop short of any real consideration of the social causes of depression or the social transformations that might address it. For the most part they have reformist and practical aims with respect to psychopharmacology, making pitches for a return to psychoanalysis and other forms of talk therapy that have been sidelined by the push for pharmaceuticals (and managed health care) or for alternative approaches such as cognitive behavioral therapy. This is no small accomplishment given the huge economy at stake, as well as the number of patients being administered to (and created) by widespread diagnosis, but it still operates within a very narrow range of approaches to healing.

VITAL FORCES: THE BIOLOGICAL AND THE SPIRITUAL

My own aim is to make conceptual space for accounts of depression that can embrace alternative medicine and healing practices as well as alternative ways of understanding depression (including other vocabularies) as the product of a sick culture. Hence my turn to acedia and spiritual crisis, which provide a vantage point on depression that foregrounds matters of faith and hope as relevant to the experience of being stuck, which can manifest in psychic and spiritual ways, as well as biological and physical ones. Acedia helps place the medical model of depression within the longer history of notions of not only health but embodiment and of what it means to be human. Psychoanalysis can provide something of the same leverage; like many cultural theorists who favor psychoanalysis over the medical model, Greenberg suggests that it fosters the rich narrative of the shape of a life that can explain periods of depression or stuckness. But psychoanalysis can still be too closely tied to modern medical models to do the work of defamiliarization, and I prefer the relative strangeness or ec-centricity of acedia as a way to open the field for other kinds of thinking.[35]

My interest in spiritual approaches to medical problems should not, however, be construed as a dismissal of science; rather it is a call for more integrated relations between science and humanities in order to transform medical cultures. Cultural historians writing about the social construction of depression are not necessarily saying science is wrong or deconstructing it in the abstract; rather, they are reckoning with it as a powerful social force and attempting to describe its institutions and social effects both with greater descriptive care and within a wider context. Jonathan Metzl warns against reading science as primary and culture as its secondary effect, and thus reinforcing, for example, a gendered binary of science as masculine and culture as the soft receptive feminine. His exploration of the role of advertising in creating "wonder drugs" reveals science to be a form of culture and one in which huge economic concerns are at stake. As a psychiatrist, though, Metzl also revisits the divide between psychoanalysis and biopsychiatry in the interest of new forms of treatment that might combine both. Using an ethnographic approach to study bipolar support groups and psychiatric hospitals, Emily Martin considers how people who have been diagnosed using psychiatric classifications make their own commonsense use of medical categories and drug treatment. As someone who lives with manic-depression herself, she uses the same strategy of some of the doctors writing popular books in depathologizing the disease by claiming it as her own. She also considers the normalizing cultural construction of mania as a desirable quality for productivity in the workplace (which is nowhere more evident than in academia, even in humanist disciplines that seek to diagnose this problem). Jackie Orr also presents herself as a patient, joining a clinical trial for Ativan and writing up her experience of panic and medical treatment as part of her research. She practices a radical sociology, whose methods include personal narrative and the use of performative writing to juxtapose personal experience with histories of medicine and cold war politics so as to challenge what counts as knowledge and disciplinary method. Studies such as these show how science and culture intersect in order to explore the social practices created by medical culture and how they are negotiated within people's daily lives.[36]

The recent turn to neuroscience within cultural studies further exemplifies the displacement of a critique of science by new collaborations between science and culture. Cultural studies scholars have been finding neurobiological inquiry into the embodiment of emotion useful to their efforts to revisit distinctions between mind and body. Cultural histories of emotion and feeling thus contribute to interdisciplinary inquiry into how feeling and sensation operate at the crossroads between embodiment and interaction with a social environment.[37] Renewed interest in vitalism and other historical discourses of affect suggest multiple resources for exploring the materiality of emotions.[38] Prominent in inspiring new dialogues between science and humanities is the work of Antonio Damasio, who, for example, invokes Spinoza's conception of the indistinguishability of mind and matter to discuss the neuroplasticity of the brain.[39] This developing body of work has taught me to revise my opening premise—"that depression should be viewed as a social and cultural phenomenon not a biological and medical one"—in order to distinguish more carefully between the medical and the biological and to consider how social and cultural approaches to depression need not preclude consideration of its biological dimensions. Countering feminist theory's fear of biological essentialisms, for example, Elizabeth Wilson calls for feminisms that forge a "critically empathic alliance with neurology" in order to build new models of the relation between psyche and soma.[40] She offers a corrective to forms of social construction that would completely dismiss biology, making room for the direct engagement with science exemplified by her use of the insights of neuroscience to articulate a "gut feminism," as well as by Metzl's work as a practicing psychiatrist and Martin's ethnographic study of psychiatrists (and now neuroscientists) to understand their culture.

But this is a two-way street: if cultural historians are renegotiating the relations between science and humanities by favoring engagement over critique, they can also do so by expanding what counts as (scientific) knowledge. The humanist embrace of neuroscience and other science cultures is only one way to consider how emotions are embodied experiences that combine psyche and soma. It's not an either/or choice between body and mind, medicine and politics, biology and culture, nature and nurture. Increasingly practitioners of alternative forms of somatic therapy, such as meditation and massage, embrace the insights of neurobiology while also drawing on bodily practices and knowledges that are not dependent on science even if they can be explained by it.[41] My turn to acedia stems from the conviction that depression can be known not just by studying the nervous system but by paying attention to what we learn through intuition or spiritual practice. Acedia, and by extension spirituality, offers another holistic perspective on feelings as the intersection of mind and body, and nature and culture. It shifts the temporal frame to the medieval and premodern period, prior even to the ascendancy of the category of melancholy, which secularized acedia and accompanied the rise of medical science's use of the category.

Looking to acedia rather than to the contemporary culture of science (or, as others have done, to the category of melancholy) as part of the historical archive of depression opens up the question of what constitutes "health" or "healing" to encompass traditions of thinking about practices of living, including the embodied knowledges of spiritual practice. Using acedia to explore depression as a political category leads to matters of spirituality that have been rendered obsolete or taboo by a secular culture that, along with medicalizing the condition of feeling bad, also cordons off the spiritual from the political. Reintroducing feelings into politics thus also entails a reconsideration of histories of secularism.

ACEDIA, LEFT MELANCHOLY, AND POLITICAL DEPRESSION

Whereas medical models of depression tend to dismiss acedia, and even many histories pass over it fairly quickly in favor of the more prevalent category of melancholy, I am not alone in being drawn to the concept, which has had a remarkable resurgence in contemporary cultural studies. Indeed, I eventually realized that I must have encountered it before in a number of different sources, especially in theories of melancholy, but the seemingly antiquated term hadn't immediately registered as relevant for my investigation of depression. With a sensibility similar to my own, Giorgio Agamben lays the groundwork for depathologizing accounts of melancholy by finding a productive representation of negative affect in Cassian and the medieval tradition of commentary on acedia.[42] Not only does he critique the endorsement of a Renaissance creative melancholy at the expense of acedia by Panofsky et al., but he links acedia to modern notions of ennui and boredom that appear in writers of the fin de siècle such as Baudelaire and des Esseintes, thus linking the spiritual and the secular and the medieval and the modern in unexpected ways. David Eng and David Kazanjian invoke these uses of acedia in their edited collection on loss and the politics of mourning, playing Agamben off Walter Benjamin to suggest that blockage in the form of acedia can occur on the brink of transition to a new society and thus that new cultures can emerge out of a sense of grief and loss.[43] Acedia is also a significant concept for Teresa Brennan in *The Transmission of Affect*, where she finds the idea of demons that visit from outside to be useful for understanding affect as shared and social rather than individual and goes so far as to consider the language of demons and sins to be an early language of affect. Although Foucault doesn't talk explicitly about acedia, Cassian plays a prominent role in his inquiries into early Christianity, which form the basis for the still unpublished fourth volume of the *History of Sexuality*. Foucault is interested in how the constant scrutiny of the self that is part of monastic life is connected to the formation of the modern subject, and he finds in practices of both chastity and confession forms of ascesis that suggest models for self-making that transform disciplinary and repressive regimes.[44] Especially important for my purposes, acedia plays a role in Benjamin's account of "left melancholy," which appears in his brief but provocative essay on the German poet Eric Kastner, and has recently been taken up by scholars such as Judith Butler and Wendy Brown to explain why the left might have a misguided sense of nostalgia for a past socialism that prevents action in the present.[45] Left melancholy points the way toward political depression and, more generally, to ways of linking emotional and political life.

Acedia's attraction for contemporary scholars certainly owes a great deal to its connections with the widespread use of melancholy, which has a long history not just within psychoanalytic discourse, where it has recently been a central category for cultural theorists interested in loss and trauma, but within humanist discourse, including the theory of the humors that is part of ancient Greek and Roman medicine and Renaissance and Romantic understandings of creative genius. Indeed, the very flexibility of the category also makes it a rather daunting one, leading scholars such as Jennifer Radden, the editor of an anthology of primary source materials on melancholy, to ask whether there is any unity at all to the diverse range of writings on the topic.[46] For example, melancholy lends itself to both histories that want to claim a continuous lineage between ancient and contemporary medicine and those that look to the past in order to chart discontinuities and constructions.[47] The medical model of depression, with its progressivist narrative of scientific discovery, places the category of melancholy in a mostly Western narrative that extends back to recognizable versions of modern medicine among the Greeks and Romans. One of the touchstones is ancient medicine, especially the theory of the humors developed by Hippocrates and Galen that links melancholy with black bile or a physiological condition. In this story, what will ultimately become a medical or scientific phenomenon is recognized by the prescient Greeks, who are our fellow traveler scientists, and picked up on during the Renaissance, in texts such as Burton's *Anatomy of Melancholy*, which in turn gives rise to eighteenth- and nineteenth-century medicine. Although there are slight nods to Arab, Byzantine, and Muslim medical discourses (whose role in the history of ancient medicine could produce alternative narratives of the constitutive relations between modernity, science, and the construction of the West and its putative others), this version of the history of melancholy largely replicates that of the Western humanist canon.[48] Moreover, it is a developmental model with modern medicine as its triumphant endpoint, and earlier histories are of interest largely because they contain versions of contemporary truth or play out a time-less conflict between biological and social explanations of illness.

The varied history of melancholy can also be a rich source of possible alternatives to contemporary medical models of depression, encouraging scholars to avoid privileging contemporary categories and opening the way for explorations of the cultural construction of very general categories such as sadness and loss. It offers a return to a time when sadness could be viewed in other ways, including as a normative part of cultural experience, and even, most notably in the case of Renaissance and Romantic understandings that have had a persistent influence, as a creative force. Not only is its connection to genius a significant nexus for historically specific understandings of melancholy as positive, but because the earlier insights of Aristotle are reclaimed by Ficino, Burton, and other early moderns in order to represent secular understandings of creativity, melancholy is also central to histories of modernity. This narrative, though, often consolidates conventional understandings of Western humanism in associating positive readings of melancholy with secular enlightenment.[49] Although the medical model and the human-ist model part paths insofar as the former constructs melancholy as a precursor to a modern disease (clinical depression) in need of cure and the latter describes melancholy as a sign of creativity, they are both in-vested in a history that is progressive and continuist.[50] This is one rea-son why the debate within the popular literature about whether a posi-tive view of melancholy might replace a negative view of depression seems somewhat artificial and doesn't necessarily constitute a clash of opposing paradigms or an alternative to the medical model.[51]

In its more psychoanalytic inflections, particularly those influenced by poststructuralism, melancholy is a less benign category, grounded as it is in presumptions about the constitutive relations between loss and subjectivity.[52] Discussions of whether melancholy is a positive or negative category for politics have been at the heart of debates within cultural studies about the politics of affect and loss. Benjamin's "left melancholy," although emerging in the specific context of German mod-ernism, resonates for contemporary critics because it gives the famil-iar psychoanalytic category a more overtly political cast and opens the way to more general discussions about feelings of political failure and disappointment within radical movements. Wendy Brown takes up the concept to describe what she calls "Left traditionalism," targeting those who are suspicious of cultural and identity politics and long for a return to a lost era of labor politics and a social welfare state. She characterizes this position in more psychological terms as that of "a Left that has become more attached to its impossibility than to its potential fruitfulness, a Left that is most at home dwelling not in hopefulness but in its own marginality and failure."[53] Brown concludes her essay by calling for attention to the affective investments that surround political dreams and to the negative and sentimental feelings that keep people attached to lost ideals. "The feelings and sentiments—including those of sorrow, rage, and anxiety about broken promises and lost compasses—that sustain our attachments to Left analyses and Left projects ought to be examined for what they create in the way of potentially conservative and even self-destructive undersides of putatively progressive aims" (464).

Political depression has a wider application than Brown's left melancholy, however, since in accusing old-school Marxists of melancholy, she implies that it could be cured by a more theoretically savvy politics, including the critique of identity politics that she favors. Moreover, Brown ultimately returns to a traditional split between feeling and politics that favors the latter when she suggests that feeling displaces politics as a response to failure and leads in conservative directions. In a slightly nervous insertion just prior to her conclusion, Brown underscores that her focus on melancholy "is not meant to recommend therapy" as a solution to the problem of sustaining political hopes and dreams. Implying that the intrusion of therapy into politics would be a bad thing, she seems to fear that talk of political feelings will lead in this direction. Even as Brown's essay breaks new ground in openly discussing feelings on the left, she ultimately retreats from a full embrace of the inevitable role of feelings in political life, failing to acknowledge that left melancholy is not just confined to "Left traditionalists" and ultimately suggesting that progressive politics needs to purge itself of bad feelings.[54]

The language of political depression developed by the Public Feelings project, by contrast, embraces melancholy with less ambivalence, following in the spirit of Douglas Crimp, for example, who echoes Brown in suggesting that we ignore or dismiss the affective disappointments and failures of politics at our own peril. Crimp's discussion of mourning and militancy, which calls for a recognition of melancholy as part of political life in the context of AIDS activism, and David Eng's rereading of Freud in order to theorize racial melancholia have been power-ful models for understanding loss as productive.[55] Their foundational work has been extended in projects that conceive of melancholy not only as an alternative to depression but as a way to rethink the relation between politics and feeling. Heather Love considers how negative feelings might be useful for politics, and for reconceptions of politics that encompass inaction or "lack of vehemence and lack of dynamism."[56] Michael Snediker calls for a queer optimism that is not bound to the psychoanalytic vocabulary of melancholy as a name for all forms of sadness.[57] Jonathan Flatley looks for an antidepressive melancholy, one that can make the aesthetic a place of action in response to the passivity or stillness of depression.[58] Flatley also takes melancholy out of a narrowly psychoanalytic frame and hence makes it more available for political uses by working in a Benjaminian tradition and reading Freud as only one of many modernists who used melancholy as a way to describe the experience of modern life.

Within these forms of contemporary cultural studies, melancholy facilitates understandings of political depression as the loss of hope in how to bring about change. Crimp finds such feelings to be inescapable even within even a vital radical movement such as ACT UP, which in its use of innovative forms of camp demonstration and cultural activism is not mired in old or new left impasses that Brown is critiquing.[59] The Public Feelings project explores the ways that affective responses, even negative ones like left melancholy, are both a necessary part of politics and a possible resource. The concept of political depression developed by Public Feelings certainly builds on the notion of left melancholy, and it shares with it a long tradition of attempting to merge politics and feeling, one version of which is efforts to think Marxism and psychoanalysis together. Even as it takes up from the familiar left position that feelings and the therapeutic institutions that address them must ultimately have a political horizon and lead to social transformation, it also seeks to move past some of the impasses that have resulted from critiques of therapy and affective politics, which often subsume feeling under the rubric of politics. It opens anew the question of how to embrace emotional responses as part of social justice projects. It is alert to the feelings that activism itself produces and with the ways that activism could change if it were to accommodate feelings, both positive and negative, more readily.

Rather than seeing negative feelings of failure, mourning, despair, and shame as getting in the way of politics or needing to be converted to something more active in order to become politics, such work attends to felt experience as not only already political but as transforming our understandings of what counts as political.[60] The encounter between feeling and politics is thus open for discussion of forms of activism that can address messy feelings rather than trying to banish them, and that can more fully embrace the role of practices that resemble "therapy" (such as "processing") within politics. It also reopens the question of the politics of therapy, recognizing its value as a way of grappling with political emotions but also alert to the need to imagine therapy in ways other than one-on-one sessions delivered through expensive or managed health-care systems. While Public Feelings can entail critiques of "therapeutic cultures" (including the forms of what Lauren Berlant calls "cruel optimism"), it also encompasses an expanded understanding of therapy and healing as manifest in the many ways in which people seek to make themselves feel better at both the micro-level of everyday life and the macro-level of organized collectivities and politics.

The recurrence of acedia within recent cultural theory revives concepts of spirituality that have often seemed outmoded in a secular age and brings the vocabulary of spiritual despair to discussions of left melancholy and political depression. Secular understandings of feeling (and discourses of feeling as the secularization of religious affect) are part of the long history of the relations between modern medicine and humanist traditions, including the splits between a scientific psychology and forms of psychotherapy, such as psychoanalysis, that remain committed to more humanist forms of storytelling. Acedia's origins within premodern religious cultures and practices serve as a reminder that the "two cultures" of science and humanities are both part of secular modernity. Rather than separating a secular, creative, and good melancholy from a religious, debilitating, and stigmatized acedia, Agamben, for example, sees the two categories on a historical continuum and embraces the persistence of sacred origins in a secular melancholy that is "the lay heir of cloistral sorrow and gloom."[61] A loss of faith in God might seem very distant or outdated, especially for queer or left activists, but if we question the tendency to secularize the spiritual to make it more palatable, spiritual forms of despair provide a suggestive comparison with other experiences of loss of ideals or commitment.

Contemporary tensions between feeling and politics can be related to secularist tendencies to banish the irrational from both medicine and politics (where "touchy-feely" therapeutic modes are often suspect). If feelings of despair are given more latitude, then other vocabularies, including spiritual ones, for both living with and battling against despair can be useful. Although described as a state of not caring, acedia is also about caring too much, and it is characterized by a restlessness of the mind as much as by apathy or lethargy. Agamben underscores this quality in order to rethink ennui or boredom as a complex political feeling. Brennan also finds this early Christian thinking relevant to the present, taking up the image of demons that pervade the mind from outside to characterize the maladies of body and soul that result from carrying other people's feelings.

Loss of hope can be like loss of faith, a form of hope that retains its religious connotations. The turn to the spiritual can emerge at moments of political crisis when organizations fail or collective goals are in doubt and "What is to be done?" becomes an expression of futility rather than a call to arms. The resistance to feeling in politics resembles resistance to the spiritual, motivated by the fear that indulgence in too much feeling (or in religion as "the opiate of the masses") will lead to selfish retreat from the political, to not working hard enough or giving up. Bringing the spiritual back to the political, by contrast, lends itself to the project of rethinking the relation between feeling and politics so that organized political collectivity or action is not an idealized or predictable horizon to which spiritual and affective life must aspire. Foucault turns to early Christianity to suggest how an art of everyday life can be a form of politics, most notably new forms of queer politics not based in rights and visibility. The concept of ascesis, a category grounded in religious life, helped him to imagine new relations between the ethical and the political and a politics of pleasure and self-making not based in modern dynamics of identity formation. If political depression, like acedia or spiritual despair, is an experience that must be acknowledged and reckoned with rather than being banished or repressed, what practices might it foster?

ACEDIA AND PERFORMANCE ART

Cassian's writing on acedia ends with the remarkable example of Abbot Paul, whose meditative practice of collecting palm leaves serves no purpose other than to keep him occupied. "Being relieved from anxiety by the date palms and a small garden, [he] had plenty to support himself, and an ample supply of food, and could not find any other work to do, which would support him," but he "regularly exacted of himself his daily task, as if he was to be supported by it" (XXIV). At the end of the year, when his cave is full of palm leaves that he doesn't need, he burns them, rendering as nothing "that at which he had so diligently laboured: thus proving that without manual labour a monk cannot stop in a place nor rise to the heights of perfection" (XXIV). The practice of renewing one's hope or faith is a daily one that is never completed, and it is also significantly physical.

   Abbot Paul's daily practice and its culmination in an annual ritual remind me of time-based performance art practices in which ordinary activities take on aesthetic significance through repetition and intentional framing.[62] This connection is not necessarily surprising given the strong Catholic influences on the embodied and durational practices of foundational performance artists such as Marina Abramović, Ana Mendieta, and Linda Montano. Abramović often repeats gestures or physical actions to the point of self-sacrificing exhaustion and collapse, and has lain on a cross made of ice blocks in *Lips of Thomas* (1975/2005) and posed naked on a bicycle seat as though suspended on a crucifix in *Luminosity* (1997/2010); Mendieta has smeared her blood on gallery walls and set fire to the traces left by her body after lying naked in sand and dirt, using ritual practice to transform the body into ephemeral spirit; and Montano has made pieces inspired by St. Theresa of Avila and Mother Theresa, and combined Catholicism with Buddhism and Hinduism to practice "the art of daily living" in performances such as the two cycles of *7 Years of Living Art*, in which she wore the same color (based on the chakras) every day for a year.[63] In her 2010 performance at MoMA, *The Artist Is Present*, Abramović sat in silence every day and, like a live religious icon, received individual visitors who could sit across from her for as long as they wanted or were able. As the title suggests, her ability to remain present during the intense physical practice of simply sitting was the work. Not only does Abbot Paul's repetitive manual labor, whose emphasis is on process without any material outcome or goal ("he performed it simply for the sake of purifying his heart, and strengthening his thoughts"), resemble performance art, it also resembles domestic habits such as crafting and forms of spiritual practice such as meditation, whose value as a way of working with depression and despair will be explored in a later chapter.

In emphasizing manual labor as a response to acedia, Cassian also points to acedia as a physical and not just a spiritual or emotional problem. The unruly presence of the body in the solitary ascetic's quest for spiritual transcendence and mental clarity is a persistent feature of Cassian's account: "It [acedia] either makes him stay in his cell idle and lazy, without making any spiritual progress, or it drives him out from thence and makes him restless and a wanderer, and indolent in the matter of all kinds of work, and it makes him continually go round the cells of the brethren and the monasteries, with an eye to nothing but this; viz., where or with what excuse he can presently procure some refreshment" (VI). With his pacing, his confinement, and his struggle to transcend the material body to achieve a state of meditative focus, the solitary who suffers from acedia may not have a biochemical disorder but he certainly has a physical one. (He also bears an uncanny resemblance to the contemporary scholar whose difficulties writing lead to either sitting around doing nothing or procrastinating by leaving the desk for other activities.) Acedia thus has lessons to offer about contemporary depression that takes the form of a breakdown in functionality. While laziness might no longer be sin in a moral sense, it is a major problem for neoliberal and market-based conceptions of the self that turn on productivity as a sign of one's identity.

agency /
function /
doing /
capacity

Cassian's focus on manual labor, as both an antidote and a corollary to the mental and spiritual demands of remaining contemplative, is suggestive for thinking about contemporary "cures" for depression. His account of a spiritual life that entails daily habits or practices that involve manual labor addresses the persistent dilemma of the relation between mind and body that pervades more medical discussions of depression. Even if depression is understood as a spiritual or political and not just biochemical disorder, it affects the body and requires physical forms of healing, whether drugs, exercise, or meditation (which has a strong physical dimension even when one is sitting still). Indeed, whether the renunciation of ordinary life takes the form of solitary retreat or collective living, asceticism, with its basis in physical habits and systems, is a form of somatic therapy.

In discussions of depression as a somatic condition, the medieval monk can thus stand alongside the figure of the *Aplysia californica*, the primitive sea snail used in research on the physiology of the nervous system.[64] While brain scans and brain-altering pharmaceuticals have become popular ways to find a "cure" for depression, the consultation of historical resources also has its value. The new vision of an integrated relation between mind and body that one finds in the best discussions of neuroscience can be joined by cultural and humanistic inquiry that crosses the divides between the modern and premodern or the secular and sacred in order to consult the wisdom of the early Christian monks and their practices for living. The integral relation between mind and body that emerges from understanding feeling as belonging to both is a lesson of spiritual practice as well as neurology.

Somatic therapies can link not just body and mind but body and soul, where soul or spirit, like feeling, is another name for the inseparability of body and mind. Somatic therapy can include not just scientific and pharmaceutical approaches to neuroplasticity but also meditation, spiritual practice, and forms of daily ritual and habit such as walking, crafting, and process-based writing that encourage physical movement as a response to psychic and spiritual blockage. The ascetic practices of medieval monks can be counted among the ways to connect psyche and soma and to talk about political depression. Not only do they belong in my version of a book about depression but they are vital to my exploration in subsequent chapters of how indigenous spiritualities cultivate emotional and somatic sovereignty as a response to genocide and colonialism, and how domestic practices of crafting and queer performance counter the tedium of modern life with the art of everyday living.

From Dispossession to Radical Self-Possession

Racism and Depression

But if whites experienced black sadness . . . (*Pause.*)
It would be too overwhelming for them. (*Pause.*)
Very few white people could
actually take seriously,
black sadness and the lives that
they livin:
livin' in denial
"Oh it couldn't be that bad"
And they have their own form of sadness
Tends to be linked to
the American Dream
But it's a very very very different kind of
Sadness.

—Cornel West in Anna Deavere Smith, *Twilight: Los Angeles*

What if depression, in the Americas at least, could be traced to histories of colonialism, genocide, slavery, legal exclusion, and everyday segregation and isolation that haunt all of our lives, rather than to biochemical imbalances? This chapter takes that premise seriously, but in doing so has to depart from most of the literature, both medical and historical, explored in the previous chapter, which, often without acknowledging it directly, tends to presume a white and middle-class subject for whom feeling bad is frequently a mystery because it doesn't fit a life in which privilege and comfort make things seem fine on the surface. Although for those whose troubles are more obvious, feeling depressed might be no surprise, they are not often the direct subjects of the books and articles in the mainstream press. To track their experi-

[handwritten margin notes:] Key experience / contributes

ences, we might have to "follow the trail of breadcrumbs" that includes the epigraph in which Cornel West invokes in an almost offhand but nonetheless chilling way an emotional color line that separates black sadness from white sadness.[1] In the space of a few sentences, he opens up the chasm of (mis)understanding that would make any white person humble about presuming to understand black sadness, and he offers, almost in passing, a beautiful diagnosis of white depression as a cultural rather than medical predicament. By linking it to the failure of the American dream, he suggests that sadness comes when the belief that one should be happy or protected turns out to be wrong and when a privileged form of hopefulness that has so often been entirely foreclosed for black people is punctured.

West is only one of many scholars of the African diaspora and critical race theory who have taken up the category of sadness in order to discuss the all too vivid afterlife—including the ghosts—of colonialism, slavery, and genocide. The "emotional color line" that he draws is not a wholly fixed one, however, given the rich body of scholarship on racial melancholy that draws on Freudian and psychoanalytic paradigms in order to describe the affective life of racialized existence and the psychic impact of racism as a form of loss and trauma.[2] Although it has most often emerged in the context of trauma studies, work on racial melancholy seems all the more relevant to the study of depression given that racism spans a spectrum that encompasses the ordinary as well as the catastrophic. As part of the revisionist theories of melancholy discussed in the preceding chapter, this scholarship formulates melancholy as a productive substitute for the concept of depression, and it also suggests alternative genealogies of melancholy that foreground the presence of colonialism and race in its Western historical lineages.

There is, however, considerable debate about the value of melancholy as a category for thinking about race, including the version of the emotional color line that constructs psychoanalysis as a problematic paradigm because it is Western or individualistic. For some critics, melancholy is associated with an irredeemably negative affect or with a dwelling in the past that remains stuck or refuses to move forward. And while for some melancholy is not politically useful because it is too sad, for others it is not sad enough and is critiqued as a sentimental embrace of the past that turns away from the real concerns of the present (although these are both versions of the same problem, a melancholic attachment to the past that prevents movement forward, whether psychic, political, or both).[3] David Eng and Shin Hee Han's work on racial melancholy addresses these reservations by suggesting that melancholy's negativity might in fact be a productive corrective to a naïve politics of hope; central to such work is a sense that we might not know what politics is, that a politics of melancholy operates when tending to feelings means the disruption of politics as usual, a need to slow down in order to see what the feelings might be.[4] As West also puts it, the challenge is to dwell in sadness, to explore its full measure without seeking immediate redemption (or, as he says, using a Christian metaphor, remaining "Saturday people") and while also not giving up a hopefulness that remains stubbornly faithful for no good reason in the midst of despair (as compared with the more rational promise of optimism, which he argues is a "deeply secular" concept; 108, 106).

This chapter is deeply informed by the convergence of psychoanalysis and critical race theory in scholarship on melancholy, but it refrains from using that more specialized terminology in favor of *sadness* and other vernacular vocabularies that can be put in dialogue with clinical or technical terms such as *melancholy* and *depression* in order to expand their meanings and lineages. In West's comments, (black) sadness is a complicated feeling, encompassing despair (but as a starting point, not an endpoint), hope, and the "*melancholia* shot through with black rage" (108) that is so frequently not heard by a "morally tone-deaf society" (109), despite its articulation by African Americans, from the singers of spirituals on Frederick Douglass's plantation to Coltrane's extended solos.[5] (And West's invocation of a psychoanalytic vocabulary suggests that he, too, acknowledges a mixed heritage for expressions of cultural sadness, as do his references to white writers such as Chekhov and Dreiser.)

One way to cross the emotional color line would be for white people, too, to acknowledge this African diaspora lineage, which makes a very different starting point for a study of depression than histories of Western medicine, the DSM, and pharmacology, or stories of white middle-class women and their anxieties, or literary and psychoanalytic traditions of melancholy. Indeed, pursuing the links between racism and depression is no ordinary research question; it requires unusual tools and imaginative forms of interdisciplinary investigation that ideally would yield not just scholarly insight but new cultural practices and so-

cial policies. Questions of interdisciplinary method and expertise are at
stake here, and race and ethnic studies and medical anthropology have
as much to say as clinical psychology, if not more, about what kinds of
therapy and social change could "cure" the psychic fallout of colonialism and slavery across a range of generations and different kinds of
people.[6]

There is a burgeoning subfield of multicultural therapy devoted to
racial difference in mental health treatment, but the starting point
tends to be not the psychic effects of racism on people of color or re-
framing understandings of mental health but rather the inclusion of
people of color within existing models of illness and treatment.[7] The
medical literature on depression, for example, explores whether rates of
depression and anxiety differ by race, but the results are often unclear,
whether because the reasons for greater rates of depression in people of
color are hard to explain (in part because they generally point in the direction of culture rather than biology and thus challenge the prevailing
medical models) or because lower rates of depression seem to indicate
methodological problems rather than actual differences. Sometimes,
for example, people of color have lower rates because they don't have
adequate health care or because depression doesn't emerge as a category independent of other health issues.[8]

One of the major areas of inquiry is thus attitudes toward medical
treatment because more general lack of access to health care prevents
accurate comparative studies, with the result that people of color are
not only underdiagnosed but undertreated. Studies show, for example,
that African Americans are less accepting of drug treatment and counseling, whereas Mexican Americans will seek counseling but not drugs.[9]
Chinese American immigrant women will seek medical help for physical but not mental ailments.[10] Many studies are based on the presumption that the medical model is the best one and that resistant or neglected subjects need to be brought more fully to mental health services
and to research projects. An article surveying research on depression
in African Americans, for example, finds that "African Americans face
a number of barriers in the recognition and treatment of major depression including clinical presentation with somatization, stigma about
diagnosis, competing clinical demands of comorbid general medical
problems, problems with physician–patient relationship, and lack of
comprehensive primary care services."[11] This list suggests that depres-

sion in African Americans opens onto the multiple and deep ways in which racism and classism manifest as health problems that require a rethinking of the medical system in general, not just a reform to provide more effective medical treatment of depression. But this body of work, suggestive as it might be, often seems relatively crude in its instruments for measuring depression and for theorizing the effects of racism. For example, the scale used to diagnose depression remains the same checklist used for everyone. And the presumption that people want to fit into the dominant culture remains relatively unexamined, with no room for alternatives to a medical model or for what "minorities" might want besides assimilation.

At the same time, though, this research, even when most committed to clinical models and quantitative data, is full of potential for more radical models for research and practice. There are some exceptions to the general trend when the research turns to how culturally specific practices ranging from healing ceremonies to understandings of history and oppression can be useful for mental health. There are, for example, studies of how religion functions within African American communities as a way to help people with depression and other mental health issues, and the research in Native communities is especially attuned to how traditional spiritual and cultural practices might have therapeutic value.[12] As the field of "multicultural psychology" addresses cultural difference more fully, it begins to challenge disciplinary and methodological boundaries.[13] It must grapple with the possibility that qualitative and ethnographic data are necessary in order to understand better the intersection of cultural difference and clinical practice.[14] Thus the fields of clinical psychology and social work move in the direction of medical anthropology by scholars such as Arthur Kleinman and Byron Good, who explore depression in cross-cultural perspective without presuming a medical model.[15] Following in their path, Theresa O'Nell examines the high incidence of depression on a Flathead reservation in Montana and wrestles with the incompatibility of the medical model with Flathead Salish understandings of depression as a cultural sadness for which one must accept responsibility.[16] Tracking between these perspectives is a reminder of the possible incommensurability of medical and cultural models and the imagination necessary to pursue the latter.

In the course of working on this project, I've been hearing hints of a different genealogy of depression in writings from the African diaspora by writers such as Harriet Jacobs, Nella Larsen, Octavia Butler, and, of course, Toni Morrison, as well as scholars such as Jacqui Alexander, Saidiya Hartman, Ruth Wilson Gilmore, and Sharon Holland. Their work chronicles long histories of "dispossession" that are both geographic and psychic, as well as imagining what Alexander calls "radical self-possession," a form of sovereignty that includes feelings and sensory experience. Although trauma can be a useful category for thinking about the psychic and transgenerational effects of slavery and colonialism, a full picture of this history must include racism's connections to more chronic and low-level feelings, such as those associated with depression. Like depression, racism is a pervasive problem that affects all levels of everyday experience, but sometimes in oblique ways that aren't overtly visible. As Sharon Holland puts it, "Racism is ordinary."[17] In its ordinary forms, racism is present, but differently so, for both white people and people of color—we are all affected by a system of differential access. Ruth Wilson Gilmore defines racism as "the state-sanctioned or extralegal production and exploitation of group-differentiated vulnerability to premature death," offering an emphatically materialist understanding of racism's inequities.[18] Can we add emotional life to this definition and consider how emotional debility can be one of the health problems that targets people for premature death? Moreover, what are the consequences for white people of living lives of privilege in the vicinity of the violence of racism? The emotional color line that Cornel West describes can itself be a catalyst for depression on both sides of the divide, including white people's feelings, sometimes unconscious, sometimes not, sometimes resentful, sometimes not, that their forms of sadness are incommensurable with those of the historically disenfranchised, an incommensurability that is lived affectively as alienation and hopelessness, as well as more clinical forms of these feelings, such as depression.

This chapter explores the relations between depression and racial histories of dispossession by considering the simultaneously ephemeral and pervasive nature of the archive of everyday racism through a particular focus on the writing of two scholars of the African diaspora, Saidiya Hartman and Jacqui Alexander, whose research on the absent archive of slavery produces forms of what I would call political depression. Whereas Hartman resists considering a return to Africa to be a form of reparation with the past, Alexander draws on indigenous practices of sovereignty that are both African and American in origin, as well as their syncretic forms, to articulate what she calls *radical self-possession,* which I read as a terminology for establishing the felt relation to body and home that (political) depression interrupts. My use of Hartman and Alexander to articulate political depression in terms of dispossession and the haunting of the past provides a framework for considering how the depression memoirs of two white writers, Sharon O'Brien's *The Family Silver* and Jeffery Smith's *Where the Roots Reach for Water,* frame depression in relation to histories of migration and class mobility.

My use of examples drawn predominantly from African American culture represents a necessary narrowing of focus for a hopelessly large project and is only one possible trajectory for the multidisciplinary project of thinking race and depression together. My borrowing from indigenous studies represents a claim for its necessary status as a resource for work on dispossession, and I hope that combining diaspora and indigeneity will inspire other comparative projects.[19] My goal is to mix it up—psychoanalysis and vernacular, black and white, indigeneity and diaspora—in order to cross the color line and make a case for a racialized understanding of depression that draws on different kinds of writing, including fusions of memoir and scholarship.

THE ARCHIVE OF ORDINARY RACISM

Following the passage from *Twilight: Los Angeles* cited earlier, Cornel West goes on to discuss the forms of expressive culture, including music and writing, that emerge from black sadness, referencing a lineage from the sorrow songs that Frederick Douglass writes about and W. E. B. Du Bois famously makes central to the "problem of the color line" up to the novels of Toni Morrison and the jazz of John Coltrane and Miles Davis. Formulating a cultural politics of emotion in the shorthand of a name check that encompasses both Anton Chekhov and Richard Pryor, West suggests that Morrison "gets at it [sadness] more / than any of the *novelists* / But / *Coltrane* / understood it" (109). Further insisting on the importance of culture, he also credits Miles Davis with facilitating that expression by standing back and letting Coltrane play for as long as he wants, in contrast with academics and politicians who are impatient to get to the point or to assert themselves. Echoing Grant Farred's argument that black public intellectuals come in many forms, West implicitly suggests that musicians and novelists may be especially well equipped to articulate the public feelings that are necessary to reckoning with the history of racism.[20]

I have thus found myself turning to art, rather than science or psychology, for complex affective stories about what racism (and depression) feels like. A persistent influence on this project, for example, has been readings of slave narrative that seek to recreate the lived experience of slavery in the face of a sketchy or absent archive, as well as the neo–slave narratives that turn to imaginative genres to do this historical work. Guided by hunches, I've also been collecting hints and resonances of the everyday affective life of racism in places where it sometimes seem less obtrusive or gets covered over by politeness—the flaring up of anger in Nella Larsen's *Passing*; Gloria Anzaldúa's discussion of *la facultad* as a form of extrasensory emotional knowledge in *Borderlands / La Frontera*; Kristina Wong's performance piece *Wong Flew over the Cuckoo's Nest*, about the high rates of depression and suicide among Asian American women; Nao Bustamante's "Neapolitan," a video installation that features footage of her crying as she watches a melodramatic love scene from *Like Water for Chocolate*, and commentary on it by José Muñoz.[21] I've been gathering moments that leap out because they provide complex accounts of what it *feels* like for people of color to live in the context of racism. Although it's a somewhat arbitrary and unsystematic collection, my hunch is that this is a necessary method in order to capture affective experiences that aren't always publicly visible, especially to white observers. It reflects what Phil Harper has called the "evidence of felt intuition," which becomes vital when there has been no public life around certain kinds of experience and the only available strategy is "speculation," the often disparaged epistemological status of "that which is not perceptible by conventional means."[22] A common thread in my examples is their focus on the domestic sphere, the landscape of everyday feelings, but from the vantage point of racialized divisions of labor where the hidden social relations and activities that keep middle-class households functioning or make them an aspirational horizon for the upwardly mobile are more visible. They highlight the dynamics of assimilation, exposing the ambivalent status of the quest for middle-class respectability that is so frequently the cause of depression or sadness for white people as well as people of color.

One such example is Octavia Butler's remarks about her inspiration for *Kindred*, her novel about a contemporary African American woman who involuntarily finds herself plunged into the scene of nineteenth-century slavery and must struggle with the everyday life of captivity, including sexual assault. Butler uses the science fiction strategy of time travel in the service of the neo–slave narrative, making the affective dynamics of servitude vivid by placing a contemporary black woman in the past. As is frequently the case in Butler's work, her heroine faces a complex ethical dilemma about sexual agency and servitude when she finds herself living the sexual relation between white slave owner and black slave woman that is her ancestry and having to choose whether to save the life of the white man without whom she will not be born in the future. In what might seem like something of a leap, Butler describes *Kindred*'s origins in her mother's experience as a maid who had to listen to racist remarks without responding to them and who is the kind of person who is misperceived as overly submissive:

> When I did *Kindred*, I really had had this experience in college that I talk about all the time, of this Black guy saying, "I wish I could kill all these old Black people that have been holding us back for so long, but I can't because I have to start with my own parents." That was a friend of mine. And I realized that, even though he knew a *lot* more than I did about Black history, it was all cerebral. He wasn't feeling any of it. He was the kind that would have killed and died, as opposed to surviving and hanging on and hoping and working for change. And I thought about my mother, because she used to take me to work with her when she couldn't get a baby sitter and I was too young to be left alone, and I saw her going in the back door, and I saw people saying things to her that she didn't like but couldn't respond to. I heard people say in her hearing, "Well, I don't really like colored people." And she kept working, and she put me through school, she bought her house—all the stuff she did. I realized that he didn't understand what heroism was. That's what I want to write about: when you are *aware* of what it means to be an adult and what choices you have to make, the fact that maybe you're afraid, but you still have to act.[23]

In contrast to her militant friend, who is so disdainful of what he sees as an earlier generation's cowardly assimilation that he is ready to kill them, Butler expresses sympathy and even admiration for her mother's survival strategies. In the intimacy of the domestic context, her mother's

livelihood is dependent on turning a deaf ear to racist remarks, and Butler suggests this might be a form of heroism in which the actions necessary for survival are accompanied by complex feelings including a mix
of fear and anger. It's telling that she faults her friend for being too cere-
bral, for his inability to "feel" Black history, whereas she uses imaginative fiction to make the complex choices of the oppressed more affectively intelligible, a task demanding enough to require the fantastic and
defamiliarizing strategies of science fiction. In making the emotional
dynamics of slavery and diaspora (as well as everyday racism) vivid,
Butler creates woman protagonists (such as Lilith in the *Xenogenesis*
trilogy) who are seen as traitors for consorting with their enemies or
oppressors. Her stories have the capacity to make the so-called traitor's
motivations understandable, often showing a willingness to negotiate
as the product of a stubborn sense of hope for the future that can take
the form of a commitment to nurturing a new mixed race.

Butler's anecdote resonates alongside the strange affective dynamics of affirmative action within the contemporary academy, one of the
places where racism now has a very ordinary life in a post–civil rights
world where acts of overt racism are supposedly no longer prevalent or
tolerated. In this context, people of color are often seen as the benefi-
ciary of policies that provide jobs, fellowships, and other forms of support, but what so often goes invisible in the polite world of bureaucratic
culture are the casual forms of racism or lack of understanding that
make this condition of so-called privilege one that is also pervaded by
anxiety and stress.

This chapter owes a great deal not only to the literary texts I've read
and taught, but also to the stories I've been privy to from my colleagues
over the years. But these stories, and their evidence of ordinary racism,
are not really mine to pass on. I've had to find traces of these often
secret knowledges in more public places and hope their resonances will
be recognizable. Phil Harper, for example, is willing to talk about how
his career is made by never saying no to requests to be the token contributor to collections, often writing essays at the last minute to meet
instant deadlines. Melissa Harris-Lacewell speaks about the injunction
against depression for middle-class black women who are instructed
to survive. Invoking the example of Fannie Lou Hamer, who ended her
years of activism alone and beaten down, she reframes the statement,

"I'm sick and tired of being sick and tired" as a comment about depression.[24]

These examples suggest that a rich vocabulary of affective life is available in the strange but ordinary situations created by racism. They speak to tensions between assimilation and radical politics and to gender's and class's refractions across racial difference, and they chart alternative modes of political response visible in everyday affective life rather than in activism or the streets. As instances of the complex links between violence and ordinary life, they also provide an important vantage point on the challenges of making links between the world of depressed white girls and national histories of trauma and mourning. (If it sometimes seems like the discussion has moved a long way away from depression, then it's a sign of work that needs to be done in order to connect disparate worlds, since the science/humanities divide is crosshatched with racial divides as well.) These examples from everyday life and from domestic scenes—these affects that look like politeness but tell other stories—are indicative of how wide-reaching the effects of racialized histories might be. They don't always appear as moments of overt violence, and the feelings that are manifest need to be seen not as repression but as a different form of publicity for anger and aggression that remains connected to earlier and more overt histories of racism. This legacy continues to pervade everyday experience—we are all living in an environment steeped with racialized violence: the land we walk on is stolen, the labor that produced the things we use is underpaid and exploited, the neighborhoods we live in are either segregated or gentrifying.

Saidiya Hartman's Political Depression

In *Lose Your Mother*, Saidiya Hartman joins the many writers and scholars who have attempted to bring slavery (and its ghosts) to life again, especially affectively, in order to demonstrate its persistent effect on the present. This is no mere scholarly exercise but one that carries deep personal significance for Hartman, as the descendant of slaves. It's also a history project that has very current political stakes. As she puts it, "If slavery persists as an issue in the political life of black America, it is not because of an antiquarian obsession with bygone days or the burden of a too-long memory, but because black lives are still imperiled and devalued by a racial calculus and a political arithmetic that were entrenched centuries ago. This is the afterlife of slavery—skewed life chances, limited access to health and education, premature death, incarceration, and impoverishment. I, too, am the afterlife of slavery."[25] Echoing Ruth Wilson Gilmore's definition of racism as "vulnerability to premature death," Hartman seeks to understand its status as the "afterlife of slavery" by exploring the connections between her own family history and a history of slavery that reaches back to Africa. Her research takes her to Ghana, where she explores the traces of the slave trade in sites such as the dungeons on the coast at Elmina, which have become part of a burgeoning industry in slavery tourism promoted by the government. Searching for the vestiges of life before slavery, she also travels inland along the trade routes that lead to the villages from which slaves were first captured, often by other Africans, in the first traumatic stages of the journey that would ultimately take them, if they survived that long, to the Americas.

Lose Your Mother is an unusual piece of scholarship that makes memoir integral to its painstaking archival research and fieldwork, not just an articulation of the personal investments that motivate it. Hartman's text thus further exemplifies the potential, explored in the previous section, for memoir to be a research method. She must write a "history of slavery that is a personal story" because one of the only ways she can convey the "slipperiness and elusiveness" of slavery's so frequently absent archive and address the dilemma of how to "write a story about an encounter with nothing" (16) is to record her own struggles and failures as a researcher. As a story about gaps in the historical record, *Lose Your Mother* sheds light on the gaps in my own efforts to track the relation between depression and the histories of slavery, genocide, and colonialism that lie at the heart of the founding of U.S. culture. I want depression, too, to be considered part of the "afterlife of slavery," but it can be hard to trace the connections between contemporary everyday feelings (especially those of white middle-class people) and the traumatic violence of the past—they might emerge as ghosts or feelings of hopelessness, rather than as scientific evidence or existing bodies of research or material forms of deprivation. Although it might seem odd to move from clinical investigations of depression in African American and other racialized communities to a memoir about a return to Africa, my claim is that cultural documents such as Hartman's memoir contain modes of thinking and feelings that don't yet exist in clinical theory and practice.

Lose Your Mother not only puts the category of depression in contact with histories of racism and colonialism but also lends itself to being read as a text of political depression. Hartman's journey to Africa is motivated by despair, by a sense of the failures of both the civil rights movement in the U.S. and the era of decolonization in Africa and of her own belatedness to those struggles. "Mine was an age not of dreaming but of disenchantment. . . . The dreams that had defined their horizon no longer defined mine. The narrative of liberation had ceased to be a blueprint for the future. The decisive break the revolutionaries had hoped to institute between the past and the present failed" (39). Hartman often represents herself as inconsolable as she resists any easy sense of belonging in the U.S. or in Africa. An ongoing sense of alienation and disenfranchisement in the U.S. makes her feel like a stranger not only among white people but among those African Americans who can sustain a hope for home or a dream of return. She also differentiates herself from the African American expatriates she meets in Ghana, the generation who came to Africa in the 1960s in the first flush of civil rights and decolonization in hopes of a better world, as well as from those tourists who look to Africa as a source of ancestors, Afrocentric culture, and welcome continuity with the past. "What had attracted the émigrés to Ghana were this vision of a new life and the promise of rebirth; what attracted me were the ruins of the old one. They were intent upon constructing a new society; I was intent upon tracing an itinerary of destruction from the coast to the savanna. They went to be healed. I went to excavate a wound. . . . My generation was the first that came here with the dungeon as our prime destination, unlike the scores of black tourists who, motivated by Alex Haley's *Roots*, had traveled to Ghana and other parts of West Africa to reclaim their African patrimony. For me, the rupture was the story" (41–42).

Hartman's marking of her generational and political distance from the era of civil rights and decolonization suggests that political depression might explain the current explosion of interest in trauma studies and public cultures of memory. She joins novelists such as Toni Morrison and critics such as Hortense Spillers (and a host of others) in returning to the past to "excavate a wound," insisting that to do otherwise is to fall prey to a historical amnesia that has consequences for the present.[26] A politics of depression is one in which the "rupture [is] the story," in which there is no celebratory connection between Africans here and Africans there, and no romance or utopia of a precolonial African past. "A growing sense of despair and an exhausted political imagination incapable of dreaming of radical change had everything to do with the busloads of black strangers looking to shed tears in a slave fort" (171). Holding fast to feelings of despair and political depression, Hartman looks to ward off melancholy attachments to the past or naïve celebrations of Afrocentrism that might be characterized as sentimental.[27] It's a difficult feeling to sustain politically and to articulate publicly; in a television interview with Tavis Smiley, she is at pains to explain what it would mean to insist on the lack of connection to Africa, in response to Smiley's desire for an uplifting story of ancestral recovery.[28] In her unrepentant crankiness, Hartman resists easy therapeutic protocols or reverse migrations that might aim to talk her out of her sense of alienation. One question this section ultimately seeks to ask, however, is whether the distinction Hartman makes between "healing" and "excavating a wound" can be rethought so that they are not mutually exclusive.

In suggesting that *Lose Your Mother* be read as an articulation of political depression, I want to reframe what might otherwise be a focus on its efforts to provide affective access to historical trauma. It's certainly the case that some of the text's most powerful moments emerge from its impossible attempts to conjure the experience of slavery, as when Hartman stands in the slave dungeons of Elmina and can't feel the past adequately or can do so only as a creepy encounter with dust: she fails to "reach through time and touch the prisoners": "The only part of my past that I could put my hands on was the filth from which I recoiled" (115, 119). Hoping to make up for the absent textual archive by staging a material encounter with history (and another reason for memoir is to document this kind of fieldwork), Hartman has a sensory experience of a different kind than she had imagined as she walks on the compacted layers of skin and shit that line the floors of the dungeon and form an all too material remnant of the past. They are ultimately, however, the scene of a missed encounter since rather than any sense of connection with the slaves who inhabited the space, she feels only a sense of loss.

Hartman's encounter with slavery's textual archive, sometimes the only recourse for recovering the past, is equally unsentimental, as she refuses any sense of easy contact with trauma's shocking realities. In recovering the archival traces of a girl whose death on the slave ship *Recovery* was the subject of a court case that was used as publicity by the British abolitionist Wilberforce in the eighteenth century, Hartman is critical of the way the girl's story leads to spectacle (in the form of an illustration of her suspended upside down and naked) rather than felt experience even in the hands of those who are sympathetic to her plight. Her efforts to find a different way than Wilberforce's to tell the story, to "save the girl, not from death or sickness or a tyrant but from oblivion," leads her to fantasize about the possibility of escape and resistance. "If the story ended there, I could feel a small measure of comfort. I could hold on to this instant of possibility. I could find a salutary lesson in the girl's suffering and pretend a story was enough to save her from oblivion" (152–53). But Hartman is skeptical of this kind of affective or archival rescue, recognizing that "it was easier to feel fully the loss of one life and to hang your hopes on one girl. Too many deaths were unmanageable" (143).

As vivid as Hartman's versions of them might be, encounters with absent archives and their reconstruction of ghost stories and other fictions have become increasingly familiar—with Toni Morrison's *Beloved* perhaps the best known—although they remain relevant and are destined to be repeated as long as slavery's afterlife of racism persists. One of the distinctive contributions of Hartman's project is the use of personal narrative to frame archival recovery as motivated by political depression and the accompanying questions this move raises about the broader political work of trauma studies' affective dynamics. Hartman is very stringent about avoiding any self-congratulatory fall into melancholic nostalgia, or a dwelling in the past that is not connected to the present. Central to her affective politics is the fraught question of how (and whether) there are connections between her own position as middle-class black intellectual and slavery's past. As she stands in the dungeons of Africa frustrated by her inability to touch the lives (and deaths) of slaves, she asks, "Could I trace my despair back to the first generation stolen from their country? Was it why I sometimes felt as weary of America as if I too had landed in what was now South Carolina in 1526 or in Jamestown in 1619? Was it the tug of all the lost mothers and orphaned children? Or was it that each generation felt anew the yoke of a damaged life and the distress of being a native stranger, an eternal alien?" (130). Hartman turns to history as a resource for understanding the despair and weariness that are frequently cited as symptoms of depression but are in this case read as the effects of racism and a sense of homelessness, not a medical disease. Uncured by the social movements of the 1960s and 1970s, Hartman's political depression leads to a journey to Africa (one that is historical as well as geographic) that is an alternative to both politics and therapy, whether pharmaceutical or psychoanalytic. She seeks an encounter with history that can be sensuous or felt because it takes place in the material specificity of a location.

Risking the charges of narcissism or self-indulgence so often leveled against writers of memoir or autoethnography, Hartman searches for the links between the experiences of slaves and her own life so as to ask crucial questions about the relation between past and present that keep the history of slavery relevant to contemporary concerns. "Why else begin an autobiography in a graveyard?" she asks (130), as she wonders what versions of utopia or political futurity might be available to her if they must emerge from the traumatic rupture that is constitutive of African American identity rather than the dream of civil rights or decolonization. Her claim that despair is historically produced is not an easy one, since she finds herself "fumbling" and a "failed witness" in her efforts "to connect the dots between then and now," but she nonetheless opens the way to an important understanding of political depression as a condition in which history shapes even the most personal experience of the present.

Despite the grimly simple fact of ongoing racist inequality, however, the connections between her own despair and past pain remain elusive for Hartman. Faced with this challenge, her narrative takes an unexpected swerve from the dungeons of Africa back to the streets of her New York childhood by way of her mother's origins in Montgomery, Alabama. The personal erupts in a surprising and potentially risky way through a story that might seem minor in comparison with the violence of the dungeons. Hartman tells an anecdote about how her mother was stopped by the police after accidentally running a red light on an icy street, and how she, as a twelve-year-old girl, yelled at the cop in a state of indignant rage despite her mother's fear of confrontation. Startled by her angry outburst, the policeman lets her mother go, and she and her mother are so shaken by the incident that they cannot speak of it. It's a story of everyday racism in the U.S., one that is notable for its ordinariness rather than its spectacularity, and Hartman unpacks it in order to show the complexity of the feelings that have been inherited by a generation brought up during the civil rights era. Explaining how her mother passed on to her, alongside hopes for political change, a dread of white policemen, Hartman exposes the underbelly of dreams of freedom and racial uplift and the emotional unconscious of a world that remains "ruled by the color line." Although Hartman's mother is "an integrationist and a striver," she has nonetheless taught her children "a set of contradictory lessons" about "infinite possibilities and absolute limitations," "spacious skies, amber waves, and niggers hanging from trees" (132). The Catholic schoolgirl with "two ponytails and ashy knees and a plaid jumper" (131) who is the recipient of these teachings is poised to respond to a minor traffic incident as though she were about to be lynched in the South or taken into slavery in Africa. This legacy of fear and suspicion even in a respectable black family—an inability to trust white people or a tendency to assume the worst in any encounter with authority—is the everyday affective life of racism that Hartman seeks to capture along with recounting the dismal statistics on imprisonment and death that are the far more visible evidence (to some at least) of ongoing racial inequality.

It might seem dangerously presumptuous to place her own experience alongside that of slaves in the past, and Hartman is wary of how a sentimental identification with slavery—"the tug of all the lost mothers and orphaned children"—can provide too easy a vehicle for inconsolable grief and suffering. She doesn't have to reach far, though, to connect the past and present, and immediately after her account of the childhood incident, she mentions Hurricane Katrina's devastations, which forcefully demonstrate her sense that slavery's past has ongoing meaning because of its urgent relation to present-day racism. But Hartman's bolder move is the intrusion of the less overtly violent episode into this account of extreme and very public suffering through her turn to a personal anecdote that is quite ordinary to describe the affective life of racism. Hartman dares to place her own racial despair alongside the gravity of the dungeons so as to avoid a public culture of trauma that substitutes the horrors of the past for a less dramatic but no less disturbing present. Without this connection to the present, trauma histories can become in their own way an exercise in self-indulgence, a substitution of the melodrama of the past for the everyday weariness of the present.

In her vigilant attention to the dark side of Africa's slave-trading past and postcolonial present and to ongoing racism in the U.S., Hartman might seem likely to refuse the reparative mode central to recent efforts within cultural studies to find alternatives to critique. But her attention to an affective afterlife of slavery that includes her own subterranean feelings of fear, anger, and hopelessness is also its own form of reparation, a way of acknowledging the value of the ordinary but complex feelings of young girls growing up in the shadows of the still to be achieved dreams of emancipation, decolonization, and civil rights. Moreover, even as she seems persistently suspicious about utopian visions of liberation, Hartman has her own version of a reparative dream. *Lose Your Mother* closes with her journey from Ghana's coast to the slave routes of the interior where she is confronted yet again not only by interminable loss but by the specter of African-on-African violence that gives the lie to a simple white-on-black exploitation or a heroically victimized African subject. As part of a research group on slavery and memory that consists largely of African scholars, she feels an increasing sense of isolation as an American of the African diaspora for whom the bitterness of slavery lives on and for whom her colleagues' tales of African resistance and survival provide no solace. But in her commitment to the epistemology of rupture, Hartman finds what she calls "fugitive dreams": "If after a year in Ghana I could still call myself an African American, it was because my Africa had its source in the commons created by fugitives and rebels, in the courage of suicidal girls aboard slave ships, and in the efforts, thwarted and realized, of revolutionaries intent upon stopping the clock and instituting a new order, even if it cost them their lives. For me, returning to the source didn't lead to the great courts and to the regalia of kings and queens. The legacy I chose to claim was articulated in the ongoing struggle to escape, stand down, and defeat slavery in all of its myriad forms. It was the fugitive's legacy" (234). Hartman seeks a utopia, not of national sovereignty or of cultural nationalism's sense of kinship, but one in which people find ways to move forward by coming together around violence and despair. "It was a dream of autonomy rather than nationhood. It was a dream of an elsewhere, with all its promises and dangers, where the stateless might, at last, thrive" (234). In her utopian "dream of an elsewhere," she can hold on to her depressive affect, even use it as a source of transformation and a way to construct a vision of how those who are depressed, alienated, lonely, or stateless can find comfort. She articulates a politics in which former slaves, conjured through memory despite inadequate archives, become comrades: "It requires the reconstruction of society, which is the only way to honor our debt to the dead. This is the intimacy of our age with theirs—an unfinished struggle. To what end does one conjure the ghost of slavery, if not to incite the hopes of transforming the present?" (170). Rejecting a politics of reparation that is locked in the past, and rejecting also the image of the slave on his knees supplicating for freedom, Hartman seeks a politics that eschews the sentimental and keeps despair next to hope. She wants to avoid an interminable sadness that remains fixed in the past and doesn't make connections to the future, but also a naïve optimism that doesn't address the past and its violence adequately and that is too easily celebratory.[29]

Radical Self-Possession and the Sacred in Jacqui Alexander

When the traces of a woman whose experience of the Middle Passage she is researching continue to elude her, Jacqui Alexander experiences political depression in the form of writer's block. Yet while Alexander fully acknowledges the ruptures in the archive that Saidiya Hartman insists on, her hopefulness about reclamation of self and history gives her process a different tone. The difference lies in Alexander's willingness to embrace the sacred, and her relation to spiritual practices that connect the African diaspora to inner-city enclaves in places like the Bronx and Brooklyn, where people may be, like Hartman, profoundly alienated but are also "living an ancient memory in a city overcrowded with errant spirits, teeming with yearning not easily satisfied in towering buildings or in slabs of concrete."[30] Whereas Hartman suggests that "history is how the secular world attends to the dead" (18), Alexander moves beyond the "secular" in order to traffic in spiritual practices that can also acknowledge the dead in the antisentimental ways that are so important for Hartman.

Alexander makes the bold claim that decolonization, which includes liberation from the internalized self-hatred, melancholia, and political depression that are among the long-term effects of histories of violence, takes the form of a "radical self-possession" that involves practices of spiritual reclamation. Noting the "geographies of suspicion" that pervade feminist and transnational theory that thinks of the spiritual as patriarchal or depoliticized, Alexander asks, "What would taking the Sacred seriously mean for transnational feminism and related radical projects, beyond the institutionalized use value of theorizing marginalization?" (326). Observing the often patronizing qualities of ethnographic studies of women of color and poor women whose spiritual beliefs are viewed as strange, or exotic, or other even when they are studied sympathetically, she wants to "move beyond the more dominant understanding of African spiritual practice as cultural retention and survival, to get inside the meaning of the spiritual as epistemological" (293). A priestess in the Vodou and Lucumí (more widely known as Santería) traditions, Alexander draws on her own experience of African diasporic practices in "taking the Sacred seriously." Refusing to see them as mutually exclusive, she tracks between the languages of spirituality and the languages of theory.

In an essay tellingly titled "Pedagogies of the Sacred," Alexander, like Hartman, incorporates into her scholarship an autobiographical account of her own research process, which includes her frustrated encounter with the absent archive of slavery and her own Afro-Caribbean spiritual practice and encounters with the sacred. And like Hartman, she turns to unconventional forms of scholarly writing, in this case a prose poem to the African spirit Yemaya and the imagined words of the African woman Kitsimba whose history she is seeking to recreate. Alexander's experimental prose is the desperate measure she finds necessitated by her own struggle with the archive of slavery that also threatens to defeat Hartman. Attempting to embark on a research project about "ways in which African cosmologies and modes of healing became the locus of epistemic struggle in nineteenth-century Trinidad" (293) and seeking to find archival traces in the colonial repositories of Britain, Alexander falls into an intellectual crisis that she also characterizes as a spiritual crisis: "Divested of the usual way of posing questions, I became vulnerable and experienced the kind of crisis that is known as writer's block" (294). She declares, "Writer's block, like alienation—or rather, writer's block as an aspect of alienation—is a spiritual problem requiring a spiritual solution" (320). She comes to understand her writer's block as "the recalcitrance that masked an unacknowledged yearning for Spirit" (294). Like Hartman, she struggles to find a research method and a form of writing that will capture the lived experience of slavery, and she draws on both her spiritual practice and the genre of memoir as her tools because the available archive is inadequate to the task.

Alexander sees the sacred as an epistemological category, a new way of producing knowledge rather than a category that is utterly outside or beyond secular ways of knowing. But it also challenges conventional modes of knowledge production and produces ruptures and shifts in her text, including, for example, a section in which Kitsimba, the woman she is researching, communicates to her the impossibility of executing her project in academic modes. Kitsimba claims, "She [Alexander] couldn't write about me unless she came to know and feel my daily life," a task all the more difficult because "she [Alexander] was not one of those who learned by feeling" (314–15). Rather than researching in books and archives, Alexander concludes that she must instead embark on a healing process that involves the body and new ways of accessing feelings. Her spiritual practice is thus also a profound response to the quest for self-possession and psychic integrity—the problem of knowledge takes affective form.

Willing to engage in the language of the sacred as a way to counter the positivism and rationalist epistemologies of the West and Global North, Alexander suggests that histories of oppression that are embedded in colonialism, genocide, and slavery are manifest in spiritual form. In her own way, she is contributing to new conceptions of neoliberalism and globalization that explore how the operations of biopower target certain populations for destruction or create states of exception and permanent war. She understands liberation to entail a reclaiming [liberation] of a self whose spirits have been depressed, a process that is a daily practice. Speaking, for example, of the accomplishments of *This Bridge Called My Back*, she says, "It was not a transcendent vision, but one that was rooted in transforming the mundaneness of lived experience, the very ground on which violence finds fodder" (279). Just as scholars have been learning to reread Western concepts of democracy, human rights, melancholy, and master–slave relations through the lens of colonial violence, so too can we read the discourse of the sacred as linked to these histories of violence.

Alexander's experience of writer's block and spiritual crisis, which I

other ways of
naming
which
don't
reduce to
medical
ailment

would suggest are other ways of naming depression that don't reduce
it to a medical ailment, is fundamentally connected to experiences of
migration, diaspora, dislocation, and dispossession, both contemporary
and historical. Like Hartman, she turns to history and global politics to
explain psychic conditions that include everyday emotions of despair
and frustration. Read as a response to multicultural psychology's approaches to depression, her work provides an alternative language for
the persistent impact of displacement. As an immigrant from the Caribbean (and hence shaped by diasporas both old and new), Alexander
is particularly attuned to spiritual work as a form of "centering" that
addresses the "misalignment" that frequently accompanies displacement. Describing the amnesiac effects of assimilation, she notes "the
perils associated with the journey: there is a cost associated with taking
refuge in the borrowed gifts of alienation that cultivate the practice of
forgetting, the refusal to pull on the ancestral cord, denying ourselves
life force" (319). Spiritual practice in the African diasporic tradition
is a way of forging a connection with cultures of origin that need not
be imaginary, nostalgic, or essentializing. In her commentary on *This
Bridge*, Alexander holds to an antinationalist, anti-identitarian notion
of "home," one that must always strive to be a house of difference, although it can include connection across difference. "We have grown
up metabolizing exile, feeding on its main by-products—alienation and
separation" (274). The project of overcoming the forms of alienation
and separation, including spiritual ones, that transnational capital produces as it moves people around the globe is a decolonization project
that belongs to all of us, although some bear disproportionately the burden of its displacements.

In proposing the sacred as a response to oppression, Alexander conceives of a politics of interiority that involves affect, the body, and practice, or a "rewiring of the senses" (328). She offers a version of "the
utopia of everyday habit" to be explored in the next chapter in her discussion of how the sacred emerges from the ordinary circumstances of
daily and domestic life. "If it [the Sacred] is to be found everywhere in
the terrain of the everyday as part of the continuous existential fabric
of being, then it lives simultaneously in the daily lives of everyone, in
spiritual work that assumes a different form from those I have engaged
here, but also in daily incidents, in those 'things' we routinely attribute
to coincidence, those moments of synchronicity, the apparently dispa-

rate that have cohesion but under another framework" (322). Even as she demystifies the sacred by connecting it to a mundane everyday, Alexander does not shy away from insisting on a notion of the sacred that transforms our understandings of political practice. (She thus echoes my suggestion, with respect to the connections between left melancholy and acedia, that in addition to offering secular explanations for the spiritual, we consider the possibility of spiritualizing the political.) Building on her long-standing rejection of easy distinctions between tradition and modernity, she insists that the sacred not be dismissed through its association with the primitive and the traditional and other conceptual frameworks that privilege the secular.[31] She translates the sacred into the language of transnational feminist theory, but without domesticating it.

Alexander uses as a foundation for transnational politics and scholarship African-based cosmologies that begin from the premise that all human beings are important and connected. For those who remain resolutely committed to the secular, this premise might be one way of understanding the meaning of the sacred—as a form of radical humanism and radical democracy that insists on the importance of every person to the collective. (For Alexander, though, a significant source for this understanding of the human is the African concept of *ase*, the life force or energy that is present in every being.)[32] She invokes the category of the "sacred" to describe new forms of knowledge production and archival practice that can counter the soul-killing effects of colonialism, which continue even now to produce forms of self-alienation that require a politics of self-transformation. The category of the sacred is a way of articulating this politics of the subject, which, like Avery Gordon's account of Toni Cade Bambara's call for a revolution of the self, is not an individualized quest.[33] The sacred is connected to everyday practices that are not glamorous or other-worldly and that suggest a rethinking of political practices that can address the self and its feelings, moods, energies, and will. Taking the risk of invoking the sacred allows Alexander to connect everyday feelings of disconnection with transnational histories, as well as to forge practices, often everyday practices of the body, that aim to address them.

SACRED THERAPIES

One of Jacqui Alexander's proposed directions for future inquiry into the pedagogies of the sacred is to establish a center for the study of indigenous spiritualities.[34] Using the category of "indigeneity" to encompass African diasporic practices is a significant move, suggesting a possible rapprochement between notions of indigeneity and diaspora that are sometimes at odds with one another because of the differences between those who can lay claim to home (including literal land claims) and those for whom it is a more imaginary concept. The study of indigenous spiritualities would enable a discussion of the syncretisms that connect indigenous and diasporic cultures and a global comparative perspective on, for example, African and (Native) American cosmologies. And if the goal is also to undo distinctions between the sacred and secular epistemologies, then American indigenous studies are an important resource for bringing the spiritual into the domains of therapy, politics, and scholarship. Hartman's and Alexander's efforts to explain despair and depression as the result of the long-term legacies of diaspora and slavery are matched by efforts to explain contemporary indigenous struggles with addiction and depression as the product of colonization, genocide, and displacement. Increasingly, "therapy" within indigenous communities includes not only historical frameworks but traditional spiritual practices as tools for healing. Theresa O'Nell, for example, describes understandings of depression on the Flathead reservation that incorporate a historical and culturally specific understanding of depression as a sadness that acknowledges transgenerational loss.[35] The social worker Maria Yellow Horse Brave Heart combines trauma theory and indigenous paradigms to develop workshops that address long-term histories of violence.[36] The wealth of work on the residential school system, including, for example the establishment of a Truth and Reconciliation Commission in Canada, proceeds from the premise that the legacy of colonization includes mind and soul and that decolonizing the mind entails a complex mix of historical, spiritual, legal, and psychic work.[37]

The debates about the category of sovereignty that have been central to Native American and indigenous studies in the U.S. and Canada are an important place where distinctions between the secular and the spiritual are challenged as claims are made for the relevance of spiritual understandings to notions of sovereignty. Dale Turner, for example, suggests that indigenous forms of knowledge, which include those which Western paradigms might classify as spirituality rather than philosophy, need to be incorporated into legal and governmental negotiations through the work of "word warriors" who can traffic between indigenous philosophy and Western political understandings.[38] He rejects liberal models of sovereignty that confine indigenous culture to a minoritarian position within a Western model of governmentality. Taiaiake Alfred also remains critical of sovereignty as a fundamentally Western concept, subjecting it to critique from the vantage point of indigenous spiritualities that cannot be contained within it as a form of cultural difference and suggesting new models for power based on indigenous concepts such as respect.[39] Like Alexander, these critical theorists offer an ambitious model for spirituality as an epistemological category.[40]

This developing body of work suggests that the psychic is also a domain for sovereignty and one that is intimately connected to questions of land rights, governmentality, and political transformation. Rethinking categories of self-possession, self-determination, and sovereignty from the vantage point of the sacred also has implications for rethinking the relations between the political and the emotional, and hence for understandings of depression. It suggests new ways of combining the cultural recognition of historical violence with contemporary therapy and politics. This work acknowledges the destructive afterlife of slavery and colonialism while also using the indigenous resources for building self and community present in indigenous American and African diaspora traditions. A truly integrated "multicultural therapy" would encompass culturally specific indigenous theories of sovereignty, which in redefining what we mean by claiming selfhood, offer a significant alternative to psychoanalytic models.

The paradigms for depression that emerge from histories of colonization and diaspora and from indigenous concepts of the sacred are suggestive for white and middle-class understandings of depression as well. A radical theory of depression aims to do justice to questions of dispossession and race in order to build a systemic framework that can be used by all. It offers alternatives to liberal forms of multicultural counseling for people of color and to therapy for white people that makes no reference to racism. Until there are more firmly established forms of radical therapeutic practice, cultural texts and practices (including spiritual ones) will remain an important resource for imagining what radical self-possession feels like.

REREADING THE DEPRESSION MEMOIR

What if we were to read the depression memoir through the critical framework provided by the preceding discussion of African diaspora, colonial genocide and displacement, and indigenous spiritualities? Over the course of writing this book, I continued reading in what is a constantly proliferating subgenre, and that question was one guide to my search for examples of the genre that I liked better than the mainstream memoirs by Slater, Styron, Wurtzel, Solomon, and others. Eventually I did find some fellow travelers, writers who took a skeptical view of the medical model and of pharmaceutical cures and who instead saw depression as the occasion for an ongoing process of adjustment, interpretation, and new ways of living (and hence well suited to the work of memoir).[41] Two writers in particular stood out because they combine scholarly research and memoir: in *The Family Silver*, Sharon O'Brien writes about her experiences on sabbatical as she traces the roots of her chronic depression in family histories marked by class, migration, and the failed quest for upward mobility, including that of her Harvard-educated father; and in *When the Roots Reach for Water*, Jeffery Smith's graduate work in environmental studies at the University of Montana informs his efforts to write a "natural history" of depression about his experiences after he stops taking antidepressants.[42] These writers offer significant alternatives to pharmaceutical treatment for depression because they understand its causes to be multiple—the result of very human and commonplace vulnerabilities, as well as long-standing historical and social inequalities.

Suggesting the capacious nature of the depression memoir, O'Brien's and Smith's messy and ambiguous conclusions about depression contrast with the much more straightforward endorsement of drugs to be found in the publicly celebrated memoirs by Slater, Styron, Solomon, and Wurtzel. One index of that difference is their different publishers and corresponding public spheres. For alternatives to the medical model, one has to seek out books published by university presses or small independent presses—*The Family Silver* by University of Chicago Press and *When the Roots Reach for Water* by North Point Press, a division of Farrar, Straus and Giroux (the publisher of *Lose Your Mother*). Within those forums, it is possible to combine memoir and critical analysis, to embark on what might seem like unwieldy or lengthy digressions, to stray from the sensational case history, to offer open-ended conclusions, to experiment with prose styles that may not be user-friendly. They also suggest uses for the memoir form other than that of the conventional medical case history or sensational confession, including its value as research report, speculative fiction, and creative articulation of public feelings.

Testifying eloquently to the specter of elite institutions and to the class aspirations fostered by academia, O'Brien and Smith can be productively read alongside Hartman and Alexander because they frame depression in terms of dispossessions of class mobility and assimilation that are at least implicitly racialized. Reading these memoirs from a more explicitly racialized perspective, particularly one focused on the entwinements of literal and psychic dispossession, underscores their emphasis on class mobility and geographic displacement (including education) as an alternative to medical models. School takes Smith away from his roots in Appalachia, and his eventual return there becomes part of his process of learning to live with depression. O'Brien's Harvard education gives her an orientation to the social geographies of Boston different from that she had as a girl in the suburbs and echoes the desire for assimilation that prompted her father to leave the working-class Irish Catholic community of Lowell, Massachusetts, in which he grew up. Although education gives them access to institutions of writing and publishing that enable their memoirs, these two writers also expose the shortcomings of academic institutions in ways that overlap with my own memoir writing and with the methodological impasses confronted by Hartman and Alexander. (Smith's experience as a social worker also gives him a critical vantage point on medical institutions.)

Sharon O'Brien's Emotional Inheritance

Sharon O'Brien's willingness to explore cultural explanations for depression provides a welcome alternative to Prozac memoirs, but I was also drawn to *The Family Silver* because of our shared biography as the children of migration histories and as girls who were saved by being smart in school but who grew up to become feminists ambivalent about academia.[43] O'Brien's critical memoir is a research and writing project catalyzed by the midlife depression she experiences when she begins to question her lifelong dedication to school and reading. When drugs and other cures don't work, she turns to family history in search of "emotional inheritance" rather than "genetic inheritance" (xiii). Although O'Brien doesn't wholly reject the genetic or the medical model—she herself relies on medication and adopts the "pragmatic" approach of embracing whatever works—she also seeks alternatives to stories that extol drugs as cure. "Because my unwelcome visitor didn't disappear as the Prozac ads had promised, I had wanted a story to explain what had happened to me; it seemed to me that being subject to human frailty and limitation—un-American attributes, human conditions—required some sort of explanation" (xii).

To write that story O'Brien uses her skills as a literary scholar who not only specializes in biography and its accompanying archival research but who has a facility for images. Her episodic memoir, while structured around the larger narrative of her mother's and father's histories, is also composed as a series of vignettes that highlight important objects and documents. One of the compelling images is that of the book's title, the family silver that is passed down from her mother's family as the one form of wealth they accrued. Equally important are the documents of her parents' academic and writerly aspirations, such as her father's Harvard application and diploma, her own forgotten application that announces her sense of being "in the shadow of Harvard Yard," and her mother's memo books, which O'Brien discovers after her death. A collector in the archive of feelings, O'Brien, like Hartman, treats family documents as materials for a research project, the results of which are both memoir and academic scholarship that contributes to fields such as American studies, feminist studies, clinical psychology, and trauma studies, as well as to the study of memoir itself.[44] Her writing displays that combination of the historical and the lyrical that makes memoir a genre well suited for public feelings.

O'Brien's depression grows particularly pronounced during her sabbatical year at Harvard, a return not only to the Boston area where she grew up, but to the school where she did both her undergraduate and her graduate work and where her father also went. She traces her sense of unfulfilled expectation to her parents' failed aspirations for themselves and especially to her father's own descent into depression upon being fired from a job that was supposed to be a big promotion. The irony is that "[her] father's midlife depression began after a professional failure; [O'Brien's], after a professional success." "Despite our differences, we had a lot in common. We were both forty years old when our depressions began, on the threshold of the second half of life, and we both found the work and meaning of our lives crumbling. We stood there, he with his failure, I with my success, looking into the abyss, all structures dissolved" (206).

O'Brien stresses the crushing pressures of the American dream and the need to disengage from its demands for visible forms of success. As she explores the significance of Harvard, which "symbolizes, concentrates, expects, and venerates the pressure to achieve," in both her father's and her own life, she comes to question how the "link between depression and seeking external approval" has governed her academic life. Seeking to turn from scholarship to more creative kinds of writing (including *The Family Silver* itself), she finds a way out of depression by detaching herself from this capitalist emphasis on the pressure to make one's identity around dissertations, books, and other markers of productivity (and in this respect, among others, her story resonates with my own).[45] Combining her Americanist knowledge of traditions of retreat such as Thoreau's with her feminist expertise, she suggests that depression can be seen as "an unconscious form of resistance to the work ethic" and seeks stories that might embrace this not as failure or weakness but as a strong choice. "I'm working on finding a new story for my life, a story that gives me hope but doesn't require the happy ending of recovery. This is a struggle in America, a culture that celebrates and practically requires individual achievement, a culture where we don't have enough stories for imagining lives that do not fit, in one way or another, the success plot" (257).

Although O'Brien does not draw on queer theories of non-normativity to imagine lives and stories that "do not fit . . . the success plot," her commitment to feminism means that gender is integral to her sociocultural narrative of depression as connected to class and migration. She especially emphasizes how the "niceness" demanded of middle-class girls keeps them silent and frustrated. Describing a photograph of herself at about the age of twelve, already the good student, she writes,

"She's the good girl, the one who follows the family plan, the one who assumes the pose. She's getting rewarded for it, and yet she looks inexpressibly sad" (37). Alert to how she was held back as a young person and to how her later feminism enabled her scholarship, including her biography of Willa Cather, to flourish, she offers a feminist account of fear as the root of depression: "fear of speaking up, fear of expressing the self fully, fear of not being . . . well, nice." "And then, fear of what you fear will follow speaking your mind, or not measuring up to what other people expect—abandonment, the ghost that had haunted me and my family for a long time" (23).

Manifesting the influence of much first-generation feminist criticism about women writers, O'Brien also places great weight on the importance of finding voice and of self-expression. Of her mother's memo books, which mix family genealogy with lists of things to do, she says, "I get a glimpse of the heroism of an elderly woman simply living her life while her health and strength were fading. I used to think of my mother's life as sadly incomplete—that was why she thrived so on my more public life—but these memo books are brimming with the on-goingness of daily life, which is what you lose when you are claimed by depression, the source of the blank patches in my life that I never let my mother see" (146). O'Brien finds in her mother's memo books the writing of everyday life that is testament to both creativity and ordinary experience. Rather than being rescued from silence by the middle-class and elite institutions of academia that give her a life different from her mother's, she finds herself still held in place by norms of femininity. But it is important to note that the norm that dictates silence for women is also marked by class and race, and a fuller account of how O'Brien's narrative concerns a specifically white and middle-class femininity would be telling.

A racialized perspective is, however, present at least implicitly in O'Brien's attention to class and migration, which are central to the multigenerational history of her family, who are descended from Irish Catholic immigrants. Boston and its surrounding area figure prominently in her narrative, as a city that encompasses both elite academic culture and the working-class white (and racially segregated) neighborhoods produced by Irish immigration. Rather than focus solely on her maternal lineage, her gendered analysis leads her to consider how norms of masculinity are adapted by the men in her family—the dashing but absentee maternal grandfather with a career as a performer and her father's rise from the factories of Lowell to a degree from Harvard. The family's earlier history in Ireland is difficult for O'Brien to trace, however, leading her to wonder about the effects not only of the experience of migration and the poverty that led to it but also of the silence around this history. "I think that we inherit our ancestors' emotional histories, particularly their unexpressed stories of suffering, exile, and yearning. . . . From what we know of trauma now, it's clear that both those who stayed in Ireland and those who left, never to return to their homeland, were marked emotionally and psychologically, and that inheritance has to have marked their children and grandchildren" (80). Linking depression to the transgenerational transmission of trauma, O'Brien discusses the history of Irish immigrants in terms that borrow from discussions of the Holocaust or African diaspora. At the end of the narrative, she returns to Ireland to look for the traces of her family lineage and is able to declare, "They don't care about how well I've done in school, or how many books I've published, or how clean my house is. They're just glad that I've made it back to this little town in West Cork and to this graveyard" (334). Like Hartman and Alexander, who trace the legacies of the African diaspora in political depression, writer's block, and ordinary racism, O'Brien takes seriously the long-term impact of migration histories on her own depression, although it is also significant that, unlike them, she can hope to find family upon her return to the places of her past.

A Natural History of Depression

Jeffery Smith's rural and more directly working-class origins give him a rather different trajectory than O'Brien's, although they both link depression to the pressures of upward (and outward) mobility. His education is nowhere close to the "shadows of Harvard Yard," instead taking him to public institutions in more peripheral locations in the Midwest and West, including Ohio University in Athens, the University of Michigan, and the University of Montana. Although my attraction to O'Brien's work was obvious, given our shared identity as feminist academics, Smith's *Where the Roots Reach for Water: A Personal and Natural History of Melancholia* was an unexpected discovery that ended up being particularly compelling for my project because it departs so emphatically from a narrative of pharmaceutical cure. He recounts how he painstakingly rebuilds his life after drugs fail to cure his depression, brought on while he himself works with psychiatric patients. As he puts it, "In my eight years as a psychiatric case manager I'd never heard of any treatment plan to guide a depressed client whose medications didn't work" (76). Like O'Brien, Smith turns to reading—from the eclectic repertoire of an autodidact that includes the history of melancholy—and to storytelling modeled after his eccentric reading in the archaic category of "natural history." Although trained as a scholar, Smith's departure from conventional medical research and customary forms of professional expertise enables him to forge an unusual path.

Moving in the directions taken by the Public Feelings project in talking about political depression, Smith writes about how the medical and scientific models of depression are linked to industrialization with its relentless demand for labor, and he dubs the current moment the "Age of Anti-Depression" (in contrast to the Renaissance and Romantic embrace of an "Age of Melancholy"), because depression counters the "efficiency," "productivity," "success," "networking," and "optimism" demanded by the modern workplace and culture, it is shunned (110). Like O'Brien's, his story is also further illuminated by being read in the context of African diaspora and indigenous perspectives on land and dispossession, since his recovery from depression is significantly enabled by his return to rural Appalachia and by an evolving understanding of nostalgia, home, and place inspired by his interest in environment and landscape.

In a move that resembles my historical turn to acedia in the previous chapter, Smith uses the literary tradition of melancholy to disrupt the medical model of depression. Casting a wide net in search of both conceptual and practical solutions after a particularly desperate descent, he conceives of his depression in terms of a human ecology that combines the spiritual and the scientific. He touches on not only melancholy but acedia as he invokes Dante's descent into the underworld (rooted in notions of Saturnine melancholy) to craft a sense of depression as a meaningful experience to be explored. He embraces the possibility, inspired by the psychologist James Hillman, that "depression is hidden knowledge" and is encouraged by his therapist to consider what depression might be trying to tell him (113). Smith takes this statement to mean that "depression has its own narrative, and our medications are obscuring it" (113). He suggests that the medical model of depression leaves us with just one story:

> Surely you know it—you've read it, or seen it on television, or heard it from a neighbor or a co-worker, or watched a family member live it; maybe you've even lived that story yourself: the quest for the proper pill that will restore the life one was leading prior to the illness. It is a moving and compelling story, and I am grateful that so many of us have been able to hear it and to live it.
>
> That is one way we might live. But we need more stories than just this one. Always and always, long as we live and breathe, this is what we need: more stories. (114)

Smith thus uses literature of all kinds as a resource and writes his way through depression in a version of the memoir genre that incorporates many disciplines and sources of information. He resembles O'Brien in his search for a different kind of story about depression than the medical narrative, and his use of a range of archives also resembles Hartman's and Alexander's turn to unusual archives, experimental research methods, and critical memoir when reckoning with the absent archive of slavery.

One of the models for this eclectic form of memoir is indicated by the book's subtitle, *A Personal and Natural History of Melancholia*. In returning to the notion of melancholia, Smith embraces an archaic method and discipline, that of "natural history," which, before the development of modern science and its separation from the humanities, was a way of collecting information about the natural world. He says, "I relish this old-fashioned phrase, have since I first heard it. I like its implication: Nature is *story*" (172). A "natural history" of depression is holistic, viewing it as part of the natural world rather than a disease to be eliminated and using "story" as a research method that keeps the humanities and the sciences, as well as humans and their natural landscapes or environments, enmeshed.

Challenging modern scientific concepts and methods, Smith assembles a compendium of different kinds of information that encompasses the scientific, the spiritual, the literary, and the personal. Like Hartman, Alexander, O'Brien, and other scholars writing memoir, he moves into the terrain of the critical essay in order to share the results of research that ranges from Peter Kramer to Thomas Merton and from Ficino to naturalists. More explicitly than most writers of popular depression memoirs, Smith shows how different genres and disciplines of writing and research, including those from the humanities and ostensibly archaic scientific discourses, merit cultural authority about depression. His ecological understanding of depression, for example, leads him to see it holistically, like the homeopath whose advice he seeks and who understands health to be a matter of restoring balance to a system (a conception reminiscent of humoral theory), rather than a single symptom to be fixed. Homeopathy can't provide instant relief; "it will not magically erase our symptoms and restore us to health," but "it can carry into our vision things long hidden" (116).

Although Smith's reading in the "natural history of melancholia" leads him primarily to sources in the Western humanist tradition rather than to discussions of diaspora and indigeneity that emerge in Hartman and Alexander, his use of these resources points in that direction, particularly insofar as his training as an environmentalist prompts him to explore, as part of the natural history of depression, its relation to landscape and geography. In his version of the transgenerational inquiry found in Hartman and Alexander, as well as O'Brien, he writes about his upbringing in southern Ohio and West Virginia, offering a cultural geography of the region that extends well beyond his own personal history. Smith characterizes his home turf of Appalachia as a region whose distinctiveness comes from having retained some of its traditional ways in the face of capitalism and from remaining proudly poor rather than upwardly mobile. "More than in any other American region, Appalachia has managed to conserve some portion of its ancient past—its handwork, its music, its stories, its religion, its traditions, its lessons. . . . These traditions are not anachronisms, nor are they wishful thinking for ye olden days. These old notions still apply" (132). Although wary of romanticization, Smith makes a plausible claim for the distinctiveness of Appalachian culture as a white settler version of an indigenous relation to land. Indeed, read from an indigenous perspective, Smith's deep attachment to Appalachia is suggestive of the relation between depression and geography and could be enhanced by a fuller history of how poor white settlement, including some of the same migrations from an impoverished Europe that brought the Irish to Boston, intersects with displacement of indigenous and histories of slavery and African diaspora settlement in the South. In the mountain borderlands

of Appalachia, where the land has been exploited by the mining industry and passed over because of the difficulty of the terrain, there are
indeed complex stories to tell about both the survival of tradition and
the ongoing effects of industrialization and its aftermath—stories that
need be neither romantically celebratory nor pessimistically grim.[46]

Concluding that leaving home, both times for college, might have
been the reason that he fell into depression, Smith explores the history
of the term *homesickness* as a way to describe his problem. "It's in the
blood," his grandmother tells him about his Appalachian home, and
he comes to understand that he needs the landscape in which he was
raised. Grappling with the possible charge of nostalgia, Smith acknowledges, "I'm not saying one place or the other is superior," but when he
returns home, he finds himself wondering, "How in the name of creation could I haul such deeply rooted blood around in some new place
and expect it to be contented there?" (131). Smith suggests that it is
not wrong to consider how being away from home might cause depression; his own depression came on during the periods when he left home
thinking that in order to "make himself" he needed to enter academic,
middle-class, and urban cultures. "We carry within our blood wherever
we go the memory of some long-familiar landscape, and that memory
might save us, might settle us into some homeplace, and hold us there"
(136). His discussion of "blood" might seem naturalizing, especially to
a reader attuned to notions of queer kinship, but his discussion of "nostalgia" indicates his own suspicion of a simple relation to origins that
could be further bolstered by a racialized history of nostalgia.[47] Not
only does his consideration of displacement as it connects to race and
class suggest a social rather than merely natural discussion of land, but
his environmental approach to what it means to be tied to a place is also
deeply social.

Smith is also careful not to presume that home can only be found
in the place where one is from, especially since he makes significant
homes for himself in Montana and Wyoming before returning to Appalachia. But even though his attunement to the land and environment
has an indigenous spirit, his version of the West seems curiously de-
void of indigenous people. During the worst of his depression, for example, he lives in Montana, where he forms a strong attachment to the
natural landscape through hiking and growing a garden, but he doesn't
explore the way the landscape is marked by a Native presence, includ-

ing the nearby Flathead reservation (which gets only a brief mention). He describes a stint (when his academic girlfriend gets a position as a temporary lecturer) in a particularly desolate area of Wyoming, whose landscape he eventually comes to appreciate. But when he writes of the "parched and unpeopled prairie" (272) of Wyoming, where coal mines have replaced the grazing lands of the bison, he doesn't mention that it would once have been occupied (and still is) by indigenous peoples who have made the High Plains landscape their own. At the same time, the seemingly barren terrain provides the inspiration for the book's title and its final image when Smith imagines the connection between the dark and hidden work of melancholy and the extensive life underground, "where the roots reach for water."

Smith's natural history of depression takes him to some suggestive areas of research, including histories of science and environment that move from Europe to the Americas. In the process of investigating the links between creativity and melancholy, he discovers that not just artists and writers but a whole cluster of scientists—including Newton, Darwin, and Lewis and Clark—exhibited forms of melancholic genius, often brought on by scientific experimentation and exploration. He turns in some detail to the stories of two relatively obscure nineteenth-century American naturalists, Francis Parkman, who set out to write a nine-volume history of the forests of the Northeast that would include the lives of Natives, and Horace Kephart, who began his career as an archivist and librarian and retreated after a breakdown to the Great Smoky Mountains, where he wrote a huge volume titled *Camping and Woodcraft*. Both men seem to have "gone native," turning to the woods when they couldn't handle civilization.

Although he does not offer an explicit discussion of colonialism and indigenous peoples, Smith's unusual archive of naturalist history suggests a specifically American lineage for thinking about melancholy and depression, thus expanding the Western European tradition. As a result of his long attachment to the southern Appalachian mountains, Kephart was a major advocate for the creation of Great Smoky Mountains National Park, the largest piece of protected land in the eastern United States, on what was Cherokee homeland. The park's southern boundaries were established through the U.S. government's complex negotiations with the Cherokees who remained on the land after the Trail of

Tears forcibly removed many to Oklahoma.[48] The land that is in Smith's blood is a complex terrain at the intersection of many American histories, and stories of white men going native are about a relation to land whose natural history also includes a rich geopolitical history. The proposal that lost homelands are a source of melancholy or depression calls for multiple histories of colonization in the Americas, which displaces both Native peoples and immigrants of all kinds, to become part of research on depression. Smith's work begins to combine a Western European genealogy that traces melancholy back to Greek medicine with discussions of land and region that are specifically American and ultimately related to indigenous cultures.

WHOSE LAND ARE WE ON?

Reading Smith and O'Brien together with Hartman and Alexander through the critical framework of indigeneity, colonization, and African diaspora brings into relief the ways their memoirs link depression to geographic displacement. Rather than dividing these texts by race or region, I place them here together in order to allow another landscape of American history to emerge, one that connects the multiple histories of displacement produced by capitalism and colonialism. These include not just the African diaspora (including internal migration from South to North) and indigenous displacement, but O'Brien's account of the Irish migration from famine and dispossession that produces white working-class cultures in Boston and Smith's account of the settlement of Appalachia by white working-class people (including the Irish) pushed westward into indigenous land and surviving the ebbs and flows of industrialization. It takes some work to relay the complex interconnections among these stories—to track the racial segregations that structure both rural and urban cultural geographies and the sometimes invisible indigenous histories that are nonetheless present on every American landscape. There are other stories as well, including past and present migrations from Asia and the Global South, and the legacies of Spanish colonialism in the Mexican American borderlands and the Caribbean. For most Americans (including indigenous people in the wake of colonialism), the story of land and where one is from rarely involves a singular history but is instead a cross-hatching of many histories that are "intimately" connected (to borrow from Lisa Lowe).[49]

If the problem of depression is linked to displacement and dispossession, then it is tempting, of course, to suggest that "cure" or "healing" or "recovery" comes from finding or returning home. The "rites of return" described in these texts, though, circumvent any simple nostalgia.[50] Hartman is the most skeptical of return and reparation, since the Middle Passage serves as a case of permanent rupture, whereas a more reparative sense of attachments to ancestors and to place is present in those writers, such as Alexander and Smith, who can invoke indigenous spiritualities or a long tradition of connection to a region. There are tensions between indigenous and diasporic perspectives that can't and shouldn't be easily papered over or resolved. But one way of doing that is through a sense of place as marked by multiple histories.

Sovereignty in the form of "radical self-possession" can also take the form of emotional, somatic, or sensory connections to place rather than nationalist or essentialist claims. Indeed, this is often the only kind of "land claim" that is possible when, as in the case of African diaspora, people remain displaced. A sovereignty of the sensory or embodied self is not necessarily about claiming land but about claiming a relation to a place or environment as a way of grounding the self. The connection to land or home need not be "natural" or in the blood to still be a relation to "nature" that connects people and places (and it can thus be queer and diasporic). Just as neurobiology (but also natural history and concepts such as acedia) shows mind and body to be deeply integrated, so too are people and places connected, and places are animated by life forces that include their previous histories. Smith's attachment to Appalachia, for example, emerges from his sense of an embodied relation to an environment that bears the wounds of history.[51] Appalachia's long traditions of folk culture and an old city like Boston can be narrated with the same density with which Hartman connects the slave dungeons at Elmina to ordinary racisms in the present. Between the radical displacement of African American culture and the claim to home and belonging of indigenous cultures is a way of thinking about depression as a "national" problem that would be "cured" by addressing racisms rather than by finding a singular or natural home.

For the writers explored in this chapter, education is a crossroads where mobility is fraught with the dangers of assimilation even as it offers the potential for new cosmopolitanisms. They use the critical memoir to question school as the only site of education and research and to craft new kinds of knowledge—based on archaic natural history methods, emotional inheritance, impossible archives, and spiritual practices—that acknowledge vulnerability and rupture. They offer forms of knowledge that can move out of the blockages and dispossessions of depression, including the framework of an indigenous epistemology that starts from the question "Whose traditional land are we on?"[52] The answers involve intimate histories of displacement and loss the acknowledgment of which can become a part of the practice of radical self-possession.

3

The Utopia of Ordinary Habit

Crafting, Creativity, and Spiritual Practice

DEPRESSION IS ORDINARY

The series of collaged shadow boxes called *War on Worries* by the visual artist Allyson Mitchell makes public the personal anxieties that claim our attention at the same time as we're worrying about war and social change (figure 3.1). Two plastic toy soldiers fight it out inside the confines of a matchbox, which is mounted on a background of fluorescent print wallpaper from the 1970s that recalls the home front. Scrawled on the silver frames in the style of a things-to-do list are labels that structure the war on worries as a series of decisions to be made: organic meat vs. cheap groceries; clean bathroom vs. visit to art galleries; serenity vs. wild partying; work vs. vacation; casserole in front of TV vs. outdoor picnic; suburban background vs. urban present; periodical upkeep vs. antipoverty actions. These conflicts of desire show the difference in scale between our political goals and what we're actually feeling and create public space for the small anxieties that keep us preoccupied but so often go underground. (I say "we" because I recognize myself in the demographic niche named here.) In her craft aesthetic of collage and glue gun, Mitchell takes up the tools of both high modernism and the stay-at-home housewife; it's a style that has lately been revitalized not only by Martha Stewart and her kind but also by hipster white girls bent on making domesticity both twisted and fun.

Mitchell's work encapsulates in visual form what depression looks like when it is taken up as a Public Feelings project. Capturing the incommensurability of everyday feelings and what's going on in the world, she suggests that, while the link between worry and war is often lived as a disjuncture, the "war on worries" is also a real one. She points to the centrality of ordinary life, especially middle-class domestic life (including the alternative versions practiced by artists, intellectuals,

3.1 Allyson Mitchell, *War on Worries*, 2001.

queers, and cultural creatives), to an understanding of depression. *War on Worries* is an apt description of my *Depression Journals* narrative, whose stories are frequently about the logistics of housekeeping and self-care and the everyday habits of living inside bodies and houses that are the intimate and material locations of depression. They chronicle forms of survival in the face of the challenges of daily life, which is where depression sets in and becomes chronic—or, to use a less medical term, pervasive or systemic—so much a part of things that it can't be isolated as a singular feeling or event. But by the same token, those humble material locations are also the spaces in which depression can be transformed through practices that can become the microclimate of hope.

Domesticity is thus a central keyword for Public Feelings work on depression, and an important theoretical foundation for that project has been rethinking the distinction between private and public spheres. The intimate rituals of daily life, where depression is embedded, need to be understood as a public arena, or alternatively as a semipublic sphere, that is, a location that doesn't always announce itself or get recognized as public but which nonetheless functions as such. My Public Feelings fellow traveler Kathleen (Katie) Stewart is very adept at capturing what she calls the private life of public culture, which holds out the dream of a cocoon-like domesticity as a sanctuary from the anxieties and terrors produced by economic crisis, war, and cultural conflict. But as the private life of public culture, the home becomes the soft underbelly of capitalism, a place where the current state of things is experienced through a complex range of feelings.

> Home is where the heart is. You can get inside and slam the door. We dream of the big, beautiful, sensate commodity-to-live-in, the bathroom done in textures of old stone and precious metals, a utopia of colorful décor. . . .
>
> The American dream takes the form of a still life: the little family stands beside the SUV in the driveway, looking up, stock portfolios in hand, everything insured, payments up to date, yards kept trim and tended, fat-free diet under their belts, community watch systems in place. Martha Stewart offers advice on the finishing touches.
>
> But then the little disappearing acts start coming up right in the middle of home's retreat, adding a different charge to things. There are times when it seems as if everything the heart drags home is peppered with a hint of addiction, aloneness, something rotten or worthless.[1]

We could add depression to the list of what comes home. Stewart describes domestic comfort as a deceptive structure of feeling, the buffer that keeps bad feelings at bay, but, as the pervasiveness of depression suggests, an atmosphere that is also haunted by bad feelings, by the awareness that something is wrong, either inside or outside. The sanctuary of the home is frequently pierced by sensational events, not just real ones, such as September 11, 2001, war, and racist violence, but also imagined ones, such as tabloid-style crime and celebrity news that make a spectacle of others' successes and misfortunes. (And it's not always easy to tell the difference between what's real and what's imagined.) But it's also pervaded by a more low-level buzz of worry and anxiety and forms of daily stress that bog people down to the point where they're so numb or weary they can't even really pay attention to anything other than what's right in front of them.

Depression is tied to the domestic because it is ordinary, and the *ordinary* is another central concept for the Public Feelings project. My previous work on how trauma manifests itself not just in catastrophic events but in the fabric of daily life has segued into my interest in depression as a chronic or ordinary feeling. Katie Stewart's acute accounts of the domestic are part of her larger effort to write about "ordinary affects," which are "public feelings that begin and end in broad circulation, but they're also the stuff that seemingly intimate lives are made of."[2] In work that has been formative for my own, she describes the ordinary as a place of intensities, potentials, and scenes that are not best understood or described as examples of big theoretical categories. The ordinary requires new genres of ethnography or storytelling that Stewart crafts through observations and writings that range across everyday life in U.S. locations that include nuclear test sites in Nevada, West Virginia hollers, and local neighborhoods where people are out walking or stuck in traffic waiting for the lights to change or figuring out what to buy at Target or Walmart. Stewart finds immanent meaning in the ordinary, turning it into stories that are "still lives," scenes of potential that can be sensational or alive with feeling without being melodramatic.

The work of representing depression as ordinary participates in the descriptive turn that Heather Love has linked to the affective turn.[3] One of the problems with medical discourses, whether about trauma or depression, is not just that they pathologize but that they homogenize and universalize a nuanced range of feelings. Along with its more technical vocabulary, the *DSM-IV*'s list of criteria for diagnosing major depressive disorder includes symptoms such as *feeling sad or empty, loss of interest or pleasure, loss of energy, feelings of worthlessness, indecisiveness*, and *recurrent thoughts of death*.[4] The appearance of everyday speech—terms like *being slowed down* rather than *psychomotor retardation*—suggests that knowledge about how to articulate depression could come from anyone, not just medical experts, and that *depressed mood* is not a self-evident category. To the *DSM*'s proliferating list could be added lethargy, numbness, being overwhelmed, anxiety, not wanting to do anything, and other variations on the official clinical symptoms. I often use the term *feeling bad* because its colloquial blandness is an invitation to further elaboration, which can consist in an anecdote (such as those in *The Depression Journals*) rather than a clinical category or even a theoretical term. Accounts of depression require new ways of talking about affective states and making them publicly significant rather than new terminologies. Thus while I use the word *depression* because of its widespread medical and popular use, when opened up to scrutiny under the rubric of Public Feelings the term folds into the vocabularies and stories of ordinary life. Depression lurks in a lot of different places, and rather than naming it as such I prefer to pay attention to the texture of lived experience and its complex combinations of hope and despair.

Public Feelings accounts of depression thus don't necessarily contain scientific evidence or medical diagnoses or big headlines about health epidemics. In my ordinary stories of trips to the grocery store or life at home, depression can't be labeled as a disease and can even be hard to pin down as an identifiable phenomenon. It might not immediately reveal its connections to capitalism and colonialism, even if it's a structure of feeling for how they are experienced. It's a sensational story of a different kind, literally sensational because it's about the impact of the world around us on our senses—which include our bodies, our feelings, and our minds. It can be hard to tell the difference between inside and outside—between what's inside your body and what's out there, between what's inside the house and what's outside in the neighborhood or on the other side of town, between your heartbreak and the misery in the world beyond. Teresa Brennan suggests, for example, that depression and other contemporary conditions that are hard to identify such as chronic fatigue syndrome and autoimmune disorders are forms of psychic and environmental poisoning caused by the transmission of bad feelings across bodies, people, and groups.[5] Floating between inside and outside, depression can be a mood, an atmosphere, or a sensibility.

Depression can be everywhere as part of the insidious effects of a culture that says people should be sovereign agents but keeps weighing them down with too much (or too little) to do. This is especially true for middle-class subjects, as well as for those living within the aspirational orbit of middle-class life. *War on Worries* suggests that domestic worry is compounded by awareness of its insularity—by the anxiety of knowing that it's both barrier and buffer against other (larger) worries and other (more real) wars. Depression stories are about people who just keep disappearing under the weight of daily life, although sometimes the feelings gather up enough force that someone goes off and it becomes a sensational story about kids, boys mostly, getting guns and killing other people or themselves—at Columbine (1999), at Virginia Tech (2007), at the University of Texas (2010), at the Safeway in Arizona (2011), at a summer camp in Norway (2011).[6] There's a story to tell there about people who get so disconnected they have to act out, but it's a story that should hit close to home and our own experiences rather than constructing psychopaths or freaks. We don't need scientific research to explain what's going on; we need better ways of talking about ordinary life, including the dull feelings of just getting by.

ARCHIVES OF SURVIVAL

This chapter proceeds in its exploratory redescription of depression not only through alternative keywords but through a collection of cultural texts that, along with Mitchell's *War on Worries*, belong to my own idiosyncratic archive of everyday feeling and depression. This archive includes the performances of the queer cabaret artists Kiki and Herb, whose cover song medleys and diva attitude express the ordinary through the melodrama of extreme feeling. It also includes the queer AIDS activist filmmaker Gregg Bordowitz's video *Habit*, whose flat affective tone and documentary disjunctions between the U.S. and South Africa perform political depression about the ongoing global AIDS pandemic. The most extended case is the contemporary practice of feminist crafting that combines art, politics, and everyday life to rework debates about domesticity. With particular attention to the work of the visual artists Sheila Pepe and Allyson Mitchell, the chapter explores crafting as a model for creative ways of living in a depressive culture and as an ordinary form of spiritual practice that I call *the utopia of everyday habit*.

Those familiar with these artists might recognize that this archive reflects the sensibility and cultural taste of the specific demographic I inhabit: a small and frequently ephemeral niche of queer and feminist bohemia centered in downtown New York and other cosmopolitan cities such as Toronto and Chicago. Although it may be a minor or eccentric archive, it offers further evidence that there are other archives besides the specific-turned-universal of medical perspectives (or the Western humanist tradition of melancholy), although it also has a different emphasis from the previous chapter's archive of diaspora and indigeneity. There is definitely traffic back and forth across race and class lines in queer bohemia, which shares with hipster culture a desire to connect with different worlds, even when it has its own problems with versions of "multicultural diversity" that are limited or superficial. Queer bohemia's relation to cultural mobility and aspiration and to middle-class privilege and assimilation takes many forms, especially since it includes artists with working-class origins. The work of the white artists who are my focus here often registers a depression-inducing anxiety about separation from real struggle, including anxiety about racial segregation, that *War on Worries* expresses. I wanted to see how the arty queer culture that sustains me brings a queer perspective to depression, one with a taste for the nonnormative and perverse. Living in close and sustained proximity with these artists and the feelings their work produces has been integral to my thinking about depression.

My method is not necessarily one of close reading or taking the examples as specific instances of a more general case; there's a methodological claim here about how depression, and even more importantly, survival, can be studied by collecting an archive that includes the queer arts. These cases are singularities or oddities whose contributions to our knowledge can't be predicted and don't follow conventional disciplinary boundaries. Theories of the case and the archive have been central to Public Feelings; my formulation of the "archive of feelings" as a critical concept is indebted, for example, to Lauren Berlant's construction of an archive that mixes high and low, queer and straight, in *The Queen of America Goes to Washington City*. This critical sensibility is also present in Katie Stewart's turn to description in order to prevent banal generalization, Sara Ahmed's construction of "unhappy archives" to disrupt conventional notions of happiness, and Heather Love's notion of a descriptive turn.[7] As Ben Highmore suggests, the description of the ordinary (or depression) requires a science of the singular, which disrupts statistical or scientific understandings that operate through generalizations.[8] My examples or cases are not applications of theory, but ways of bringing new knowledge to the table and resisting a general theory of depression. They are dense or complex enough to speak back to a medical theory of depression, to create problems for it, to transform it.

In particular, my examples are reparative ones, which tell us something not just about depression but about ways of living. They emanate from the insurgent and experimental genres of queer cultures—performance, activist documentary, crafting, and installation art—that attempt to make things, to be creative, to do something. They are the creative accompaniments to this essay's ambitions to provide a way of thinking that does not have to be scientific or to marshal evidence in the form of generalizable data to constitute knowledge. They taught me that depression is ordinary—as is its "cure," which resides not in medical treatment but in the art of daily living.

THE DEPRESSION ARCHIVE:
KIKI AND HERB AND MATERNAL MELODRAMA

> Do you wanna stay in bed all day?
> Do you remember feeling any other way?
>
> —Le Tigre, "Much Finer"

My depression archive includes these lines from Le Tigre, which provide a gratifyingly public statement of feelings of withdrawal that would seem to resist being shared.[9] The riotgrrrl and zine culture of the 1990s out of which Le Tigre emerged sustained the feminist conviction that going public with your feelings can make a difference both to how you feel and to the state of the world. Le Tigre's expression of lethargy seems like the opposite of the emotional extravagance of Kiki and Herb, but their live performances also served as an important accompaniment and backbeat to my thinking while writing this book.[10] Embodying the characters of Kiki, an aging alcoholic cabaret artist staging her comeback, and Herb, her longtime piano accompanist, Justin Bond and Kenny Mellman regaled East Village audiences with their ingenious medleys of popular songs and autobiographical monologues (followed by wider visibility in an off-Broadway theatrical run and Carnegie Hall show) before parting in 2008 (figure 3.2).[11] Although I could unapologetically claim that Kiki and Herb are in the depression archive simply because, like Le Tigre, they have made me feel better on so many occa-

3.2 Justin Bond and Kenny Mellman as Kiki and Herb, 2007. Photo courtesy of Liz Ligouri.

sions, their capacity to do so prompted my thinking about the relation between expressions of mute withdrawal like Le Tigre's and more melodramatic modes of articulating depression's ordinary feelings.

The art of the domestic looks different when it leaves the confines of the normative white middle-class home, the breeding ground for what gets classified as depression, even if it must ultimately be understood as an equal opportunity form of misery. Not only is the domestic transformed by feminists, especially queer ones, but it looks different again when taken up in Kiki and Herb's twisted cabaret show, in which maternal melodrama meets the cover song and child abuse is never far from the discussion. ("Ladies and gentlemen," Kiki declares, "if you were not abused as a child, you must have been a very ugly child.") Although I'm wary of how sincerity can fall out of the picture when gay male camp culture reframes and ironizes feminine genres such as the maternal melodrama and the women's film, I can't help loving Kiki and Herb for how they mine the maternal melodrama as an archive of depression, giving voice to otherwise mute feelings, sometimes in high-concept stories that are heartbreakingly funny and sad, and sometimes just in a guttural shriek.

Although Kiki's over-the-top emotions can seem just the opposite of the mute darkness of the depressed, the multilayered life history that emerges in her sometimes extended between-song monologues hints that she has likely been laid low by depression on numerous occasions. Rather than dwelling there, she has found a way to go public with the pain, swigging another rye and ginger ale, telling another story about her lost or dead children, and exorcising her demons in songs that are loud, long, and full of anguish. Kiki revitalizes the tradition of maternal melodrama in the serial drama of her relations with Brad, her oldest child, a homosexual decorator who lives in San Francisco's Russian Hill; Coco, who was washed overboard while Kiki was on a Mediterranean cruise after a big comeback show in Monte Carlo; and Misty, her younger daughter, who was taken from her by child protective services and now lives in foster care, although Kiki occasionally visits her in Delaware and has vague dreams of reconciliation. Despite her dubious maternal skills, Kiki makes poignant her loss and her love, demonstrating the affects of motherhood to be far more complex than the sentimental representation of a natural and unsullied attachment. She offers a shrewd cultural analysis of bad mothering as a systemic rather than individual problem. In addition to regaling us with her own personal woes, an ongoing theme of her monologues (through references to Columbine and other current events) is public hypocrisy about children, who are sentimentalized on the one hand and abused on the other. The culture that would exorcise or scapegoat bad mothers like Kiki is only providing an alibi for its own violence, and one of the cathartic dimensions of a Kiki and Herb show is that, rather than wallowing alone in its blues or being encouraged to forget them, the audience makes contact with the harshness of the world at large in the intimate company of a cabaret setting.

This potent affective brew is achieved through a combination of music and story, when, as in the musical, Kiki turns to song to express the affective excess that can't be contained in her narrative. In addition to speaking bluntly about domestic life, she uses song to express the swirl of affects that are so feebly named by depression, and she demonstrates why melodrama has given voice to the silent and disenfranchised. The affective experience of the show is often wrenchingly

exhausting, as it oscillates between stories and carefully crafted medleys that move from one emotional register to the next at breakneck
speed. Both the medley and the cover song are important ways of incorporating multiple affective registers—cover versions, especially of
pop songs, can craft new and very personal meanings from even cliché
expressions of emotion. Kiki and Herb are masters of the art of covers
as they range from popular favorites, such as Britney Spears's ". . . Baby
One More Time," whose line "my loneliness is killing me" acquires new
emotional profundity, to obscure tunes by bands such as the Geraldine
Fibbers, to independent classics that are unlikely cover material for a
lounge act, such as PJ Harvey's "Rid of Me" or Nirvana's "Smells Like
Teen Spirit."

Kiki's delivery (and Herb's arrangements) bring out the emotional
content of the songs, twisting them to express feelings you might
not have known were there. The medleys further enhance the cover
songs' emotional dynamics as abrupt and sometimes surprising musical segues create unusual combinations and collisions of feeling. This is
melodrama, but it is melodrama that has so many emotional registers
that it begins to do justice to what it means to feel bad, including what
it means to be depressed, rather than merely transforming it into over-
wrought or reductive sentimentality. Kiki provides sustenance for those
in search of the soundtrack for political despair and, by performing
femininity in all its queerness, reveals anew the art of women's genres.
As a prelude to a discussion of how a Public Feelings approach to depression draws on the legacies of feminism, I invoke Kiki and Herb's
performances as a model for how popular women's genres maintain
their power to express the complexity of everyday emotional life.

PUBLIC FEELINGS AND LEGACIES OF FEMINISMS

Allyson Mitchell's *War on Worries* is an apt visual emblem for the Public
Feelings project of tracking the intertwined histories of feminism and
depression. The gendering of mental health is referenced in her place-
ment of the toy soldiers inside the enclosure of the matchbox-size domestic interior and then again inside the frame of the shadow box. She
reverses the usual relation between home front and battlefront—the
soldiers are now in the home—and thus articulates the links between

female ailments ranging from hysteria to depression and a masculinized history of shell shock, combat fatigue, and PTSD. Mitchell provides a visual rendition of arguments like Jonathan Metzl's, for example, about the prominence of women in the successive marketing of drugs such as Miltown, Valium, and Prozac as pharmaceutical treatment for depression.[12] Although the ultimate goal of such critiques might be to consider the feelings of other demographic niches, the middle-class white woman has been central to medical histories of mental illness.

Critiques of the connections between women and madness have thus been foundational for feminism, which has promoted the idea that feelings of unhappiness that get classified by categories such as depression are better served by social revolution than by medication. In the early days of second-wave feminism, books like Betty Friedan's *The Feminine Mystique* cast feminism as a cure for a domesticity whose problems manifested as bad feelings—housewives needed to leave the repressive confines of the home that was making them crazy. In Friedan's account of "the problem that has no name," feminism is the answer to the "strange feeling of desperation" that plagues so many middle-class women and gets falsely represented as a medical or social pathology; her analysis encouraged women to name "desperation" as a public feeling that could become the catalyst for a political movement.[13] For the generation that followed, leaving the home for the workplace hasn't quite proven to be the solution that middle-class women sought; antidepressants seem to be most frequently prescribed not for mad housewives but for working people who need to be able to function amid the high levels of stress and ambition created by the simultaneous demands of career and family. But the everyday lives of middle-class women, now trying to juggle work–life balance, remain a point of departure for exploring social problems as problems of feeling, all the more urgent when the neoliberal gutting of social welfare that assigns affective labor to the family or privatized intimacies creates challenges even for alternative kinships.

In trying to use white middle-class women's distress as an entry point into systemic inequalities and violence, feminism has butted up against some intractable problems. It has been a challenge to hold on to the felt experience of depression, of an everyday life that produces sentiments such as "I don't care," "I am worthless," or "I don't know what to do," without getting hamstrung by the incommensurability of small-scale anxiety and global problems. In calling for a revolution in feeling or a "war on worries," feminism has often critiqued affective solutions to affective problems as a substitute for more properly political solutions. The result is various forms of depressive impasse—the sense that our feelings, both good and bad, don't matter and that any effort to transform the sense of feeling bad about oneself that is so endemic to capitalism is too insignificant to make a difference. The nagging buzz of critique is ready to question good feelings as a class privilege that ignores or exploits others or an inadequate form of politics that is merely cultural; efforts to make change are never enough, there is always more to be done.

Lauren Berlant (who along with Katie Stewart has been one of the most important Public Feelings fellow travelers for this project) offers one of the most sophisticated versions of a critique of women's culture as a "sentimental bargain," the marketing of strong feeling, including romance and melodramatic suffering, as a comfortable refuge not only from social transformation but from feeling the actual conditions of one's life or the larger world. The term *juxtapolitical*, which Berlant coins to describe the way that cultures of feeling frequently opt out of conventional politics as an arena of social change, articulates the limits of many alternative public cultures, including those based around art and creativity.[14] One of the strengths of her analysis lies in her persistent attention to "the unfinished business of sentimentality," the places where "the sentimental bargain" to be found in the history of discourses of domesticity, such as Harriet Beecher Stowe's politics of abolition and the melodrama of the women's film, continues to thrive.[15] In subsequent work that takes up the category of political depression that emerged from Feel Tank and Public Feelings, the "sentimental bargain" morphs into the more general category of "cruel optimism," which describes the affective condition of an everyday life in which the ways people seek to flourish turn out to be bad for them.

The focus on intimacy drawn from women's culture continues to play a role in Berlant's analysis since one of the paradigmatic forms of "cruel optimism" is the turn to romance (and other forms of bad attachment) as a source of solace when it becomes impossible to imagine how the "better good life" might emerge from something other than an attachment to normative forms of kinship. Especially powerful, though, in Berlant's vision of politics as embedded in the domestic, the intimate, and the complexities of desire and attachment is her focus on the everyday act of eating. Honing in on scenes of ordinary domesticity, she frequently describes sentimental culture in terms of eating what is bad for you, a graphically material metaphor for the desire for immediate gratification: "As when a refrigerator is opened by a person hungry for something other than food, the turn to sentimental rhetoric at moments of social anxiety constitutes a generic wish for an unconflicted world, one wherein structural inequities, not emotions and intimacies, are epiphenomenal."[16] One of her paradigmatic cases of "cruel optimism" is the obesity epidemic, which she describes as a form of "slow death," to describe how capitalism affects people at the level of daily somatic practice by offering them forms of immediate gratification and comfort that are ultimately killing them. (Antidepressants can also be understood as a prescription for "cruel optimism," the pills that are handed out to be ingested internally as a substitute for transforming the world.) Berlant risks the charged race and class politics of stigmatizing the obese for their fatness in order to focus attention on the systemic prevalence of junk food and the impossibility of conceiving of somatic sovereignty as dependent on individual agency or choice. She is thus also skeptical about the forms of public culture, such as fat activism, that emerge from reclaiming the pathologization of overeating (like the reclamation of the stigma of trauma or queerness) by asserting agency.

Berlant can often seem like the exemplary case of Sara Ahmed's "feminist killjoy" in her redescription of what seems like pleasure as in fact contaminated and in her insistence that "shifts in affective atmosphere are not equal to changing the world."[17] Yet while her attentiveness to the ways that social life is lived as a relation to body and eating seems harsh at some points, it also emerges from her relentless curiosity about how to describe intimacy and attachment without being reductive or dismissive. She slows down the analysis of ordinary life to challenge understandings of sovereignty that presume a rational subject in control of her desires and to surprise us with accounts of people moving laterally, spacing out, or just keeping up.

In the spirit of slowing down, I want to look at how people find ways to live better in bad times, including countering "slow death" with "slow living." I turn to contemporary practices of crafting, which emerge from the ambivalent status of women's culture as the site of both struggle and renewed opportunity for feminist politics (or of what

I have elsewhere called "mixed feelings"). Engaged in a deep dialogue with women's culture through forms of practice that perform thinking by doing, crafting self-consciously questions what constitutes feminism and what constitutes the political; that engagement and its ambition to provide forms of therapy and self-help that address conditions such as depression provide a suggestive laboratory for the concerns of Public Feelings.

Crafting practices inhabit the epidemic of feeling bad that is one form of insidious slow death spawned by neoliberal capitalism, especially among the middle classes who, despite fewer material obstacles to thriving, are still bogged down by worry and—to invoke a concept that is both psychic and somatic—stress. Unlike forms of self-sovereignty that depend on a rational self, crafting is a form of body politics where agency takes a different form than application of the will. It fosters ways of being in the world in which the body moves the mind rather than the other way around, or in which, echoing neurobiological views in another register, body and mind are deeply enmeshed or holistically connected. It produces forms of felt sovereignty that consist not of exercising more control over the body and senses but instead of "recovering" them from the mind or integrating them with it. Crafting emerges from the domestic spaces that are at the heart of women's culture to provide a model for ways of living that acknowledge forms of structural inequity while also practicing modes of bodily and sensory life that incorporate or weave them into the fabric of a daily life that literally includes texture, color, and sensory pleasure.

Crafting is about a way of being in the world that requires not just knowledge but practice, or the "pedagogy of recognition" that Eve Sedgwick, herself a crafter, describes in relation to Buddhism.[18] The craft of slow living is not exclusively middle class, since it takes up the manual labor often associated with working-class and precapitalist ways of living and working. And lest crafting seem pervaded by nostalgia for the past, it is important to note that it belongs to new queer cultures and disability cultures that (along with animal studies) are inventing different ways of being more "in the body" and less in the head. As a practice, and not just an ephemeral feeling, crafting is not the homology or first step or raw material for some form of political change beyond it. It is already a form of self-transformation, although it can also be a way to build the spiritual warrior self necessary for doing other kinds of work in the world, including organized political activism.

THE DEPRESSION ARCHIVE: CRAFTING

When you're making crafts you're spicing up the world
Face it pretty girl, you're . . . craftastic!
You're following no plans, you're building it with hands
Let's do a dance because you're . . . craftastic!
Let's get together and share supplies
Your craftsmanship deserves top prize
Glue it, cut it, stitch it, felt it,
Paint it, bead it, dough it, dye it,
Embroider it, solder it, hotter it.
Let's go walking (walk, walk)
Let's get talking (talk, talk)
Let's craft talk, craft talk
You can build me whatever you want.

—"Craft Talk," Leslie Hall

A big woman who sports a gold lamé jumpsuit, larger-than-life hair and makeup, and 1970s-style oversize glasses, Leslie Hall, a performance artist and front woman for Leslie and the Lys, sings rap song anthems about gold pants and bedazzled sweaters.[19] She collects gem sweaters from thrift stores and has accumulated a collection large enough to be housed in a mobile home she has turned into a museum. During her show, audience members wearing their own gem sweaters in homage to her passion are invited onstage to bow to her and have their sweaters christened with original names. With her queer femme drag and an astounding array of merchandise she makes herself, including rainbow shoelace headbands, spandex jumpsuits, and a stunning collection of self-designed T-shirts, Hall has crafted an exhilarating and poignant character and a world that surrounds her (figure 3.3).

Leslie Hall's gem sweaters are only one of many signs of a recent resurgence of interest in crafting: neofeminist publications like *Bitch* and *Bust* provide a heady mix of consumerism and politics with stories

3.3 Leslie Hall, Stargazer. Photo by Rena Hall.

about artists and designers and activism, instructions for cool stuff you can make yourself, and ads for things to buy from independent artisans taking advantage of web-based sales. Annual gatherings such as the Renegade Craft Fair that bring craft makers together to promote their wares and connect with one another have become regular ongoing events. When I visited Stitch in Austin, for example, the large convention hall was filled with booths displaying T-shirts with hand-drawn designs; handbags quilted, patched, and sewn from colorful fabrics; and clever renditions of household items, such as potholders and dishtowels.[20] The programming also included a DJ, a fashion show, and an area where you could make your own crafts, thus promoting crafting as a full-fledged cultural scene, not just an individual taste or hobby or a marketing trend. The documentary *Handmade Nation* (2009) and an accompanying book show how crafting has emerged as a locus for alternative ways of living and political projects.[21] The craft movement has also established an online community through sites such as Etsy, where crafters can sell their work and also create social networks over much longer distances. And crafting has even made its way into Public Feelings programming; for an event in Austin to discuss the war in Iraq, we created a crafting table where participants could make political stickers, drawings, and other objects while they talked.

The tensions between two different versions of feminism (often cast as a generational difference), one that repudiates the home and one that returns to it, can be seen in contemporary practices of crafting, which have become the public articulation of new forms of feminist sensibility and collectivity. Born from the DIY aesthetics of punk subcultures, especially their feminist incarnations ranging from riotgrrrl to Ladyfest, crafting provides opportunities to make art that is usable (although often by lending a decorative finesse to mundane objects and activities), accessible to all, reproducible (albeit manually rather than mechanically), and marketable. It presents itself less as an alternative to market culture and more as an alternative market culture. The knitting store has now joined the feminist bookstore of the 1970s and the sex toy store of the 1990s as a public space for feminist thinking and activity. Such stores blur the boundaries between producers and consumers, since what is often being bought are materials for DIY projects, and people are sharing work and using commercial space as public space for organizing, learning, and community building.

Crafting forges a complex set of relations to the historical past, situating itself in dialogue with both second-wave feminisms of the 1970s and post–Second World War domestic cultures, as well as with longer histories of women's culture and industrial culture extending back to the eighteenth and nineteenth century. Although with its emphasis on artisanal rather than mass production it is tempting to see crafting as the expression of the desire to return to a period before commodification, it is more accurate to think of it as a return to a different form of commodification or to different periods of commodification, exemplified by the taste for retro styles from a prefeminist era, including knitted scarves, quilted tote bags, and kitchen gear, such as potholders, aprons, and dish towels. The spirit of William Morris, himself on the hinge between art and design (and distinctions between high and low culture) and between industrial and handmade production, is present but it's filtered through the post–Second World War culture of Betty Crocker cookbooks, *Ladies' Home Journal* and other women's magazines, and McCall's and Simplicity home sewing patterns, as well as the discarded styles of more recent decades. That longer history of efforts to forge forms of industrial production hospitable to the aesthetics of craft and to embrace previous historical styles (such as the medieval) rather than making a modernist break with the past offers a valuable context for contemporary crafting.[22] It is a reminder that this movement should be seen not as outside of consumerism or previous generations of feminism but rather as another moment in a long-standing set of constitutive tensions about the relation between the premodern and the modern, women's culture and feminism, and handmade and industrial modes of production.

Crafting thus stages a dialogue with both feminism and its putatively prefeminist past, acknowledging the way that women's culture persists across both moments, and doing so in ways that are charged with intense feelings about this history. A feminist camp humor often accompanies the rehabilitation of domestic hobbies such as needlepoint, rug hooking, and paint by numbers, which combined art and mass production in order to encourage women in particular to express their creativity by following detailed instructions and reproducing images designed by someone else through the painstaking labor of repetitive motion. Thrift store finds provide inspiration for a vast repertoire of images—floral arrangements, landscapes, animals, especially cute ones, and sad-eyed girls, with an emphasis on bright, even garish color—which crafters are now recirculating in ways that bridge the past and the present and are saturated with affect. The scarves and sweaters that have been rendered obsolete by microfibers and other new fleecy materials can now be recreated in high-quality cotton and pure wool yarns that are significantly different from the acrylics and synthetics increasingly marketed in the postwar period. The domestic textile arts that once gave women many forms of creative outlet but gradually became defunct (at least for middle-class housewives) because women were too busy going to work and buying for convenience have now been reclaimed as a way of indicating that one has leisure time for hobbies and for creativity. In many cases, the items being made, such as purses and kitchen accessories, are associated with forms of femininity that have often been repudiated by second-wave feminism, and they can signal a disidentification with critiques of the domestic, the feminine, and the cute. They are often, if not luxury items, accessory or decorative items that aren't strictly functional, as evident by their frequent status as collectibles. Because craft produces objects that are both useful and exceed the necessary, it is readily available to commodified proliferation, but it is also about art in everyday life.

Crafting's heterogeneity makes it rich terrain for cultural politics, and one of the most important dreams attached to the current crafting scene is that it gives rise to new forms of collectivity and politics. Knitting circles and other groups in which people share information and make their labor more social easily lend themselves to other forms of collectivity, including activism or what, in a redescription of the political, some are calling "craftivism." The Revolutionary Knitting Circle, a Canadian group that has knitted large banners for its appearances in demonstrations and marches for progressive causes, has a mission statement that includes "speeding forward the revolution through knitting," a nonviolent and "constructive revolution" dedicated to "creating community and local independence which, in this corporate society, is a truly revolutionary act." In 2004, the Cast Off group in London staged an event at the Victoria and Albert Museum in which over four thou-

3.4 Lisa Anne Auerbach, *Body Count Mittens*, 2005.

sand knitters took over the space (thus bringing grassroots crafting to the preeminent design museum, whose history includes contributions by William Morris).

Using the web as a point of distribution, political knitters such as Lisa Anne Auerbach provide patterns for projects such as the Body Count Mittens, in which the knitter documents the dead in Iraq by knitting the body count at the start of the project on one hand and the number dead when the project is finished on the other. The time-based practice of knitting gets connected to the time of mortality, and the sustained process of knitting the number becomes an act of mourning that gives the knitter a chance to contemplate the dead (figure 3.4). Auerbach also adapts knitting's domestic use for clothing and fashion to make public installations of sweaters and skirts that bear political messages subtly embedded in the beautiful colors and patterns. For an installation at the Nottingham Contemporary that engaged with the history of Lud-

3.5 Lisa Anne Auerbach, *Take This Knitting Machine and Shove It*, installation at Nottingham Contemporary Museum, 2009.

dite rebellion in the clothing industry, one dress bore a slogan borrowed from Diderot's revolutionary writings, "Strangle the last king with the entrails of the last priest," and another announced "We are all heroes" on the front and "We are all terrorists" on the back as a way of reappropriating political discourse and T-shirt identifications (figure 3.5). Practices such as knitbombing take knitting into public spaces often with the aim of transforming the industrial into the "cozy" by covering objects with knitting. In Austin, Magda Sayeg of Knitta Please covered the trees outside the Blanton Art Museum on the University of Texas campus (with the state capitol in sight; figure 3.6), the reflector signs of an underpass in a major traffic throughway, and lampposts outside an alternative bookstore, as well as the corporate offices of Etsy in Brooklyn and a statue near the Eiffel Tower in Paris. These are only a few examples of knitting-based activism, which continues to proliferate in public spaces and to inspire new collective formations.

3.6 Magda Sayeg and Knitta Please, *Knitted Wonderland*, installation at Blanton Museum, Austin, Texas, 2011. Photo by Shawn P. Thomas.

Although these new forms of crafting ostensibly take knitting out of isolation and into collectivity by taking it out of the home and into the street, crafting has long been a mode of socializing. As with other forms of manual labor, it's possible to talk or listen while the hands do the work. Thus while a more self-conscious sense of the relation between crafting and politics has created new formations, crafting's basis in collectivity and its connections to working-class culture have long been part of its social power. Although craftivists often worry about what circumstances make knitting and other crafts count as politics, they are also reinventing what we might mean by the term.[23] Betsy Greer articulates a craftivist mission: "Because we create to connect beyond ourselves. Whether it's next door or across the globe. Craft and activism both take and inspire passion. When used as a joint force, they can quite possibly begin to slowly challenge and change things. Atrocities are happening in our front yards and on our televisions and we need to find ways to react against what is happening without either giving up or exploding. This is less about mass action or more about realizing what you can do to make things around you better. . . . In promoting the idea that people can use their own creativity to improve the world, craftiv-

3.7 Betsy Greer, *These Are Dangerous Times*, 2004.

ism allows those who wish to voice their opinions and support their causes the chance to do just that . . . but without chanting or banner waving and at their own pace."[24] Greer's vision for changing the world through crafting integrates the personal and the political; the creativity fostered by crafting is itself meaningful because the political is constituted by the small local gestures embodied in knitting projects or her own cross-stitching works (figure 3.7).

Sheila Pepe's Common Sense

Craft culture is a sprawling version of what Katie Stewart would call a "little world," and although craftivism might seem like the most obvious place to look for crafting's political potential, crafting's interventions in the art world are central to the reclamation of feminist cultural politics, as well as to crafting's redefinition of what counts as politics to include sensory interactions with highly tactile spaces and with other people—or, in other words, feelings.[25] My archive of depression includes the work of two lesbian artists, Sheila Pepe and Allyson Mitchell, whose ability to render in visual and material form the relation between craft and public feelings has enabled my thinking. While Pepe's work is seemingly more abstract and conceptual and immersed in a fine art tradition, and Mitchell's emerges from DIY and activist cultures that have intruded upon gallery spaces, one of their points of convergence is that they both claim a connection to Judy Chicago, who has often been the stigmatized and sensational touchstone for critiques (including those by other feminists) of feminist celebrations of craft.[26] Not only does their work embody a reparative response to conflicts within feminism and between art and craft, but the utopian spaces of their large-scale installations produce a reparative experience of depression by literally engaging the senses in a way that makes things feel different.[27]

Since 2000, the New York–based artist Sheila Pepe has been suspending huge crochet pieces from gallery walls and ceilings to make her site-specific installations. She has sometimes combined these delicate and unpredictable cobwebs with pencil drawings, which she calls doppelgängers, that respond to the shadows that the hangings cast on the walls. The results are both sensual and abstract, material and conceptual, referencing feminist textile arts of the 1970s and also making popular crochet the stuff of art world sculpture and installation. Some of Pepe's inspirations are humble ones; she is interested in the local and the ordinary, naming the junk drawer in the kitchen, Woolworth's (or Walmart), and her family (her mother, for whom her first crochet installation, *Josephine*, was named, taught her how to crochet) as sources for her materials, which include shoe strings (her grandfather had a shoe repair shop), industrial rubber bands, and nautical ropes (a nod to her studio's location near the Gowanus Canal in Brooklyn).

Although Pepe's site-specific installations are often very large, they also have an intimate scale that insinuates the domestic into the modernist architectural spaces of galleries and museums in sensuous and unexpected ways. Heavier materials such as ropes and industrial rubber bands are counterbalanced by the smaller intricacies of shoelaces and yarn, and individual sections of the pieces have their own visual density and autonomy that adds to the cumulative impact of the whole. Completing her installations on site, Pepe wraps around corners and doorframes, up staircases, and into atriums, adapting to the space rather than requiring a blank white box that won't compete with the work. (Her background as an art installer and a museum guard plays a role in her respectful attention to the spaces in which she works.) Each piece is ephemeral, not only because it is assembled for the occasion, but because it is suspended by seemingly invisible supports and thus floats as if by magic in the space. As the color plates featuring both entire pieces and details from them demonstrate, Pepe also experiments with different color palettes in each installation. While the neutral black of the rubber bands used in *Lap* (figure 3.8) are prominent in some such as *Gowanus* (plate 1), there are also feasts of color, such as the bright blues of *Terminal* (plate 6) and the purples and greens of *Your Granny's Not Square* (plate 5). Pepe combines the bold blue of nautical ropes with bright orange in *Mind the Gap* (plate 3) or deep purple with black and white in *Under the F&G* (plate 4) to create color studies that are reminiscent of abstract expressionism as well as textile arts, but abstraction can also carry humorous representational meanings in pieces such as *Greybeard* (plate 2).

In her new ongoing series *Common Sense*, Pepe constructs the large-scale installation on a more intimate scale by making it accessible to public participation of a very literal and tactile kind, as the name suggestively indicates. The first of these was a crochet installation in Austin for Fluent-Collaborative's testsite, a house that has been converted into a gal-

3.8 Sheila Pepe, *Lap*, 2001.

3.9a and **3.9b**
Sheila Pepe, *Common Sense*,
a collaboration with curator
Elizabeth Dunbar, testsite/
Fluent-Collaborative, Austin,
2009. Photos by Kate Watson.

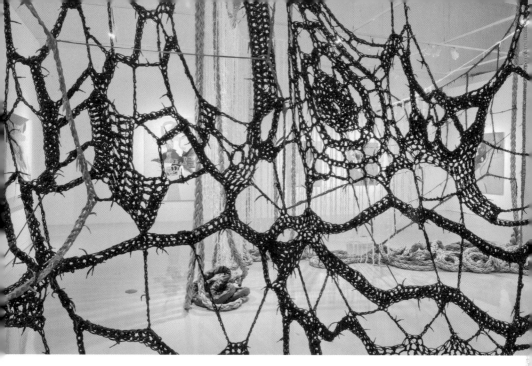

Plate 1. Sheila Pepe. Detail from *Gowanus*.

Plate 2. Sheila Pepe. Detail from *Greybeard*.

Plate 3. Sheila Pepe. *Mind the Gap.*

Plate 4. Sheila Pepe. *Under the F&G.*

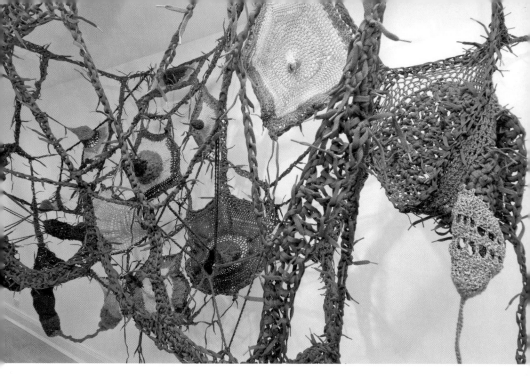

Plate 5. Sheila Pepe. Detail from *Your Granny's Not Square*.

Plate 6. Sheila Pepe. Detail from *Terminal*.

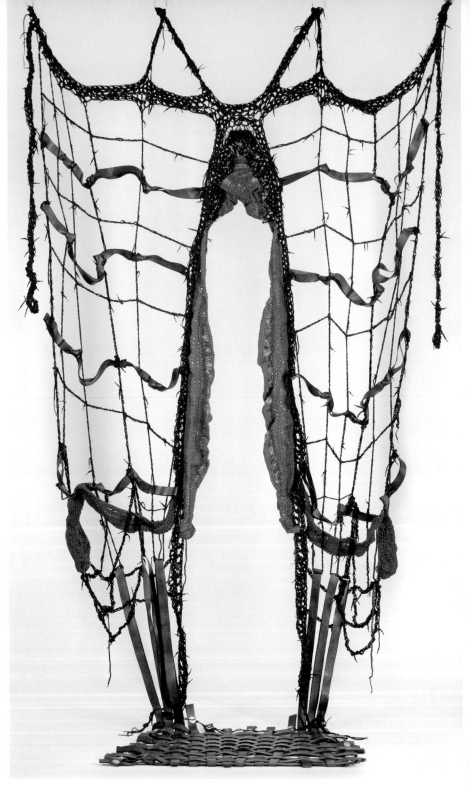

Plate 7. Sheila Pepe. *Mr. Slit*.

Plate 8. Allyson Mitchell. *Hungry Purse: The Vagina Dentata in Late Capitalism*.

Plates 9, 10, and 11. Allyson Mitchell. *Hungry Purse*.

Plates 12–14. Allyson Mitchell. *Ladies Sasquatch*.

3.9c and **3.9d**
Sheila Pepe, *Common Sense II*,
Contemporary Arts Museum,
Houston, 2010. Photos by the
author.

lery space for experimental projects (figures 3.9a and 3.9b).[28] Pepe uses regular yarn this time around, unlike in some of her earlier pieces, but the clusters of colored yarn explode the neat geometry of crocheted squares typical of such materials. As with the larger installations, there's something magical about their appearance in the midst of the living-room furniture and across the dining-room table, carefully tailored to the space so that visitors can still sit or move around. In a collaborative and performative process of making and unmaking, viewers were invited to become crafters and use the yarn to knit and crochet their own projects, thus dismantling the piece over the course of the exhibition. In a second version of *Common Sense*, at Houston's Contemporary Arts Museum in 2010, crafting transformed the more conventional gallery space as viewers sat on stools within and under the installation in order to make their own pieces, enfolded into the piece through direct interaction rather than standing outside of it (figures 3.9c and 3.9d).[29] As the work literally unraveled over time, with strands of red and gray hanging down, its somewhat bedraggled appearance became an invitation to participate. Enacting what she calls "preparation for the end of ephemera," Pepe traces her interest in ephemerality not only to high art traditions of conceptual and performance art but also to her experience growing up working in a deli where lavishly prepared food disappears when eaten.[30] In *Common Sense*, she produces a reparative solution to the problem of ephemerality because disappearance, or unraveling or becoming undone, is an occasion for making something new. As with the monk collecting and then burning his palm leaves, the process and rhythm of the work is what matters, and the activity of the people who are simultaneously unmaking and making creates the magic of the commons.

Refusing to choose between the domestic and the public, the intimate and the monumental, craft and fine art, Pepe provocatively names as her influences both Judy Chicago and Eva Hesse, slyly referring to them as the parents who didn't speak to one another and expressing a conviction that work that can be simultaneously sexy and abstract.[31] (One of her exhibitions was titled "Hot Lesbian Formalism!") Pepe embraces Chicago and lesbian feminism, but she also affiliates herself with the minimalist art practice of Hesse, whose relation to the history of feminism has been revisited in recent retrospectives.[32] For example, in a piece titled *Mr. Slit*, a black crochet hanging with a red-rimmed labial opening, Pepe invokes both vaginal art and the more amorphous sen-

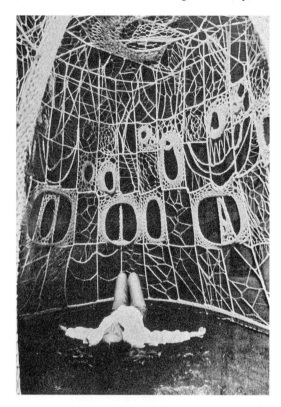

3.10 Faith Wilding, *Crocheted Environment (Womb Room)*, 1972. Rope and yarn, 9′ x 9′ x 9′, Womanhouse, Los Angeles.

sual shapes of Hesse's latex sculptures (plate 7). Pepe's work also recalls that of Faith Wilding, whose *Crocheted Environment (Womb Room)*, which was part of the Woman House project in Los Angeles in 1972, epitomizes the forms of feminist textile installation that have been critiqued as essentialist but are now acquiring renewed visibility (figure 3.10). Pepe refuses divisions within feminism and the art world, and she is also unapologetic about claiming an identity as an artist without feeling obliged to be an activist or critical of the gallery system to count as politically engaged.

In the Hungry Purse with Allyson Mitchell

Somewhere between Sheila Pepe's art world practice and Leslie Hall's pop culture performance lies the capacious and eclectic oeuvre of Allyson Mitchell, whose *War on Worries* is just one of her many projects that draw inspiration from crafting. Although her work is now being exhibited in galleries and museums, she comes out of feminist and queer DIY subcultures rather than formal art training, and her background includes collaborative filmmaking (including lots of animation), fat activist performance with Pretty Porky and Pissed Off, music and recording as Freeshow Seymour, and a Ph.D. in women's studies. She has often expressed the sensibility of Public Feelings, in series such as *55 Things That Tried to Kill Me*, for example, where portraits of sad-eyed girls are labeled with problems ranging from "academic jargon" and "grant applications" to "cellulite," "always hungry," "wet diary," and "white pant period." The serial practice that is often characteristic of crafting leads to multiple images that give each indignity, no matter how small, its own moment of publicity. Ordinary feelings acquire melodramatic status through the big eyes and bold colors that use the aesthetics of girly cuteness as a form of diva expression (figure 3.11).

A self-described "maximalist," Mitchell often finds the materials for her art in thrift stores, where she has collected shag rugs, crocheted

3.11 Allyson Mitchell, *55 Things That Tried to Kill Me*, 2000.

afghans, ceramic figurines, fake fur, and macramé plant holders. While some versions of crafting reject mass production in favor of handmade or artisanal production, Mitchell's work engages with the marketplace of commodities, but often in its more abject forms. Recycling objects and styles associated with previous generations, Mitchell is drawn to that which has been rejected as outmoded or déclassé (and hence a trigger for deep feelings). For her, the strong and frequently negative feelings attached to objects that are sentimental, cute, garish, cheap, or excessive resemble the feelings associated with both fat girls and feminisms, and this reservoir of shame, abjection, and mixed feelings is a resource for queer reparative strategies. Collecting the lost objects that others left behind to be thrown away or sold for cheap, and collecting in massive quantities that reveal consumption's popular trends, she creates new worlds out of discarded ones.

Like Pepe, Mitchell makes large-scale installations, including a series featuring the Ladies Sasquatch, a band of giant lesbian monsters whose overblown size is inspired by Mitchell's fat activism (plates 12–14). They are made of fun fur, the material of stuffed animals and kitschy costumes, whose garish colors and lavish textures Mitchell embraces. (She also used fun fur for a series of wall hangings inspired by paint by numbers and soft porn that turned large-bodied women into fat feminist sex symbols.) The Ladies Sasquatch are joined by the Sasquatch familiars, a tribe of protective totem animals with pink fur and garishly exposed nipples, teeth, and claws who are both cute and slightly grotesque. Simultaneously frightening and seductive, the Sasquatches offer a queer twist on gothic monstrosity and fairy tales, indigenous culture and colonialist myth, and lesbian feminist traditions of goddess worship.[33] The lady monsters hover between being overwhelming and being approachable—if they are scary, it's in the way that big female flesh has been scary, and Mitchell transforms that version of monstrosity into an erotics of the monster. Their luscious asses are unapologetically big and ask to be touched, but although fun fur maintains the tactility of many of the materials used in crafting and textile arts, the "artificial" more than the "natural" is being fetishized. If the monster is made sexy and attractive, it is not, however, domesticated, at least not in the sense of being defanged or tamed; the Ladies Sasquatch retain the power of their size and voluptuous proportions to become lesbian feminist icons.

For *Hungry Purse: The Vagina Dentata in Late Capitalism* (2006, 2008,

2010), Mitchell created a room-size female womb whose over-the-top abundance of textiles and colors is (quite literally) hysterical and touching.[34] Actively embracing what might seem like clichés about feminist art's focus on wombs, cunts, and the female reproductive body, Mitchell's sex-friendly dyke attitude transforms those traditions to make them less solemn. The doorway to the space is lined with crocheted afghans in multiple shades of pink and brown, which are draped in the shape of labial folds; to enter it one has to push past a hanging macramé sculpture that resembles a clitoris (plate 8). Inside the room is a riot of colors with shag rugs upholstering the floor and walls, blankets covering the ceiling, and throw pillows scattered about (plates 9 and 10). At one end stands a throne covered in shag-rug owls and framed by stuffed animal heads in pink fun fur (plate 11). Whether one sits in the chair, curls up in a corner to survey the room, or wanders around touching the space, the sensurround experience fosters a variety of feelings. With her maximalist sensibility, Mitchell does not try to fend off the obsessive-compulsiveness of overconsumption and she embraces the full range of joy and sadness, comfort and pain familiar from the melodrama and sentimentality of domestic genres. In its tactility, *Hungry Purse* is loaded with history, including history as the dust and dirt of the items that come from other people's pasts.

Mitchell's art practice finds its theoretical expression in her "Deep Lez I Statement," a manifesto in which she acknowledges critiques of lesbian feminism but refuses to repudiate it. Instead she sees it as part of a utopian vision for contemporary queer culture whose "both/and" sensibility embraces multiple histories and perspectives. "Deep Lez" thinking aims to acknowledge and address histories of conflict; one catalyst for the statement, for example, are the tensions between lesbian and trans identities and communities:

> Deep Lez was coined to acknowledge the urgent need to develop inclusive liberatory feminisms while examining the strategic benefits of maintaining some components of a radical lesbian theory and practice. This project is carefully situated not to simply hold on to history, but rather to examine how we might cull what is useful from lesbian herstories to redefine contemporary urban lesbian (and queer) existence. In so doing, "lesbian" is resurrected as a potential site of radical identification, rather than one of de-politicized apathy (or worse, shame).[35]

Just as the thrift store provides material for recycling rather than being a refuse pile, so too does Mitchell find a world of possibility in earlier generations of lesbian feminism, which can be used flexibly and creatively.

A striking example of this rehistoricization is Mitchell's recent collaboration with Judy Chicago as the curator of a retrospective of her textile art, which was accompanied by an exhibition of work by younger artists who use craft, such as Cat Mazza and Ginger Brooks Takahashi.[36] Naming as political feelings the "apathy" and "shame" that the failures and conflicts of feminism can produce, Mitchell seeks to avoid political depression by seeing the past as a potential ally and resource. Using crafting as a metaphor for her mix of theory and practice, Mitchell describes the Deep Lez sensibility as a "macraméd conceptual tangle for people to work through how they integrate art into their politics and how they live their lives and continue to get fired up about ideas. Deep Lez can offer alternative ways of imagining the world and who we are." In this unabashedly utopian vision, "macramé" de-

3.12 Allyson Mitchell, *Menstrual Hut Sweet Menstrual Hut*, 2010.

scribes the process of bringing together potentially disparate materials in unpredictable combinations and the refusal to separate art and politics or feminist generations.[37] Especially important is the Deep Lez version of the "art of daily living," where a craftivist focus on practice means that politics is integrated into how people live their lives. *War on Worries* is one of my favorite manifestations of this sensibility because it doesn't try to transcend the mundane but instead works with it. In *Menstrual Hut Sweet Menstrual Hut*, another space upholstered in shag rugs where visitors can watch Mitchell's video animations, the soft textiles forms of craft and the virtual forms of mass media are combined, and media consumption becomes a collective and material experience (figure 3.12).[38] In installation works such as *Menstrual Hut Sweet Menstrual Hut*, and *Hungry Purse*, Mitchell seeks to create alternative spaces and built environments in which daily life can be literally felt and sensed differently.

Both Pepe and Mitchell thus offer a newly invigorated picture of the use of craft and the domestic in feminist art of the 1970s, ambivalence about which stigmatized figures such as Judy Chicago, and the generational narrative emerging from their work does not celebrate the "third wave" at the expense of the "second wave." Their reparative and bighearted relation to 1970s feminisms also characterizes their relation to the art world, which is seen as a home for craft rather than an institution to be rejected or deconstructed in favor of some putatively more radical or activist practice. Rather than approach the politics of crafting with the paranoid skepticism of the cultural critic through some calculus whose results we already know—in the words of Eve Sedgwick (again, herself an avid crafter and textile artist), "kinda subversive, kinda hegemonic"[39]—they encourage us to get inside the "little world" that they create, a world of textures and colors that are handmade with love and attention.

Indeed, at a Public Feelings event in Toronto, we did so very literally, gathering in *Hungry Purse* for a discussion of art and utopia that included a group sing-along of cover songs ranging from Britney Spears's ". . . Baby One More Time" (in homage to the version sung by Kiki and Herb as much as to Britney herself) to Joni Mitchell's "The Circle Game" (for Canadian content). As we huddled together in the slightly too close embrace of shag rugs and crocheted afghans, it felt like there was room both to express loneliness and to feel a little less lonely. Although we might have been using the currency of Berlant's "sentimental bargain," through the afghans that blanket distress with warm fuzzy feelings and bright cheery colors and the pop songs that express both inchoate and intense feelings, we were also creating a poignant sense of collectivity in a version of what Jill Dolan calls the "utopian performative."[40]

THE UTOPIA OF ORDINARY HABIT

In addition to its productive use in both activism and art, what particularly interests me about crafting is the process itself, especially the forms of repetition that it requires—how knit, purl, knit, purl, over and over again, becomes a creative act. In this respect, crafting is connected not only to creativity, art, and politics but to spirituality and sacred ritual. It requires modes of attention that resemble those of meditation: having something to do with your hands keeps the attention both focused and free, and you can remain on task in the midst of other distractions.[41] Knitting and meditation share a rootedness in ordinary and daily life; the extension of "spiritual practice" to encompass knitting or other textile-based crafts is possible because both can involve the repetitive and regular motion of the body and its use for activities that can also be time-consuming and boring. Crafting is a way of making something creative out of the habitual nature of domestic life, a knowledge long embodied in its more traditional forms and now reclaimed to fit the changing context of everyday life.

I write about crafting in the context of depression because, as a form of daily activity (whether individual or collective) that can soothe the mind and even raise the spirit, it presents an alternative to treating depression with drugs. It also reframes what we mean by treatment since crafting and other activities like it may not be cures or antidotes but ways in which depression and related affects are lived with rather than banished. It reflects the sensibility of my depression memoir, which explores how politics are lived at home and in the body by chronicling activities such as preparing food, creating a built environment, and moving through space. And it participates in both these ordinary forms of creativity and the more specialized forms demanded by writing and other modes of intellectual and artistic production. No doubt one of crafting's appeals for those who do primarily mental labor is the return to more concrete forms of manual activity. Moreover, it also conveys a DIY conviction that creativity, and even art, is available for everyone and that the results need not be special to be meaningful, and hence it challenges the perfectionism and hierarchies demanded and fostered by academic work.

Thus my investigation of depression is also an exploration of pleasure, joy, and vitality. The links between the ordinary habit of knitting and spiritual practice, and between crafting (as well as creativity more generally) and depression, lead to a cluster of keywords such as *hope, happiness, optimism,* and especially *utopia* that have been revived by the Public Feelings project and its various fellow travelers such as José Muñoz, Avery Gordon, Jill Dolan, Michael Snediker, and Sara Ahmed.[42] Deeply skeptical about conventional forms of happiness, such as the heteronormative family, or fantasy forms of utopia such as colonial paradise, these critics nonetheless formulate an educated hope that fully recognizes the sorry state of the world and maintains plenty of room for unhappiness, melancholy, depression, and other bad feelings. There are definitely differences among them, which itself suggests that utopian sensibilities are a complex brew of "mixed feelings": Dolan is probably the most optimistic about the experience of hope and of "how utopia feels" that she finds at the theater (in contrast to Berlant's claim that "changes in affect can't change the world"); Gordon's utopia of African American survival strategies is decidedly unsentimental, while Snediker finds affirmation in the virtuosity of queer lyric poetry; Muñoz and Ahmed claim the bitchy queen and the feminist killjoy as modes of critical pleasure when critiquing conventional understandings of hope and happiness, but, like Dolan, Muñoz is drawn to queer performance worlds as a touchstone for "concrete utopia." Discussions of utopia and other related concepts have been part of queer theory debates about the "antisocial," which have circulated most prominently in connection with Lee Edelman's rejection of futurity as reproductive heteronormativity.[43] Central to this discussion has been the question of whether it is possible to sustain a commitment to the utopian without falling into the pastoralizing or romanticizing tendencies that Edelman (echoing Leo Bersani) critiques. It should be noted, though, that queer work on the utopian generally embraces negativity, finding the utopian in perversion, abjection, failure, depression, and struggle, and hence refusing easy or binary distinctions between positive and negative affects.[44]

My contribution to this discussion is to insist that daily life in all its ordinariness can be a basis for the utopian project of building new worlds in response to both spiritual despair and political depression. As forms of practice, rituals such as crafting, knitting, and other hobbies, as well as yoga, running, and other forms of exercise, belong to what I want to call a *utopia of ordinary habit*. Although the term *practice*, a repeated action whose meaning lies in the process of performing it, might seem more appropriate here, especially because of the connections between daily practice and spiritual practice, the positive and negative connotations of the term *habit* are also relevant. Habit encompasses both the desirable and healthy regularity of practice and the putatively unhealthy compulsions and obsessions of addiction. We try to break bad habits and give up addictions, and we can feel dulled by the routine of habit; moreover, building good habits can seem like the internalization of regimes of discipline and self-formation that make us good or docile subjects. Using the term *habit* in connection with utopia, however, suggests that habit can be a mechanism for building new ways of being in the world because it belongs to the domain of the ordinary, to activities that are not spectacular or unusual but instead arise from everyday life.[45] When a habit becomes a practice, a repeated action that is actively and consciously pursued, it has not left its everyday status behind. Ordinary activities or habits can be the ground for a practice, not just the specialized activities, such as reciting mantras or sitting still, that constitute spiritual practice or the carefully refined movements and skills that form the basis for artistic, athletic, or creative practice. The *utopia of ordinary habit* would be a version of Avery Gordon's "usable utopia," a utopia of the "here and now" that is "oriented toward the future" but "doesn't treat the future as either an off-world escape or a displacing fetish," as do the forms of utopia often found in the otherworldly exoticisms of science fiction and colonialist dreams.[46] It is also reminiscent of Foucault's interest in traditions of asceticism and "practices of the self" that provide a model for new ways of inhabiting the disciplinary regimes that constitute the modern self. It reconceives the rational sovereign subject as a sensory being who crafts a self through process and through porous boundaries between self and other, and between the human and the nonhuman (including animals and things).[47]

In addition to knitting and crafting, the *utopia of ordinary habit* can include the practice of writing that forms the basis for my depression memoir. Writing is presented, for example, as a form of spiritual practice in popular books such as Julia Cameron's *The Artist's Way*, which recommends daily "morning pages" as the foundation for creativity; Nathalie Goldberg's Buddhist *Writing Down the Bones*, which suggests the practice of regular writing as a way of staying focused on the present; and Anne Lamott's *Bird by Bird*, which encourages a writing process in which the act of writing is more important than the product and "shitty first drafts" are welcome. The habit of writing also belongs to ordinary practices such as keeping a diary, the everyday or popular genre that has been a mainstay of girls' culture, or maintaining a blog, the capacious new genre that is so well-suited to documenting the everyday and the present in painstaking detail. Across these various forms of writing practice, the emphasis is on writing as something that is ordinary because anyone can do it and because, as a regular habit, it makes creativity a part of everyday life. In the process of demystifying writing to construct it as an ordinary activity, writers such as Cameron, Goldberg, and Lamott implicitly suggest that spiritual practice take the humble form of ordinary habit. Even if this form of spiritual experience also partakes of the transcendent and extraordinary, it is rooted in the ordinary. It is about paying attention to what is immediately present and hence about valuing the ordinary and the detail. If the spiritual is about a connection with something beyond or outside the self, the route to that form of utopian feeling is the simple act of observing or noticing what lies in one's immediate vicinity (an act for which writing serves as a tool). And if it is about creating the sense of self-worth that comes from acknowledging the divine within, free writing facilitates the valuing of all thoughts and feelings without judgment that is also a form of ordinary habit. In these theories of writing, then, spiritual practice is a variant of ordinary habit (and vice versa), in part because they understand spirituality (like the concept of utopia) as something that is not transcendent or beyond but rooted in the here and now.

The *utopia of ordinary habit* is forged out of the loss of connection—to the body, to a meaningful sense of work, to relations with others—

that characterizes depression. It suggests that within current forms of domestic life are the simultaneously utopian and ordinary desires and activities that can remake the affective cultures of nuclear family life, consumerism, mass media, and neoliberal culture. But it does not seek to gloss over the dire state of contemporary politics, nor to deny the feelings of sadness, apathy, isolation, or anger that are often manifest in the practice of small daily gestures. As an example of this idea, I turn to Gregg Bordowitz's video *Habit*.

THE DEPRESSION ARCHIVE: HABIT

> I think at the end of the day I make work so I can understand my own historical present. To me that's a very important thing—to be able to understand my own moment . . . for me, not in any kind of global sense, not for you, not for anyone else. I feel disturbed when for long periods of time I don't make the effort to somehow produce a cosmology for my self. —Gregg Bordowitz, *Habit*

Gregg Bordowitz's autodocumentary video *Habit* (2001), a follow-up to *Fast Trip, Long Drop* (1993), reflects on his daily life as a long-time HIV survivor in an era of globalized AIDS pandemic.[48] It explores the contradictions between habits that deaden, such as answering email and being inured to the stories of AIDS as global crisis, and habits that create awareness or facilitate life, such as meditating daily or taking pills for survival. Bordowitz is interested in questions of will and agency, of what makes it possible to do anything when the specter of death looms large and makes depression a seemingly inevitable condition of daily life.[49] *Habit* risks being boring in its depiction of ordinary routines of daily life; the video opens and closes with scenes of Bordowitz getting up in the morning and taking his pills, while also making coffee and staring out the kitchen window, and interspersed with the more conventional activist documentary footage about South African AIDS activism and global pharmaceutical projects are domestic scenes of Bordowitz on his computer, mowing the lawn, and hanging out with his girlfriend Claire in bed and in the backyard. A recurrent image is that of the many pills that he takes every day. Presenting habit as both a problem and a solution, the video explores ways of reworking habit in relation to daily life. While habit can take you away from paying attention to the world, and Bordowitz is quite open about his depressive anomie, he also considers the ways that habits such as art and meditation can foster agency and will. As he embarks on the weekly ritual of placing his pills into the large plastic container that organizes them by day and time, he explains that the regularized compartments help to relieve "stress and worry" that he might otherwise have about whether he's taken all of his meds (figure 3.13).

Habit also takes on the problems of incommensurability that are present in *War on Worries*, risking the disparity between Bordowitz's domestic life in Chicago, which, however routinized, includes the comforts of groceries in the kitchen and daily pills that can be taken, and the realities of life for HIV survivors in other parts of the world. It moves between the daily life of AIDS as chronic disease in Chicago and the global AIDS conference in South Africa in 2000, the activism of Zackie Achmat and Treatment Action Coalition, and the urgency of a widespread pandemic whose face has shifted considerably from the days of North American queer AIDS activism in the 1980s. Rather than offer some reassuring solution to the question of how to connect these worlds, Bordowitz makes no synthetic links and instead underscores the "impasse" of his own quest for agency and meaning and the smallness of his contact with a South African movement. He remains modest in his goals, enacting depression as the failure to be able to mediate between widely disparate worlds. South African AIDS activism represents both an exhilarating moment of possibility, including its significance as a resurgence and expansion of AIDS activism, and a daunting challenge, given the widespread nature of the pandemic, the economic inequities it foregrounds, and the need to develop new activist strategies.

In refusing to mediate between these disparate realities or to offer some neat solution, *Habit* remains both emotionally and intellectually honest, and not without its utopian moments. The most hopeful moments in the films include not just the heady triumphs of a new South African AIDS activist movement at the World AIDS conference in Durban in 2000, but also the depiction of daily practices of survival in Bordowitz's immediate vicinity, which combine art and spirituality in suggestive ways. Bordowitz's partner, Claire Pentecost, is seen both making

3.13 Gregg Bordowitz,
stills from *Habit*, 2001.

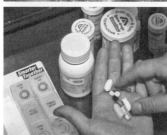

art in her studio and practicing kundalini yoga, and Bordowitz also continues an ongoing conversation about art and mortality with Yvonne
Rainer (an older mentor to Bordowitz not only as an artist but as a long-
time cancer survivor) that was also part of *Fast Trip, Long Drop.*

In one of the video's final scenes, longtime friends and fellow AIDS
activists Daniel Wolfe and Richard Elovich talk about their regular
practice of morning prayer as they lounge in their meditation nook,
which includes an altar of photos and spiritual icons. Their spiritual
practice is not presented as a perfect solution or transcendent moment;
rather it is embedded in daily life and is discussed in modest terms.
Their practice of praying together is "like taking a morning swim," and
Richard describes prayer as necessary to his sobriety but also jokingly
mentions praying for safety when copping drugs as an addict. Emphasizing the ephemeral, Daniel describes "moments of spiritual connection" as "fragile like dreams," as "powerful but precious and breakable,"
and as something that can't "withstand the scrutiny or skepticism" of
others and around which he draws a protective circle in order to preserve it as meaningful. Through their comments, Bordowitz dares to
combine spirituality and politics, so often seen as mutually exclusive
realms of personal and social transformation, and moreover does so in
a way that doesn't suggest that the viewer has to share a set of beliefs
or belong to a particular tradition or collective to be able to understand
these practices.

Indeed, we don't know if Bordowitz himself agrees with the artists
and activists he documents; he uses video to combine different perspectives and vastly different worlds so as to create a "cosmology for
[him]self" and to be able to "understand [his] own historical present."
In 2000, his personal "cosmology" encompasses both Kofi Annan addressing the United Nations about the global pandemic and footage of
himself at the kitchen counter pouring a glass of orange juice and swal-
lowing pills while he waits for the coffee to brew in his own version
of the forms of repetition that Richard Elovich describes as one of the
attractions of prayer, which works because, not unlike a pill, he says,
"[It is] something literal in my hand that I could hold onto." Bordowitz's
notion of cosmology is another way to describe how capitalism feels;
his process involves gathering bits and pieces (or an archive) that are
important to him, not creating a master narrative of neoliberalism or
pious injunctions to political activism. Depression is far too thin and

undescriptive a term for what it means to live with AIDS (and AIDS activism) in a globalizing culture.

SPIRITUAL PRACTICE (OR, THE SACRED EVERYDAY)

I don't believe in The Rapture
Don't want to go flying through the air
Leaving my friends all here behind
Turning my back on humankind.
Why don't we stay here and try to make things work?

—Gretchen Phillips, "In Case of Rapture"

My invocation of the concept of *spiritual practice* as a version of the *utopia of ordinary habits* and a possible response to political depression will no doubt be troubling to some readers, given the resolute secularism of so many academics.[50] But the persistent presence of the category of *spirituality* across my argument—not just in Bordowitz's *Habit*, but in Cassian on acedia and Jacqui Alexander on the pedagogy of the sacred—signals the failure of conventional ways of linking emotion and politics and also names different ways of connecting them. As "something literal in my hand I could hold on to," prayer or spiritual practice is often a very ordinary form of sustenance, a small gesture of faith or hope in the midst of prohibitive circumstances.

For those who are skeptical of matters spiritual, there are many ways to demystify the concept of *spiritual practice*. It may be easier to think of it as daily habit or in terms of the more secular category of *creative practice*. Its ties to the ordinary and the repetitive and its fragile and ephemeral presence in places where feelings of despair and hopelessness are also powerfully present suggest that it is not necessarily a form of transcendence or escape from the messy realities of the here and now. Like creative practice, spiritual practice is a daily activity whose meaning resides in the process itself, not in results that happen somewhere else. Because spiritual practice involves forms of embodiment or rituals with physical dimensions—lighting a candle, chanting a mantra, sitting in silence—it can be described in sensory and affective terms. Although spiritual practice can take the form of becoming aware of a spiritual presence or divinity that is immanent in the present or in ordinary experience, moments of spiritual transcendence are often simply moments of heightened feeling, both psychic and somatic.

Yet even as the spiritual is rendered ordinary through notions of habit and practice, such demystifications don't capture its full resonance if they ultimately secularize the spiritual and take away its qualities of enchantment and magic.[51] Instead, to invoke again Jacqui Alexander's question from the previous chapter, what would it mean to take spirituality seriously in academic scholarship? Why does it keep appearing so insistently amid this project's efforts to view depression through the lens of public feelings? As a category often taken up by those who reject organized religion, spirituality can seem insufficiently orthodox for those who embrace a particular religious tradition, irrationally superstitious for those who are avowed secularists, and wildly ungrounded or touchy-feely to both. Frequently associated with cultures that are deemed premodern or outside modernity, spirituality comes under suspicion as a domain of cultural otherness that is either inaccessible to secular modern subjects or appropriated by those attracted to its exoticism. The "new age" cultures of white middle-class spirituality are an especially easy target for critique on the grounds of cultural appropriation, as well as individualism, consumerism, and sentimentality.[52]

Yet, cordoning off white middle-class spirituality from serious consideration can perpetuate problematic racial divides as much as it calls attention to them. Spiritual practices have often been placed outside the domain of organized religion because they have been literally condemned or suppressed or have been the subject of an epistemic violence that doesn't grant them the status of religion. Responses to colonialism present in African diasporic practices, syncretic versions of Catholicism and indigenous cultures, and the reclamation and preservation of indigenous ways of thinking, all of which trouble any strict equivalence of modernity and secularism, suggest the intersections of spiritual practice and affective politics. Rather than being cause for critique, the ongoing impact of such traditions and practices in mainstream popular culture indicates the salience of those traditions, an investigation of which entails attention to feeling. Given how common yoga and Buddhist meditation, new world Catholicisms, African diaspora practices, and indigenous spiritualities have become for many people (including, whether they publicly articulate it or not, lots of academics), standing alongside trips to the gym and the therapist as part of the practices of daily life, it seems inadequate to dismiss them as forms of cultural appropriation.

Indeed, spirituality stands at the conceptual crossroads of distinctions between the religious and the secular that are central to histories of feeling and the public sphere. The history of affect is a history of secularization (and vice versa), which includes the processes through which religious feeling got transferred to sanctioned forms of feeling within the home, the family, and the marketplace (and the truth of deep personal feelings came to replace the feeling of connection to God).[53] If the attention to the affective, as opposed to rational, public sphere that has been enabled by gender studies is to complete its project, it must consider the residual forms of religious feeling in the eighteenth- and nineteenth-century cultures of sentimentality and abolition that promoted a humanism of fellow feeling. Another important arena for discussions of religion and emotional life is the contemporary moral panics around sexuality that, as queer scholars have suggested, indicate that the state is far from secular.[54] Spirituality often takes the form of the return of the repressed, emerging in cultural formations where distinctions between the religious and the secular are messy or unresolved or breaking down.[55] Although still at the margins even of scholarship on religion and affect, spirituality shares with these categories the capacity to put pressure on the category of the secular. Scholarship in religious studies often remains secular and critical in its perspective, even as it pursues important work in folding religion into culture, but another direction for inquiry would be to hold on to forms of "enchantment" (and other related feelings) rather than demystifying religion as cultural expression.

My aim here is to suspend the tendency to dismiss spirituality, even in its "new age" manifestations, in order to reckon with the resources it has to offer for Public Feelings. The spiritual can help articulate a politics of feeling that is manifest not just in the overt or visible social movements of conventional politics but in the more literal kinds of movement that make up everyday life practices or forms of cultural expression. Thinking about everyday habit and spiritual practice together provides resources for thinking about depression as a problem that requires new ways of living. Embracing their connection obviates the need to apologize for or excise the spiritual resonances that often accompany utopian claims for the aesthetic or performative as an alternative form of politics.[56] The ways of living cultivated by spiritual practice may entail significant social transformation, but they are also practices of the body, which are available in the here and now. Spiritual practice consists of attention to the present and awareness of or orientation toward it as immanently meaningful or sufficient. Such awareness may resemble a version of modernist epiphany, which, like women's culture, is another long-standing laboratory for this concept. But the ordinary is extraordinary in a full range of places, from the popular or everyday to elite culture, whereas modernist practices, in the process of converting everyday experience into aesthetic form, often take the ordinary out of the extraordinary.[57]

Connecting the spiritual with the everyday helps transform the model, so central to cultural studies, and sometimes so hard to avoid, of assuming that the expression of feeling has to become something else to make it count as political—that it is the first step or the raw material for social change, or an individual experience that has to become collective to matter. When the spiritual, like utopia, is conceived of not as transcendent but as available here and now (through practice) and, analogously, when social critique does not take the form of looking for a deeper meaning or a "real" politics that lies elsewhere, emotional expression doesn't have to be converted to something else called "politics" to be meaningful.

Spiritual practice is also a way of becoming open to what we don't know. It's often described as a way to connect to that which is beyond or larger than the self (although sometimes divinity is said to be immanent or present within the self and daily experience) and hence as that which exceeds our current thinking (although the unknown might be manifest as a feeling). Spiritual experience or practice lends itself to ways of thinking and feeling that differ from the usual model of cultural criticism, which demands that we be able to track the concrete steps that connect the emotional and the political. In spiritual practice one cultivates a willingness to encounter impasse or lack of knowledge, to not know how things will turn out and to go with that feeling, to practice accepting or welcoming it rather than being scared by it. (The embrace of fear, or anxiety, or not knowing is central to the popular Buddhism of, for example, Pema Chödrön and Thich Nhat Hanh and is also described in compelling ways by Eve Sedgwick.)[58]

In *Habit*, the visual artist Claire Pentecost is seen practicing a kunda-lini yoga meditation called *sat kriya*, which includes recitation of the mantra *sat nam* (truth is my identity). In the kundalini tradition, medi-tation is considered to be a spiritual technology, one that involves mind and body and the energetic centers that combine them. The chanting of the mantra that creates mental concentration is accompanied by clasp-ing the hands over the head (which can be very tiring) and a sharp pumping of the navel point, which affects all of the organs and facili-tates the fuller breathing that opens up not just the mind but a spiri-tual body that is dispersed across the seven energy centers, or chakras. I recognized Pentecost's meditation practice because it's the same one I do every morning for eleven minutes in order to prepare for the day. It helps with the war on worries by honing my attention, not only pull-ing it away from the distractions of so many things to do and the dis-asters in the world, but also setting me up to be oriented toward them in a calmer way. It is a technology for developing spiritual warriors who will have the sensory tools (both cognitive and emotional, both mental and physical) to focus and be present even in times of crisis. But it has to be repeated every day because the lesson is never done—the mind will always wander, the body will be blocked by stress, the spirit will be dampened.

I have found intellectual support for the value of the concept of spiri-tuality in the disparate archive of fellow travelers I have assembled for this project. The fourth-century desert monk Cassian writing on acedia as one of the deadly sins offers a remarkably accessible account of the despair that can plague the modern intellectual or activist who loses faith in a particular project or set of ideals. Jacqui Alexander speaks of the "disconnection" that is the postcolonial condition and the sacred practices that can heal both writer's block and a daily sense of despair. It is not surprising that the early Christian ascetic and the contempo-rary postcolonial intellectual would both point in the direction of the spiritual, since both belong to traditions that have been shaped by and on the margins of Western secular understandings of the rational. In order to retrieve the spiritual, we often have to look to both geographic and historical peripheries and to vernacular practices that have been cast as irrational and superstitious. Along with the feminist crafter, the early Christian ascetic and the postcolonial intellectual provide forms of knowledge that are not scientific, knowledges that come from the body and from practices rather than texts, as well as from immaterial sources that some would call the domain of spirit.

These disparate sources of wisdom have helped me see how the combined forces of the ordinary and the spiritual can be an antidote to despair, alienation, and depression. The labor of habit or practice—gathering palm leaves, performing rituals from diasporic and indigenous traditions, knitting and crocheting, writing—forges new understandings of the political. It also generates a reparative relation to depression and alternatives to the medical model of depression as something to be diagnosed and known. The experience of depression or being stuck can be an invitation to that which we don't yet know and a way of reminding us why cultural studies matters. Like spiritual practice, creative practice—and scholarship as creative practice—involves not knowing, trusting to process and to a holistic intelligence that encompasses body, mind, and senses in order to see what happens, rather than having an answer to writing a dissertation, transforming depression, or planning a life.

Lynda Barry, *What It Is*.

IS THIS GOOD? DOES THIS SUCK?

> Is this good? Does this suck? I'm not sure when these two questions
> became the only two questions I had about my work, or when making
> pictures and stories turned into something I called "my work"—I just
> know I'd stopped enjoying it and instead began to dread it.
> —Lynda Barry, *What It Is*, 123

These two questions constitute a refrain in *What It Is*, Lynda Barry's
how-to manual for writers, which is also a meditation on the creative
process, a memoir about her own development as an artist, a philosophical inquiry into how memory is embedded in places that are "spots
of time" out of which images emerge, and a genre-bending graphic narrative in which the relation between text and drawing is integral to the

story.[1] Telling the story of her own childhood pleasure in drawing, she cites the moment when judgment from others sets in as the killer of the creative impulse. Two evil twins, whom Barry draws as impish blobs with stick legs, one telling her she's great and the other telling her she sucks, take up residence and prevent her from simply making things for the pleasure of it, without knowing "what it is." They are the monstrous counterparts to the animal familiars whom she doodles over and over as part of her process, including her guardian cephalopod, who reminds her of the lesson she repeatedly forgets and has to be reminded of through practice: "to be able to stand *not knowing* long enough to let something alive take shape!"[2] (See figure on page 211.)

Barry's demons of the creative process have certainly haunted me throughout the writing of this book, especially the memoir material. To Barry's questions I would add the voice in my head that said "You're a full professor, you can do whatever you want!" When I was stuck, this voice adopted a more overtly shaming tone: "You're a full professor, what's your problem?" Other variations included "This is not scholarship" or, a variant on that theme that can carry an even bigger barb for some of us, "What makes you think this is going to change the world?" Although many people told me so, it didn't *feel* like I could do whatever I wanted, and the tension between the material reality of privilege and the lived experience of fear created another "war on worry" that became the project of this book.

Some readers have wondered about the afterlife of *The Depression Journals* since I've obviously gone on to a successful career, not only publishing that first book and getting tenure but maintaining an active life as a scholar. Just beyond the horizon of the story, for those who know me at least, are also twenty years of a happy relationship and a fantastic network of queer friends. But the path is not that simple. Writing this book took place during one of the worst periods of anxiety I have experienced since completing my first book. Although one "cure" was getting the time to write it, that simple practical solution did not come easily. I was turned down three times for internal funding at my university (the only way to get a research leave since we do not have sabbaticals), and I suspect one of the reasons was because interdisciplinary work on feelings, especially in the form of critical memoir, does not look like serious research.

While sabbaticals and research leaves can be considered a luxury enjoyed by faculty at Research I institutions, they are also a life-saving respite from the obligation to write more, teach more, mentor more, and do more that is part of the speed-up in the workplace in academia and elsewhere. The struggle to protect that privileged position from being eroded by budget cuts and constant slams against not only radical cultural studies but the humanities in general can lead to the extreme weariness known as burnout.[3] If even those of us in the most senior or prestigious positions are experiencing our labor conditions as crushing, what does that mean for the many who have far less power, security, or freedom over their labor time? I consider my experience to be business as usual in the academy—an ordinary story, not an exceptional one. Thus, although one implicit message of *The Depression Journals* is that it is possible to come out on the other side of a period of blockage, struggle is also ongoing.

One solution to the challenges writing this book presented was to turn doggedly to thinking of my scholarship as creative work whose only importance might be that it mattered to me. Or as Lynda Barry astutely puts it, "We don't create a fantasy world to escape reality, we create it to be able to stay."[4] Her writing tips are much like those that I drew on while writing this book—free writing, lack of self-censorship, calling up concrete memories of images and place—all quite common within creative writing practice or even beginning composition instruction but not always accepted practice for advanced academic scholarship. Barry's recommendation to keep moving, not just by never picking up the pen from the page when free writing, but also by turning to drawing or doodling is ingenious. The pages from her daily notebook that she reproduces at the end of *What It Is* are a brilliant example of how process is the material, as she not only writes and draws key phrases and images, but makes the seemingly meaningless doodles that are incorporated into the design of the pages of the final book.

DOES IT REALLY GET BETTER?

> But if you really learn how to pay attention, then you will know there are other options. It will actually be within your power to experience a crowded, hot, slow, consumer-hell type situation as not only meaningful, but sacred, on fire with the same force that made the stars: love, fellowship, the mystical oneness of all things deep down.
>
> —David Foster Wallace, "Real Freedom?"

Although my invocation of utopia and spiritual practice in chapter 3 may seem to imply respite or solution or a happy ending, the final message here can't really be construed as "It gets better," to quote from the recent video campaign that aims to talk queer youth out of suicidal despair.[5] If depression is a version of Lauren Berlant's slow death, then there is no clean break from it. The bad feelings that hover around daily practices of survival are always there, especially if it's a political depression, which won't end until there is real economic justice and a better reckoning with histories of violence. But just because there's no happy ending doesn't mean that we have to feel bad all the time or that feeling bad is a state that precludes feelings of hope and joy.

The It Gets Better campaign, along with some of the cases that catalyzed it, including the suicide of Tyler Clementi at Rutgers, is an interesting study in depression and how to combat it. It's not hard to find problems with the campaign's earnest belief in being able to make a difference, and it has generated some important queer cultural critique.[6] As Jack Halberstam succinctly puts it, in the unapologetically cranky rant of the Bully Blogger, "It gets worse."[7]

But it is perhaps hasty to generalize about It Gets Better since it has gone viral so quickly and there are not only hundreds of videos, many of which are more complex than the original Dan Savage video, but the multiple and unpredictable effects they generate. Nonetheless, I fear that one of the potential problems with the campaign is that no matter how heartfelt, injunctions to stay alive, whether mediated or direct, are so often doomed to fail. Commanding someone to stay alive is, unfortunately, not a performative statement, however much we wish otherwise, and expressions of love don't necessarily translate, except haphazardly, into a cure for the insidious habit of self-hatred or feeling bad about oneself that lies at the root of so many addictions. Many of us have no doubt tried to encourage someone—an alcoholic brother, a depressed sister, a drug addict cousin, a desperate student, our queer friends—to keep on living or just to remember that they are loved. But because knowledge and recognition aren't the same thing, because staying alive is a practice and not just a momentary feeling, those moments of reassurance can be ephemeral, whether they come from a friend or a celebrity, from a live conversation or a YouTube video (or a book in the library, the lifeline of many queer adolescents before the Internet).

Although as the queer pundits have pointed out, the desire to help those who are younger often stems from the sometimes sentimental and patronizing belief that childhood and adolescence should be protected, it can also be motivated by the grim and sometimes secret underbelly of our own experiences of suicidal wishes and desperation. Along with worrying about all the adolescent and college-age queers who are more anxious than ever, this book is haunted by the memory of many people for whom growing up didn't necessarily mean getting better, people who couldn't figure out how to wait until things got better, people who are not that different from me.[8] My friend Lora Romero, the same one who provided the inspiration that helped me finish *Mixed Feelings*, is one of the ones who didn't manage to survive the long slow descent into unrelenting despair.

Being an adult—or white or male or middle class or professionally and creatively successful—is no guarantee of protection from despair. Consider, for example, the case of David Foster Wallace. He was neither a kid nor a queer when he died, but his brilliant ability to describe the numbing effects of normative white middle-class life suggest why he might have gone under. It Gets Better can be juxtaposed with his celebrated commencement speech, a genre whose mode of address is also that of an older person offering wisdom and advice to a younger person. But Wallace turns the genre on its head, eschewing the usual pieties about using one's youthful potential and enthusiasm to address world problems in socially responsible ways, and reminding us that the high points of a college degree and the brink of adulthood are often not so far from the anxieties of adolescence. Wallace gets down and dirty with the deadening power of "boredom, routine, and petty frustration" that will likely confront these future college graduates. In the nuanced detail of the immersive realism for which he is known, he describes a scene that also appears in *The Depression Journals*—the humbling experience of a trip to the grocery store:

> By way of example, let's say it's an average adult day, and you get up in the morning, go to your challenging, white-collar, college-graduate job, and you work hard for eight or ten hours, and at the end of the day you're tired and somewhat stressed and all you want is to go home and have a good supper and maybe unwind for an hour, and then hit the sack early because, of course, you have to get up the next day and do it all over again.
>
> But then you remember there's no food at home. You haven't had time to shop this week because of your challenging job, and so now after work you have to get in your car and drive to the supermarket. It's the end of

the work day and the traffic is apt to be: very bad. So getting to the store takes way longer than it should, and when you finally get there, the super-market is very crowded, because of course it's the time of day when all the other people with jobs also try to squeeze in some grocery shopping. And the store is hideously lit and infused with soul-killing muzak or cor-porate pop and it's pretty much the last place you want to be but you can't just get in and quickly out; you have to wander all over the huge, over-lit store's confusing aisles to find the stuff you want and you have to maneu-ver your junky cart through all these other tired, hurried people with carts (et cetera, et cetera, cutting stuff out because this is a long ceremony) and eventually you get all your supper supplies, except now it turns out there aren't enough check-out lanes open even though it's the end-of-the-day rush. So the checkout line is incredibly long, which is stupid and infuriat-ing. But you can't take your frustration out on the frantic lady working the register, who is overworked at a job whose daily tedium and meaningless-ness surpasses the imagination of any of us here at a prestigious college.

The passage goes on at length in the humorously excruciating detail that characterizes Wallace's art of "the descriptive turn," which is cen-tral to his conception of compassion as the capacity to imagine (in equally excruciating detail) the troubled lives of people he finds su-premely annoying. With his extraordinary ability to document the feel of ordinary life, he implicitly suggests the connections between every-day experience and more spectacular forms of despair, such as suicide and its near-cousin homicidal violence.[9]

Wallace's extended account of tedium culminates in the observations quoted at the beginning of this section in which he offers his version of advice for how to fight the "war on worries" of a mind so full of its own boredom, aggression, and anxiety that it can't ever get outside of the hamster wheel of narcissistic self-loathing long enough to have any attention or compassion for others. Surprisingly for someone who might seem to epitomize the straight white critical secularism of the postmod-ern American novel, Wallace mentions the sacred and worship, and his recommendation for "paying attention" resembles a Buddhist training in mindfulness and the sacred everyday. Attention is a difficult and on-going practice, he seems to be saying, not the result of a college degree and getting older; cultivating the "freedom" to see sacred meaningful-ness even in the grocery line is the hard work (or art) of daily living. The default setting of numbness that Wallace warns against includes critique (such as cursing the owners of SUVs and their consumerism), but even as his essay critiques critique and the smugness of being smart or right, it also manifests compassion (and despair) for how easy it is to succumb to it. That he couldn't himself practice it suggests how difficult it is; being able to think one's way out or offer a beautiful description of thinking's impasses isn't necessarily enough.

FLOSS YOUR TEETH AND KEEP ON LIVING

> As they become known to and accepted by us, our feelings and the honest exploration of them become sanctuaries and spawning grounds for the most radical and daring of ideas. They become a safe house for that difference so necessary to change and the conceptualization of any meaningful action. Right now I could name at least ten ideas I would have found intolerable or incomprehensible and frightening, except as they came after dreams and poems. This is not idle fantasy, but a disciplined attention to the true meaning of "it feels right to me."
> —Audre Lorde, "Poetry Is Not a Luxury"

> I just want to be frank about what you will be really living through. You'll be living through flossing. Years of it, both in the mirror and away from it, both with girlfriends and alone. Girlfriends will be really excited that you floss your teeth, because they should and they think it's really inspiring that you do that and they will ask you if they can do it with you because it's easier that way, bumping their hips and thighs against you while you keep peering at yourself under the shitty bathroom light. —Eileen Myles, "Live Through That?!," 219

My friend Nancy's two-point plan for getting through depression is simple: (1) Keep moving. (2) Help other people. Despite being extraordinarily ambivalent about self-help books and their can-do lists, this book has its own aspirations to the genre. In keeping with the niche marketing that allows the genre to proliferate endlessly in order to keep up with new identities, diagnoses, and demographics, my self-help book for depression would be directed to an audience of academics and queers, especially those who remain curious about the genre despite their reservations and disidentifications. I have some fellow travelers in the queer self-help subgenre, including Kate Bornstein, whose *Hello*

Cruel World: 101 Alternatives to Suicide for Teens, Freaks, and Other Out-laws provides its wisdom with a combination of humor and perversity that avoids the sentimentality of It Gets Better.[10]

My dream advice manual would include the comments of the many thinkers and writers who have offered me wisdom and solace, not by wishing away the hard stuff but by facing it head-on and being willing to take us there. By way of closing, the quotations above pair the words of Audre Lorde and Eileen Myles, each in her own way a fierce dyke warrior-poet, on the need to take care of one's own body and feelings, to craft a "radical self-possession" in order to fight larger battles.

For Lorde, poetry is not a luxury because the energy for social transformation is dependent on the access to the feeling of one's own truth that creativity cultivates. There is a perhaps surprising overlap between her wisdom and that of David Foster Wallace, a connection that suggests that there is no identitarian claim on this wisdom, which can be derived from many sources. Both of them emphasize that the practice of living doesn't come from new ideas—Wallace readily admits that much of what he says is present in clichés that are so ubiquitous that we become numb to them. Lorde has the righteousness of the oppressed on her side, pitting a black matriarchy of feeling against white patriarchal rationality, and can thus perhaps more easily claim the practice of old traditions (which include the hard-won survivals of the African diaspora) as a victory:

> Sometimes we drug ourselves with dreams of new ideas. The head will save us. The brain alone will set us free. But there are no new ideas still waiting in the wings to save us as women, as human. There are only old and forgotten ones, new combinations, extrapolations and recognitions from within ourselves—along with the renewed courage to try them out.
>
> For there are no new ideas. There are only new ways of making them felt—of examining what those ideas feel like being lived on Sunday morning at 7 a.m., after brunch, during wild love, making war, giving birth, mourning our dead.[11]

Alongside Lorde's more solemn form of inspirational sermon, Eileen Myles's meditations on brushing her teeth as a commitment to living suggest the ordinary power of the daily ritual. Published in a queer feminist collection called *Live through This*, on the use of creativity to counter self-destruction, her essay gave me a thrill because she affirmed my sense that visits to the dentist were among the many tiny but important ways in which the desire to live manifests itself. Health care might be a middle-class luxury, but Myles resists the working-class fate of a father who "lost his teeth at 40 and then he died at 44," and chooses dental care over therapy as the secret to longevity: "In my twenties when I had never gone to therapy I decided that I would always privilege the dentist over the therapist and that I was really getting a two-in-one service when I went to the dentist but still when I drank I would often pass out before I could floss."[12]

Barry's free writing and notebook doodles, Wallace's grocery store routines, Lorde's Sunday morning rituals, and Myles's daily flossing—I collected these insights on the art of daily living in part because I was so delighted to see echoes of *The Depression Journals* in these other places. My routines include both the spiritual beyond and the mundane dirt of the dust bunny, both writing and cleaning the cat box. But no matter how hard I try, I still can't seem to make myself floss every day.

Lynda Barry, *What It Is*.

Notes

1. Core members of the group in Austin have included Sam Baker, Alyssa Harad, Neville Hoad, Deborah Kapchan, Ann Reynolds, Janet Staiger, Kathleen Stewart, many of our graduate students, and, as this book was being finished, Craig Campbell, Josh Gunn, Heather Hindman, Randy Lewis, Sofian Merabet, and Circe Sturm.

2. For more on Feel Tank Chicago, see Berlant, "Critical Inquiry, Affirmative Culture." Feel Tank members have included Lauren Berlant, Deborah Gould, Vanalyne Greene, Mary Patten, and Rebecca Zorach. The group helped organize a conference at the University of Chicago called "Depression: What Is It Good For?" in March 2004, and a conference called "Anxiety, Urgency, Outrage, Hope . . . A Conference on Political Feeling" in October 2007. See http://politicalfeeling.uchicago.edu/ (accessed 15 March 2012). For a review of the conference, see Carmody and Love, "Try Anything."

3. Gordon, "Something More Powerful Than Skepticism."

4. See Clough and Halley, *The Affective Turn*, and Gregg and Seigworth, *The Affect Theory Reader*.

5. Rather than attempt an exhaustive list, I will name here some of the sources that have been most influential or productive for my thinking. I do so in the interest of acknowledging fellow travelers, many of whom have had direct connections with Public Feelings events and programming, and thus to use affiliations, influences, and networks as the way of creating a bibliography rather than some putatively more objective standard of coverage or completeness.

Among those with direct ties to Public Feelings are Baker, *Written on the Water*; Berlant, *The Queen of America Goes to Washington City*, *The Female Complaint*, *Intimacy*, *Compassion*, *Cruel Optimism*, and many others; Boler, *Feeling Power*; Cobb, *God Hates Fags*; Duggan, *Sapphic Slashers* and *The Twilight of Equality*; Gould, *Moving Politics*; Hoad, *African Intimacies*; Jakobsen and Pellegrini, *Love the Sin*; Joseph, *Against the Romance of Community*; Love, *Feeling Backward*; Luciano, *Arranging Grief*; Manalansan, *Global Divas*; Muñoz, *Disidentifications*, *Cruising Utopia*, "Between Psychoanalysis and Affect: A Public Feelings Project," "Feeling Brown," and "Feeling Brown, Feeling Down"; Reynolds, *Robert Smithson*; Soto, *The De-Mastery of Desire*; Staiger, *Perverse Spec-*

tators; Stewart, *A Space on the Side of the Road* and *Ordinary Affects*; Torres, *Black, White, and in Color*; Woodward, *Statistical Panic*.

For earlier work of mine, see Cvetkovich, *Mixed Feelings*; "Public Sentiments" (coedited with Ann Pellegrini); *An Archive of Feelings*; "Public Feelings"; and Staiger, Cvetkovich, and Reynolds, *Political Emotions*. It is hard to imagine the work of Public Feelings without the writings of Eve Kosofsky Sedgwick, ranging from *Between Men* to *Touching Feeling*. As this book goes to press, the posthumously published *The Weather in Proust* is contributing to discussions of the "affective turn."

Other important books on affect, feeling, and emotion include Abu-Lughod and Lutz, *Language and the Politics of Emotion*; Ahmed, *The Cultural Politics of Emotion*, *Queer Phenomenology*, "Happiness," and *The Promise of Happiness*; Boym, *The Future of Nostalgia*; Brennan, *The Transmission of Affect*; Butler, *The Psychic Life of Power*, *Precarious Life*, and *Frames of War*; Crimp, *Melancholia and Moralism*; Dolan, *Utopia in Performance*; Eng, *The Feeling of Kinship*; Eng and Kazanjian, *Loss*; Flatley, *Affective Mapping*; Gordon, *Ghostly Matters*; Halberstam, *The Queer Art of Failure*; Holland, *Raising the Dead*; Koestenbaum, *Humiliation*; Lutz, *Unnatural Emotions*; Massumi, *Parables for the Virtual*; Moten, *In the Break*; Ngai, *Ugly Feelings*; Probyn, *Blush*; Reddy, *The Navigation of Feeling*; Salecl, *On Anxiety*; Seremetakis, *The Senses Still*; Snediker, *Queer Optimism*; Taussig, *The Nervous System*; Terada, *Feeling in Theory* and *Looking Awry*; Warner, *Publics and Counterpublics*.

Other foundational works include Benjamin, *Illuminations*, *Reflections*, *The Arcades Project*, and *Selected Writings*; Habermas, *The Structural Transformation of the Public Sphere*; and Williams, "Structures of Feeling."

Further relevant works are listed in notes on specific subtopics; for additional work on queer theory, see note 13; on trauma, see note 17; on race and affect, see note 18; and on feminism, gender, and women's genres, see note 19.

6. In addition to Clough and Halley, *The Affective Turn*, see Gregg and and Seigworth, *The Affect Theory Reader*, for a compilation of this work. Gregg and Seigworth trace the affective turn to the combined influence of Eve Sedgwick and Larry Grossberg, as well as Brian Massumi, who has been one of the major disseminators of Deleuze's work. An important use of Deleuzian affect theory within queer theory has been Puar, *Terrorist Assemblages*, as well as more generally the ongoing body of work by Elizabeth Grosz, including *Time Travels* and *Becoming Undone*.

7. For more detailed discussions of these distinctions, see Gregg and Seigworth, *The Affect Theory Reader*; Flatley, *Affective Mapping*; Gould, "On Affect and Protest."

8. See "From Surface to Depth, between Psychoanalysis and Affect," Muñoz's introduction to "Between Psychoanalysis and Affect: A Public Feelings Project," as well as the entire special issue of *Women and Performance* more generally, for a discussion of the complementary rather than mutually

exclusive relation between affect theory and psychoanalysis. See also Brennan, *The Transmission of Affect*, for an example of psychoanalytically inflected work that is also attentive to the somatic nature of affect and its intersubjective qualities, as well as Sedgwick's turn to Sylvan Tompkins for alternatives to psychoanalysis in Sedgwick and Frank, *Shame and Its Sisters*.

9. The fellow traveler relation between Public Feelings and the Deleuzians is a friendly and intimate one, though, visible, for example, in Clough's presence in Muñoz's "Between Psychoanalysis and Affect," Berlant's and Stewart's inclusion in *The Affect Theory Reader*, Stewart's own use of Deleuze in *Ordinary Affects*, and Gould's use of Deleuzian distinctions between affect and emotion in her essay "On Affect and Protest."

10. This book's working subtitle, "A Public Feelings Project," was changed after the manuscript was submitted. This designation has also been used by me and my coeditors Janet Staiger and Ann Reynolds in conjunction with *Political Emotions*, a collection based on a conference at the University of Texas in 2008; by José Muñoz for the special issue of *Women and Performance*, "Between Psychoanalysis and Affect"; and by Lauren Berlant in *Cruel Optimism*; and this book remains "A Public Feelings Project" in spirit.

11. Sedgwick, "Paranoid Reading and Reparative Reading, or, You're So Paranoid, You Probably Think This Essay Is about You," *Touching Feeling*, 123–52.

12. Stewart, *Ordinary Affects*. Stewart has, however, been making this argument throughout her career, not only in her first book, *A Space on the Side of the Road*, but also in earlier essays such as "On the Politics of Cultural Theory."

13. See Sedgwick, *Touching Feeling*, and Sedgwick and Frank, *Shame and Its Sisters*; and in addition to works cited in note 2 by Ahmed, Cobb, Butler, Crimp, Dolan, Duggan, Eng, Gould, Halberstam, Hoad, Jakobsen and Pellegrini, Joseph, Love, Manalansan, Muñoz, Soto, Snediker, and Warner, see also work on queer temporalities such as Dinshaw, *Getting Medieval*; Freeman, "Queer Temporalities," and *Time Binds*; and Halberstam, *In A Queer Time and Place*, which in its concern with the affective relations between past and present has been a rich source for queer affect theory.

14. This debate has circulated around Edelman's *No Future*. See Caserio, Dean, Edelman, Halberstam, and Muñoz, "The Antisocial Thesis in Queer Theory" and Muñoz, *Cruising Utopia*, as well as Weiner and Young, "Queer Bonds."

15. See Snediker's critique in *Queer Optimism*, especially 21–25, of "queer pessimism" as exemplified especially by Edelman, but also by my own work on trauma.

16. See Eng, Halberstam, and Muñoz, "What's Queer about Queer Studies Now?" and Murphy and Ruiz, "Queer Futures," as well as Muñoz's account of the dismal state of mainstream gay politics (and Edelman's version of antisociality) as inspiration for *Cruising Utopia*.

17. See Cvetkovich, *An Archive of Feelings*. Key texts in trauma studies include Caruth, *Trauma* and *Unclaimed Experience*; Eyerman, *Cultural Trauma*; Felman and Laub, *Testimony*; Hirsch, *Family Frames*; Kaplan, *Trauma Culture*; LaCapra, *Representing the Holocaust, History and Memory after Auschwitz*, and *Writing History, Writing Trauma*; Leys, *Trauma*; Miller and Tougaw, *Extremities*; Sturken, *Tangled Memories*; Young, *The Texture of Memory*.

18. This body of work on race and affect includes, in addition to Ahmed, Eng, Gordon, Hoad, Holland, Manalansan, Moten, Muñoz, and Soto, cited in note 2, Cheng, *The Melancholy of Race*; Eng and Han, "A Dialogue on Racial Melancholia"; Gilroy, *Postcolonial Melancholia*; Hartman, *Scenes of Subjection* and *Lose Your Mother*; Khanna, *Dark Continents*; and Zwarg, "Du Bois on Trauma."

19. Important work on feminism and women's genres includes Armstrong, *Desire and Domestic Fiction*; Barnes, *States of Sympathy*; Berlant, *The Anatomy of National Fantasy* and *The Female Complaint*; Brown, *Domestic Individualism*; Burgett, *Sentimental Bodies*; Cherniavsky, *That Pale Mother Rising*; Cvetkovich, *Mixed Feelings*; Davidson, *Revolution and the Word*; Davidson and Hatcher, *No More Separate Spheres!*; Halberstam, *Skin Shows*; Hendler, *Public Sentiments*; Merish, *Sentimental Materialism*; Radway, *Reading the Romance*; Romero, *Home Fronts*; Samuels, *The Culture of Sentiment* and *Romances of the Republic*; Sanchez-Eppler, *Touching Liberty*; Sedgwick, *Between Men*; Stern, *The Plight of Feeling*; Tompkins, *Sensational Designs*.

20. The "unfinished business of sentimentality" is the subtitle of Berlant, *The Female Complaint*. My claims for the generational specificity of Public Feelings owe something to my shared graduate school training with Berlant at Cornell in the early 1980s, where her work on romance and sentimentality began along with my own on sensationalism.

21. Kleinman, Das, and Lock, *Social Suffering*; McLagan, "Principles, Publicity, and Politics," and "Introduction: Making Human Rights Claims Public"; Keenan, "Mobilizing Shame"; Berlant, *Compassion*.

22. One of the other initial groups from the Chicago and Barnard meetings in 2001 was Feminist Pundits, spearheaded by Lisa Duggan, whose collaboration with Berlant on the collection *Our Monica, Ourselves* is an example of this kind of queer and feminist public commentary. More recently, Duggan has teamed up with Muñoz, Halberstam, and Tavia Nyong'o in the blogosphere to produce Bully Bloggers at http://bullybloggers.wordpress.com/.

23. Although the affective turn is sometimes characterized as a turn away from theory or even a sign of the exhaustion of theory, this is certainly not the case for Public Feelings or more generally, for the scholarship generated by the affective turn remains inspired by cultural and social theory. Theoretical insights may, however, be embedded in particular cases and local examples, discovery of and accounting for which can be the result of larger theoretical questions. My focus on depression as a Public Feelings project, for example,

constitutes an effort to use depression as a way of investigating larger questions about everyday life and politics. The languages of theory can include memoir and the personal essay or archival materials that address large transhistorical concerns, including methodological questions about what constitutes an archive or evidence.

24. At the University of Chicago in January 2001, organized by Janet Jakobsen and Lauren Berlant. Public Feelings emerged as a topic for future discussion and was one of the five subgroups for the second national meeting at Barnard College in late September 2001 (a meeting significantly dominated by discussions of September 11, 2001).

More recently, in March 2009, the "Rethinking Sex" conference at the University of Pennsylvania, organized by Heather Love, combined reflections on Gayle Rubin's influential essay and the infamous Barnard conference on Sexuality in 1982 with sessions on the politics of feeling, thus forging a connection between these cultural moments and movements. Some of the proceedings from the conference have been published as Love, "Rethinking Sex."

25. Gilbert and Gubar, *The Madwoman in the Attic*; Chesler, *Women and Madness*.

26. See, for example, Benjamin, *The Arcades Project*, especially "Paris, Capital of the Nineteenth Century," 3–26; Williams, *Culture and Society, 1780–1950* and *Marxism and Literature*; Taussig, *The Nervous System*, especially "Tactility and Distraction," 141–48; Stewart, *A Space on the Side of the Road*; Seremetakis, *The Senses Still*; Gordon, *Ghostly Matters*.

27. Duggan, *The Twilight of Equality?*

28. Ehrenberg, *La fatigue d'être soi*, translated as *The Weariness of the Self*.

29. On permanent war and states of exception, see, for example, Foucault, *"Society Must Be Defended"*; Agamben, *Homo Sacer* and *State of Exception*. On neoliberalism, see Harvey, *A Brief History of Neoliberalism*, and Brown, "Neoliberalism and the End of Liberal Democracy."

30. See Williams, *Keywords*, as well as Bennett, Grossberg, and Morris, eds., *New Keywords*, and Burgett and Hendler, *Keywords for American Cultural Studies*.

31. Feel Tank Chicago made a Wiki for collaborative accounts of keywords.

32. See Berlant, "Slow Death (Sovereignty, Obesity, Lateral Agency)."

33. Or as Eve Kosofsky Sedgwick puts it, "As far as I can tell, current popular thought seems to understand depression in terms of a kind of chronic natural gloominess, on the one hand, or alternatively as a completely exogenous malady, from who knows where, that is liable to descend on its unsuspecting host until heroically routed by medicine and positive mental hygiene" ("Teaching/Depression").

34. See Duggan, *The Twilight of Equality?* For more on the dismantling of public education and the university, see Readings, *The University in Ruins*; Newfield, *Ivy and Industry* and, especially, *Unmaking the Public University*.

35. As part of her affective turn to Sylvan Tompkins, Melanie Klein, and the reparative, Sedgwick also seizes upon this blockage in her critique of how *Mixed Feelings* exemplifies the routinized regimes of theory's paranoid position. See the discussion of *Mixed Feelings* in Sedgwick and Frank, *Shame and Its Sisters*, 15–19. In retrospect, I find it interesting that Sedgwick so astutely identifies the problem with which I was struggling, but in failing to notice the gestures toward the reparative in *Mixed Feelings*, she herself remains in the critical mode. Among other things, my work on depression and public feelings is the result of a long period of pondering this encounter with Sedgwick in order to view with more compassion the blockages that accompanied my fledgling version of the affective turn. For a discussion of the persistence of the paranoid mode in Sedgwick's critique of it, see Love, "Truth and Consequences."

36. See Romero, *Home Fronts*, and also the way the reparative is used in Davidson and Hatcher, *No More Separate Spheres!*

37. See "Starved," *SAQ*, 434, and republished in Halley and Parker, *After Sex? Impasse* is a central concept for Berlant's *Cruel Optimism*, which was published just as this book was going into production. Here and elsewhere, I have retained references to the articles that preceded *Cruel Optimism*, since my discussion was shaped by those sources. A version of the passage cited here appears in *Cruel Optimism*, 199, and *impasse* is also introduced on 4–5.

38. For a medical theory of depression as "being stuck," which combines both traditional and alternative medicine, as well as a Jungian framework, see Gordon, *Unstuck*. Thanks to my acupuncturist, Laura Mathews, for drawing this book to my attention.

39. Ahmed's phenomenological approach to affect in *Queer Phenomenology* and *The Promise of Happiness* is relevant to thinking about depression as impasse, including the relation between being stuck and what she calls "sticky" feelings, which combine the material and the psychic.

40. See, for example, Freeman, *Time Binds*, as well as, more generally, "Queer Temporalities"; Halberstam, *The Queer Art of Failure*; Love, *Feeling Backward*; Stockton, *The Queer Child, or Growing Sideways in the Twentieth Century*.

41. Sedgwick, "Queer and Now," 19.

42. The phrase "coming to know each other through our depression" comes from comments made by José Muñoz at the wrap-up session of the conference partially sponsored by Feel Tank Chicago on Depression: What Is It Good For? at the University of Chicago, March 2004.

43. Dolan, "From Flannel to Fleece."

THE DEPRESSION JOURNALS: *Reflections*

1. For more on this strategy, especially as it applies to the tendency to critique women's genres such as the domestic and sentimental novel, which, like the memoir, are based in the public expression of feeling, see Cathy Davidson and Jessamyn Hatcher's introduction to *No More Separate Spheres!*, 7–26.

2. For an intelligent example of the debate about memoir, although one that doesn't grapple with the queer, academic, and diasporic memoirs that inform my practice and analysis, see Yagoda, *Memoir*.

Although terms such as *creative nonfiction* have dignified memoir as a genre that merits literary recognition alongside fiction, it has also been seen as competition for fiction and has been cast as encouraging a desire for the sensationalism of "true" stories that compromises aesthetic values. The controversy over the revelation that James Frey's addiction memoir, *A Million Little Pieces*, was fictionalized is only one in an ongoing series of discussions about the extent to which memoir's value (whether aesthetic, social, or economic) is grounded in its claims to truth. Because Frey was featured on Oprah's Book Club, the revelation of his book's fictional status produced huge publicity and led to the drama of her confrontation with him on her show. Oprah subsequently apologized to Frey, perhaps in recognition that dismissing him as a liar was scapegoating him for a larger set of issues about memoir and truth.

Other high-profile cases, such as the faked identity of novelist JT Leroy and Binjamin Wilkomirski's false Holocaust memoir, *Fragments*, suggest that the sensationalism of memoir in turn gives rise to sensational stories about its veracity, stories that remain fixated on questions of truth and falsehood rather than the larger social issues often embedded in even suspect memoirs. These public scandals about false memoirs are reminiscent of the false memory syndrome debates around incest, and it would be valuable to remember, as Janice Haacken has argued, that even putatively false stories can provide testimony to experiences of oppression or injury, and that even in the register of truth, memoir must be read as a form of fiction. See Haacken, *The Pillar of Salt*.

3. Queer memoir operates across multiple genres and often in the experimental interstices of genres such as solo performance, graphic narrative, installation art, historical fiction, and creative nonfiction. Cherríe Moraga, Audre Lorde, Minnie Bruce Pratt, Dorothy Allison, Amber Hollibaugh, Joan Nestle, and Leslie Feinberg, to name just a few crucial writers, represent a generation of working-class and woman of color dykes who participated in and were shaped by lesbian feminist culture but who also used memoir and accompanying forms such as the anthology to critique homogenizing understandings of lesbian and queer identities. Examples that have been important to me include Allison, *Two or Three Things I Know for Sure*; Bechdel, *Fun Home*; Kron, *2.5 Minute Ride and 101 Humiliating Stories*; Lorde, *The Cancer Journals*;

Moraga, *Loving in the War Years*; as well as autoethnographic film and video, such as Jean Carlomusto's *Monte Cassino* and Marlon Riggs's *Black Is / Black Ain't*, and works by Gregg Bordowitz, Richard Fung, Alex Juhasz, and Ellen Spiro, among others.

On queer autobiographical performance, see Hughes and Roman, *O Solo Homo*; Muñoz, *Disidentifications*. On video, see, for example, Pidduck, "Queer Kinship and Ambivalence: Video Autoethnographies by Jean Carlomusto and Richard Fung." A crucial foundation for the memoir within lesbian feminist print culture has been the presses, such as Firebrand, Seal, Crossing, and Kitchen Table, that published and distributed work when it otherwise would not have had a public forum, and the network of feminist bookstores that gave it space and programming. On the history of feminist bookstores as public culture, see Kristen Hogan, "Reading at Feminist Bookstores: Women's Literature, Women's Studies, and the Feminist Bookstore Network."

4. Illness narratives, though, can both affirm and critique medical discourse. Many popular depression memoirs, for example, significantly reinforce current medical wisdom by endorsing the power of pharmaceuticals, but they have the power to do so because the patient's voice is a crucial form of evidence, providing a case history that offers a qualitative account of what it feels like to be both ill and under treatment.

On AIDS memoirs, see Tougaw, "Testimony and the Subjects of AIDS Memoirs."

On illness narratives, particularly the way they reconceptualize illness as a form of access to new identities and empowerment, see Couser, *Recovering Bodies* and *Vulnerable Subjects*; Hawkins, *Reconstructing Illness*; Charon, *Narrative Medicine*. Also relevant is the burgeoning field of disability studies which provides resources in the genres of both memoir and theory for transformed and reparative understandings of so-called "disability," and includes queer perspectives such as McRuer, *Crip Theory*.

5. See Gayatri Spivak, "Can the Subaltern Speak?," revised as the chapter titled "History" in *A Critique of Postcolonial Reason*; Scott, "The Evidence of Experience"; and Hartman, *Scenes of Subjection* and *Lose Your Mother*. See also Franklin and Lyons, "Special Effects: The Testimonial Uses of Life Writing"; Schaffer and Smith, *Human Rights and Narrated Lives*.

6. See Brison, *Aftermath*; Davidson, *Thirty-Six Views of Mount Fuji*; Gallop, *Feminist Accused of Sexual Harassment*; Hirsch, *Family Frames*; Hirsch and Spitzer, "'We Would Not Have Come without You': Generations of Nostalgia"; Kacandes, *Daddy's War*; Miller, *Getting Personal, Bequest and Betrayal*, and *But Enough about Me*; Passerini, *Autobiography of a Generation*; and Sedgwick, *A Dialogue on Love*, among others; and Miller and Rosner, "Writing a Feminist's Life: The Legacy of Carolyn G. Heilbrun," which explores the importance of work such as Heilbrun's *Writing a Woman's Life*.

Important feminist scholarship on autobiography includes Brodzki and Schenck, *Life/Lines*; Smith and Watson, eds., *Getting a Life* and *Women, Autobiography, Theory*; Gilmore, *The Limits of Autobiography*.

7. For a critical discussion of the academic memoir, though, see Franklin, *Academic Lives*, which discusses Cathy Davidson and Eve Sedgwick, along with Jane Gallop and bell hooks, among others. While Franklin sees potential in the academic memoir as a form of institutional critique, she is also wary of its personalist tendencies.

8. For a history of riotgrrrl, see Marcus, *Girls to the Front*.

9. See, for example, Goldberg, *Writing Down the Bones* and Lamott, *Bird by Bird*.

10. I am grateful for workshops sponsored by the Michigan Womyn's Music Festival, the Throws Like a Girl Series produced by Jill Dolan and Rude Mechs in Austin, and the Austin Project. For more on the latter, see Bridgforth, Jones, and Moore, *Experiments in a Jazz Aesthetic*.

11. See, for example, work by Taussig such as *What Color Is the Sacred?* or *My Cocaine Museum* that combines theory and story in writerly ways. Stewart's *Ordinary Affects* also uses the format of the brief mini-essay or illumination.

12. Lorde, "Poetry Is Not a Luxury," 37.

13. In *Writing Down the Bones*, for example, Natalie Goldberg insists on the importance of writing by hand in order to sustain a sense of writing as embodied movement, and while I often write by hand for this reason myself, I also find free writing on a computer to be equally valuable in its own way, in part because of the speed with which one can both draft and revise.

14. See Sedgwick, "Queer Performativity," 15. A version appears in *Touching Feeling* but without the concluding paragraphs that include this oft-quoted phrase as well as its counterpart, "good dog/bad dog criticism."

15. In this respect, I have been influenced by my Public Feelings fellow travelers, especially Katie Stewart on ordinary affect, Heather Love on flat affect, and Lauren Berlant on melodrama and de-dramatizatized affect. See Staiger, Cvetkovich, and Reynolds, *Political Emotions*.

CHAPTER 1. WRITING DEPRESSION

1. Cassian, *De Institutis Coenobiorum*, translated by Edgar C. S. Gibson as "The Institutes of John Cassian," in the 1894 edition of *The Works of John Cassian* in *The Select Library of the Nicene and Post-Nicene Fathers of the Christian Church*, 267. In addition to books on each of the "eight principal faults" that serve as the source for the "deadly sins," the *Institutes* includes books on the dress of the monks, the system of nocturnal and daily prayers, and the renunciation of worldly life. Further citations will be included in the text by chapter number and refer to Book X of this edition, titled "Of the Spirit of

Accidie," 266–75. There is a more recent translation (2000) of the *Institutes* by Ramsey.

2. My source for the Latin is the online version of the *Patrologia Latina Database*, Book 49, which includes the complete Latin text of *De Coenobiorum Institutis* as written by Joannis Cassiani.

3. Dinshaw, *Getting Medieval*. My use of queer medieval studies to discuss acedia is not accidental, since there is a methodological analogy between my approach to histories of medicine and depression and histories of sexuality that track same-sex sexualities and intimacies that precede modern understandings of homosexuality. For further examples along these lines, see Freccero, *Queer/Early/Modern*; and Lochrie, *Heterosyncracies*.

4. My sources on acedia are primarily Jackson, *Melancholy and Depression*; Bloomfield, *The Seven Deadly Sins*; and Wenzel, *The Sin of Sloth*, none of which operates with a cultural studies or genealogical framework. See Wenzel, 62, for a discussion of acedia as "spiritual dryness," a translation derived from the Latin "*taedium cordis*" and note 6 below about Chaucer's use of "anguish of a troubled heart." Despite their dated frameworks, Jackson, Bloomfield, and Wenzel continue to be a source for contemporary work (including my own), and a study of acedia that proceeded from more recent cultural studies methods in medieval studies that link past and present would be extremely valuable.

5. Cassian's eight faults, *gastrimargia/gula, fornicatio/luxuria, avaritia/ filagylia, ira, tristitia, acedia, cenodoxia*, and *superbia* (gluttony, lust, avarice, wrath, dejection, acedia, vainglory, pride), each of which gets a chapter in *De Institutis Coenobiorum*, became Gregory's seven sins: *superbia, ira, invidia, avaritia, acedia, gula, luxuria* (pride, wrath, envy, greed, sloth, gluttony, lust). See Bloomfield, *The Seven Deadly Sins*, especially 69–77.

6. Within the history of English literature one of the important representations of *accidie* is Chaucer's "The Parson's Tale," where, echoing Cassian, it is described as "the angwissh of troubled herte." The legacy of acedia in medieval texts is beyond the scope of this project, and I confine myself to a reading of Cassian's text in order to suggest the potential value of a revisionist account of acedia for histories of melancholy and depression.

7. Solomon, *The Noonday Demon*, 292–95.

8. Klibansky's, Panofsky's, and Saxl's *Saturn and Melancholy* is a paradigmatic text for the history of the category of melancholy, not only for the embrace of its Renaissance formulation but also for a methodology of iconographic reading that assumes the investigation of historical sources (of Dürer's engraving of melancholy, for example) will yield the meaning of a cultural image.

9. Solomon, *The Noonday Demon*, 25. At this writing, for example, the National Institute of Mental Health reports that 9.5 percent (20.9 million) of Americans age eighteen or over have a mood disorder, including 6.7 percent (14.8 million) who have a major depressive disorder. Major depressive dis-

order is the leading cause of disability in U.S. adults ages fifteen to forty-four. See "The Numbers Count: Mental Disorders in America," on the NIMH website, http://www.nimh.nih.gov/.

10. The WHO website (accessed 15 March 2012) reports, "Depression is the leading cause of disability as measured by YLDs (years lived with disability) and the 4th leading contributor to the global burden of disease in 2000. By the year 2020, depression is projected to reach 2nd place of the ranking of DALYs (Disability Adjusted Life Years) calculated for all ages, both sexes. Today, depression is already the 2nd cause of DALYs in the age category 15–44 years for both sexes combined."

11. As might be expected, statistics are a common feature of journalistic accounts of depression and mental illness as well as scholarship in the sciences and social sciences. But they are also used as important background in cultural studies books such as Ross, *The Aesthetics of Disengagement*; Orr, *Panic Diaries*; Lane, *Shyness*.

12. See, for example, Whybrow, *A Mood Apart*, which combines current scientific knowledge about mood disorder with case histories; and Karp, *Speaking of Sadness*, which is based on interviews with those suffering from depression in order to explore how depression feels from the patient's perspective.

The success of the pharmaceutical industry has also led to a publication boom on the hot topic of antidepressants. Popular books on antidepressants, especially Kramer's, were followed by a wave of books critiquing them, including Breggin and Breggin, *Talking Back to Prozac*; Valenstein, *Blaming the Brain*; Glenmullen, *Prozac Backlash*.

The books published in the mid-1990s that brought these authors to prominence in the wake of public attention to the supposedly revolutionary power of SSRIs have been followed by more recent publications that continue to situate their authors as visible public experts on depression and mental illness. See Kramer, *Against Depression*; Whybrow, *American Mania*; Karp, *Is It Me or My Meds?*

13. Although it is about manic-depression, Jamison's *An Unquiet Mind* appeared in the context of debates about antidepressants and makes a persuasive case for pharmaceutical treatment of mental illness. Karp's *Speaking of Sadness* also discusses his own struggle with depression, although he is a sociologist, not a medical doctor.

Like those cited above, Jamison also continues to publish on mental illness, especially its links with creativity, but remains within the framework of a medical model; see Jamison, *Exuberance*.

14. Memoirs by O'Brien, *The Family Silver*, and Smith, *Where the Roots Reach for Water*, that present alternatives to medical models of depression will be explored in the next chapter. Other depression memoirs and related literary texts that have informed my discussion include Casey, *Unholy Ghost*; Manning, *Undercurrents*, which chronicles the author's treatment with shock therapy;

Blackbridge, *Prozac Highway*, a lesbian/queer novel about depression and on-line communities, which is discussed in some detail in Metzl's *Prozac on the Couch*; Danquah, *Willow Weep for Me*, which has the distinction of being one of the few memoirs by a woman of color in what is a predominantly white middle-class genre; Harris, *An Ocean of Despair*, a graphic narrative by a dear friend published locally in Austin; Barber, *Songs from the Black Chair*, another memoir by a writer with professional medical expertise (as a social worker) that offers a suggestive counterpart to his critique of antidepressants in *Comfortably Numb*; Mays, *In the Jaws of the Black Dogs*, which uses Foucauldian theory to link depression to modernity and capitalism; and the remarkable work of David Foster Wallace, whose efforts to find a syntax for depression as the experience of everyday life include the story "The Depressed Person" and his commencement address at Kenyon College in 2005, published as *This Is Water*, and discussed briefly in this book's epilogue.

15. Solomon, *The Noonday Demon*, 133.

16. A significant number of important popular books about depression were first published in these venues, which serve as a major platform for popular views about science that carry authority. For example, Kramer's *Against Depression* appeared as an article in the *New York Times Magazine*, "There's Nothing Deep about Depression," on 17 April 2005. Other significant articles over the past five years in the *New York Times Magazine* include Daphne Merkin, "My Life in Therapy," 4 August 2010, which uses the author's own experiences to question the value of long-term psychotherapy, and "A Journey through Darkness: My Life with Chronic Depression," 6 May 2009; Bruce Stutz, "Self-Nonmedication," 6 May 2007; David Dobbs, "A Depression Switch," 2 April 2006. Virtually all of these articles focus on variations of a medical model, especially pharmaceutical treatment, even when they question its limits and problems.

17. See Berlant, "On the Case." For a discussion of the complex imbrication of humanities and science, and fiction and nonfiction, in the mutual history of the novel and the case history, see Tougaw, *Strange Cases*.

18. Dudley, *Antidepressants*, 14.

19. Solomon, *The Noonday Demon*, 31.

20. See Greenberg, "Manufacturing Depression."

21. Healy, *The Creation of Psychopharmacology*, 4. For versions of this story, see especially Healy's chapter 3, as well as Shorter, *A History of Psychiatry*, and Dudley, *Antidepressants*. Healy is one of the most detailed (and prolific) historians of psychopharmacology because of his own intimate relation to the field, including his controversial rejection from a position at the University of Toronto because of his public criticism of pharmaceutical companies for their inadequate reporting of the risk of suicide by users of antidepressants. See his *Let Them Eat Prozac*. Other significant books by Healy include *The Antidepressant Era* and *The Psychopharmacologists*, a series of interviews.

For versions of this story that provide more cultural and social context, see Ehrenberg, *The Weariness of the Self*; Metzl, *Prozac on the Couch*: Orr, *Panic Diaries*.

22. Shorter, *A History of Psychiatry*, 255.

23. See Morrison, "The Discovery and Development of the First Modern Antidepressants."

24. Healy, *The Creation of Psychopharmacology*, 104. Also, for a history that offers a social context for psychopharmacology that includes gender politics and cold war politics and that understands scientific research to be a cultural formation, see Orr, *Panic Diaries*.

25. See Orr, *Panic Diaries*.

26. Metzl, *Prozac on the Couch*.

27. See Kirk and Kutchins, *The Selling of DSM,* and Horwitz and Wakefield, *The Loss of Sadness*, as well as discussions of the DSM classifications in Shorter, *A History of Psychiatry*, and Metzl, *Prozac on the Couch*. See also Orr on panic disorder in *Panic Diaries*, Lane on social anxiety disorder in *Shyness*, and Martin on manic-depression and bipolar illness in *Bipolar Expeditions*.

28. See Shorter, *A History of Psychiatry*; Lane, *Shyness*, which includes extensive interviews with Spitzer; and Orr, *Panic Diaries*, who also interviewed Spitzer.

29. See *Diagnostic and Statistical Manual of Mental Disorders*, 3rd edition (1980) and 4th edition (1994).

30. On PTSD, see Young, *The Harmony of Illusions*; on GID, see Bryant, "Making Gender Identity Disorder of Childhood."

31. The productive links between histories of sexuality and histories of medicine are evident in, for example, the scholarship of Steven Epstein, who has moved from studying the role of patient-activists as medical experts during the AIDS crisis to more general work on social difference and the politics of medicine and public health. See his *Impure Science* and *Inclusion*.

32. Barber's *Comfortably Numb* recommends alternatives to pharmaceuticals, such as cognitive behavioral therapy and neuropsychology; Blazer's *The Age of Melancholy* calls for a return to a social psychiatry that can understand depression as a historical problem; Horwitz and Wakefield's *The Loss of Sadness* criticizes the overly expanded reach of the DSM diagnosis and calls for reform of its categories; and Kirsch's *The Emperor's New Drugs* revisits pharmaceutical research to suggest that many antidepressants have a placebo effect. In response to this skepticism about antidepressants, Kramer wrote a 9 July 2011 *New York Times* op-ed piece, "In Defense of Antidepressants," that continues to keep the pharmaceutical debate alive.

33. Horwitz and Wakefield, *The Loss of Sadness*. Although this discussion is useful, particularly because it critiques psychiatry from within the field, its understanding of the history of depression before modern psychiatry and medicine largely follows the contours of Jackson's *Melancholia and Depres-*

sion, and the conception of "normal sadness" has its own normalizing tendencies.

34. See Menand's review of Greenberg and Kirsch, "Head Case: Can Psychiatry Be a Science?," *New Yorker*, 1 March 2010.

35. There are some signs of a turn toward spiritual and somatic practices within the medical and psychoanalytic literature. See, for example, the cluster of essays in *Contemporary Psychoanalysis*, which includes Solomon's account of writing *The Noonday Demon*, "Depression, Too, Is a Thing with Feathers," as well as essays that question Solomon's commitment to medical models and propose alternative understandings, including those that incorporate the social and the spiritual, by O'Leary, "Putting It Together While Falling Apart"; Horwitz and Wakefield, "Noonday Demons and Midnight Sorrows"; and Blechner, "Interaction of Social and Neurobiological Factors in Depression." See also a number of the essays in Chambers and Elliott, *Prozac as a Way of Life*, especially Squier, "The Paradox of Prozac as Enhancement Technology"; Chambers, "Prozac for the Sick Soul." Gordon, *Unstuck*, combines conventional and alternative medicine, including spiritual practice.

Other books that more fully embrace spiritual practices and that have been especially useful to me in thinking about alternative therapies include Huber, *The Depression Book*, which is Buddhist in orientation, and Greenspan, *Healing through Dark Emotions*, which draws on Buddhism, Judaism, and progressive politics.

36. See, for example, Cohen, *A Body Worth Defending*, for a genealogical history of immunity that seeks to expand the concept beyond its medical meanings, as well as other work in the European tradition of the history of science and biopolitics, represented by scholars such as Daston (with Galison, *Objectivity*), Latour (*We Have Never Been Modern*), Stengers (*Cosmopolitics* I and II). The burgeoning field of science and technology studies, evident in collections such as Clarke et al, *Biomedicalization*, suggests the importance of humanities-based scholarship on the history and culture of science but my goal here is to suggest that we also continue to explore alternatives to scientific understandings.

37. See Reddy, *The Navigation of Feeling*, for the use of anthropology to combine cultural and scientific approaches in the study of emotion. Although sympathetic to studies of the discursive construction of emotion, Reddy criticizes cultural histories of emotion that refrain from saying what emotions are.

38. On vitalism, see Bennett, *Vibrant Matter*, and on materialisms, see Coole and Frost, *New Materialisms*.

39. See Damasio, *Looking for Spinoza*, as well as his influential earlier books such as *The Feeling of What Happens* and *Descartes' Error*. This work has been taken up in popular books such as Husvedt, *The Shaking Woman, or A History of My Nerves*, that do for neuroscience what a previous generation of

books has done for antidepressants and medical models of depression and has also had a notable impact on literary studies, especially narrative theory, in books such as Young, *Imagining Minds* and Zunshine, *Why We Read.* Thanks to Jason Tougaw for encouraging me to pursue this developing literature in neuroscience, and for the inspiration of his memoir in progress, *The One You Get: Portrait of a Family Organism,* an excerpt from which has been published as "Aplysia californica."

40. See Wilson, *Psychosomatic,* 29, and "Underbelly." For another example of this "biological turn," see Grosz, *Becoming Undone.*

41. For an example of discussions of the science of meditation, see Khalsa and Bhajan, *Breathwalk.*

42. Agamben, *Stanzas.*

43. Eng and Kazanjian, "Introduction: Mourning Remains," in *Loss,* especially 12–14, which include mention of Cassian.

44. See Foucault, *Religion and Culture,* especially "The Battle for Chastity (1982)," 188–97, and "About the Beginning of the Hermeneutics of the Self (1980)," 158–81. For further discussion of Foucault's plans for "The Confessions of the Flesh," the unpublished fourth volume of *The History of Sexuality,* see Carrette, *Foucault and Religion*; Halperin, *Saint Foucault*; and Boyarin and Castelli, "Introduction: Foucault's *The History of Sexuality*," part of a special issue of *Journal of the History of Sexuality* on the late ancient Christian source materials for Foucault's unpublished work.

45. Brown, "Resisting Left Melancholia." For Benjamin's writing on left melancholy, see "Left-Wing Melancholy." For more on Benjamin and melancholy, see Pensky, *Melancholy Dialectics.*

46. See Radden, *The Nature of Melancholy,* which, in addition to surveying key primary texts in the field ranging from Aristotle and Burton through to Freud and Klein, contains a very helpful synthesis and summary of key themes and problems in the literature on melancholy. Radden is especially attentive to the question of whether melancholy and depression can be linked, seeking to explore the way the concepts overlap without assuming their equivalence. The other important survey is Jackson, *Melancholy and Depression,* which surveys the literature from a vantage point that is inclined to see continuity between the past and present.

47. There is a difference between seeing the present in the past, as is the case with the search for precedents, however crude, to the medical model, and looking for the past to speak to the present through its differences and alternatives. I'm more interested in melancholy and depression not as equivalents but as importantly different, using models of historical scholarship that emphasize both the alterity of the past and its dynamic relation to the present. I've been particularly influenced by models of queer temporalities that emphasize an affective relation to the past and queer connections to the present.

(See Freeman, "Queer Temporalities.") Such work encourages us to ask what melancholy represents that has been lost by the medical model of depression and what resources might exist in these earlier models that can help us to rethink the present. Christine Ross also suggests that melancholy has been replaced by depression and that the notion of melancholy as central to creativity and to normal experience has now been displaced by a pathologizing medical model (see *The Aesthetics of Disengagement*, chapter 2).

48. The most salient example is Jackson's *Melancholy and Depression*, which serves as a basis for Solomon's chapter on the history of melancholy and depression in *The Noonday Demon*.

49. See in particular Klibansky, Panofsky, and Saxl, *Saturn and Melancholy*, with its discussion of the apotheosis of creative melancholy in Dürer's famous engraving of melancholy. See also Babb, *The Elizabethan Malady*. The work on gender cited earlier challenges this model of heroic or romantic melancholy as the sign of creative genius.

50. See Wilson, *Against Happiness*, for an example of this use of a humanist tradition of melancholy to counter the medicalization of depression. Those who draw from more psychoanalytic traditions, such as Ross, tend to offer a less benign sense of melancholy.

51. See especially Kramer, *Against Depression*, for the most explicit rejection of the links between creativity and depression explored by writers such as Eric Wilson.

52. Embracing the work of the unconscious, constructing loss as constitutive, and promoting other forms of therapy besides pharmacology, psychoanalysis serves as an important intervention against contemporary medical understandings of depression. The psychoanalytic tradition has inspired a rich body of work on melancholy that has taken up the category in order to gender it, racialize it, and queer it. Feminist theorists have explored the gendered dimensions of representations of loss and melancholy in, for example, Kristeva, *Black Sun*; Schiesari, *The Gendering of Melancholia*; Enterline, *The Tears of Narcissus*.

Psychoanalytically based notions of melancholy have been used productively in discussions of colonialism, race, and social history, thus enlarging the psychic to embrace the social. See, for example, Cheng, *The Melancholy of Race*; Eng and Han, "Dialogue on Racial Melancholia"; Gilroy, *Postcolonial Melancholia*; Holland, *Raising the Dead*; Khanna, *Dark Continents*; Muñoz, *Disidentifications* and "Feeling Brown, Feeling Down" and other essays that are part of the book in progress, *The Sense of Brown*; Moten, *In the Break*; Zwarg, "Du Bois on Trauma."

53. Brown, "Resisting Left Melancholia," 464.

54. See Love, *Feeling Backward*, 149–52, for an argument that echoes mine here. Love credits Brown for aiming "to diagnose, not to punish" left melan-

choly but points out that Brown ultimately seems "to shade into the kind of chin-up neoliberal polemics that she abhors" (149, 150). Love's use of Carla Freccero on Benjamin's "angel of history" to counter Brown's call for a seemingly voluntarist hope that separates itself from a melancholic relation to the past is suggestive, pointing in the direction of the spiritual categories explored here. Conceiving of political life in terms of the forms of spiritual practice inspired by the concept of acedia makes it possible to embrace more fully the "politics of passivity" that intrigues Love and Freccero; acedia also cleaves melancholy from psychoanalysis and restores it to the religious lineages that some readers resist, thus multiplying its meanings and refusing the pressure evident in Brown's work to make it into a "good" feeling rather than a "bad" one. Anne-Lise François's theory of "recessive action" helps extend the discussion of the politics of passivity. See *Open Secrets*.

55. See Eng and Kazanjian, *Loss*; Crimp, *Melancholia and Moralism*. See also Butler, *Precarious Life*, for consideration of the relation between mourning and politics, which also draws on Butler's ongoing consideration of the role of melancholy in gendered subject formation.

56. Love, *Feeling Backward*, 162. For other rich treatments of loss, melancholy, and history that are especially attuned to queer histories, see Dinshaw, *Getting Medieval*; Freeman, *Time Binds*; Luciano, *Arranging Grief*; Nealon, *Foundlings*.

57. Snediker, *Queer Optimism*.

58. Flatley, *Affective Mapping*. See also Ross, *The Aesthetics of Disengagement*, for a suggestive argument about the relation between melancholy and depression in contemporary art practices.

59. See Crimp, *Melancholia and Moralism*.

60. In addition to Crimp, *Melancholia and Moralism*, see also Love, *Feeling Backward*; Berlant, *Cruel Optimism*; Gould, *Moving Politics*; Halberstam, *The Queer Art of Failure*.

61. Agamben, *Stanzas*, 13.

62. A late discovery during the writing of this chapter was Norris, *Acedia and Me*, a memoir-based account of acedia as a modern spiritual category, which opens with a discussion of Abbot Paul's ritual and also notes its resemblance to performance art. Norris spent a year at a Benedictine monastery in order to cure depression, and her ability to articulate the relevance of this spiritual category to contemporary life is remarkable. Even as she links acedia to depression, though, she ultimately preserves the distinction between depression as a medical disease and acedia as a concept that describes spiritual matters of loss of faith, boredom, and ennui.

For another account of contemporary retreat that considers the relation between acedia and depression, see Maitland, *A Book of Silence*. My thanks to Alyssa Harad for drawing this book to my attention.

63. See Abramović, *Marina Abramović: The Artist Is Present*; Viso, *Ana Mendieta*; and Montano, *Letters from Linda M. Montano.*

64. See Barber, *Comfortably Numb*, 191–210; Greenberg, *Manufacturing Depression*, especially 315–37; and Tougaw, "Aplysia californica."

CHAPTER 2. DISPOSSESSION AND SELF-POSSESSION

The source of this chapter's epigraph is Smith, *Twilight: Los Angeles, 1992*, 108. The video version of the play does not include the full text of West's comments as they appear in this published version of the script.

1. "Following the trail of breadcrumbs (in my head)" is a phrase that I borrowed from Kathleen Hanna to describe the methodology of *An Archive of Feelings* and it remains relevant to this project.

2. This body of work includes Muñoz, *Disidentifications*, "Feeling Brown," and "Feeling Brown, Feeling Down"; Holland, *Raising the Dead*; Cheng, *The Melancholy of Race*; Eng and Han, "Dialogue on Racial Melancholia"; Eng and Kazanjian, *Loss*; Moten, *In the Break*; Khanna, *Dark Continents*; Gilroy, *Postcolonial Melancholia*; Zwarg, "Du Bois on Trauma."

3. This was a central issue at the "Melancholic States" conference organized at University of Lancaster by Anne-Marie Fortier and Gail Lewis, 27–29 September 2007. Especially significant for the discussion was a presentation by Gaye Chen and Nandita Sharma titled "Good Grief! Recognizing Imposed Identities and Transforming Our Imaginary of Change," which focused on how melancholy lends itself to a nostalgic or sentimental sense of lost origins and questioned whether it could be salvaged as a form of "good" grief.

4. See Eng and Han, "Dialogue on Racial Melancholia." Love's *Feeling Backward* is also useful for its discussion of the politics of negative affect, as is Flatley's *Affective Mapping*, which considers nondepressive forms of melancholy, including the work of Du Bois.

5. For more on music, especially experimental jazz and bebop, as an articulation of racial affect and African diasporic histories, see Moten, *In the Break.*

6. See Kleinman and Good, *Culture and Depression.* For more recent work that approaches mental health from the perspective of medical anthropology and cultural and social history, see also DelVecchio Good, Hyde, Pinto, and Good, *Postcolonial Disorders.*

7. See, for example, Sue and Sue, *Counseling the Culturally Different.*

8. See Stephanie A. Riolo, Tuan Anh Nguyen, John F. Greden, and Cheryl A. King, "Prevalence of Depression by Race/Ethnicity: Findings from the National Health and Nutrition Examination Survey III," *American Journal of Public Health* 95 (2005), 998–1000, which indicates that major depressive disorder rates are higher for white people than for African Americans and Mexican Americans but that the latter have higher rates of dysthymic disorder, particularly low-education, non-English-speaking Mexican Americans.

The survey results show that poverty makes a bigger difference for whites than for people of color.

V. Lorant, D. Deliege, W. Eaton, A. Robert, P. Philippot, and M. Ansseau, "Socioeconomic Inequalities in Depression: A Meta-Analysis," *American Journal of Epidemiology* 157, no. 2 (2003), 98–112, explores whether rates of depression are higher for those with low socioeconomic status. The results appear to be positive but are not definitive, in part because of methodological problems with strict diagnoses and measurement and with lack of access to health care for people of color. See also C. H. Carrington, "Clinical Depression in African America Women: Diagnoses, Treatment, and Research," *Journal of Family Practice* 55, no. 1 (2006), 30–39, which argues that it's hard to compare rates of depression in African Americans and whites because of a lack of research on African Americans in general and African American women more specifically.

9. See Lisa A. Cooper, Junius J. Gonzales, Joseph J. Gallo, Kathryn M. Rost, Lisa S. Meredith, Lisa V. Rubenstein, Nae-Yuh Wang, and Daniel E. Ford, "The Acceptability of Treatment for Depression among African-American, Hispanic, and White Primary Care Patients," *Medical Care* 41, no. 4 (2003), 479–89. See also Alessa P. Jackson, "The Use of Psychiatric Medications to Treat Depressive Disorders in African American Women," *Journal of Clinical Psychology* 62, no. 7 (2006), 793–800, who argues that "culturally based attitudes or resistance to pharmacology can complicate the use of psychoactive medicines, often a first-line approach in primary care clinics" (abstract).

10. Yu-Wen Ying, "Explanatory Models of Major Depression and Implications for Help-Seeking among Immigrant Chinese-American Women," *Culture, Medicine, and Psychiatry* 14, no. 3 (1990), 393–408.

11. A. K. Das, M. Olfson, H. L. McCurtis, and M. M. Weissman, "Depression in African Americans: Breaking Barriers to Detection and Treatment," *Journal of Clinical Psychology* 62, no. 7 (2006), abstract. See also E. L. Barbee, "African American Women and Depression: A Review and Critique of the Literature," *Journal of Clinical Psychology* 62, no. 7 (2006), 779–91, and Jackson, "The Use of Psychiatric Medications to Treat Depressive Disorders in African American Women." These articles are part of a special section of the journal titled "Clinical Depression and African American Women: Issues of Diagnosis, Treatment, and Research."

12. Christina G. Watlington and Christopher M. Murphy, "The Roles of Religion and Sexuality among African American Survivors of Domestic Violence," *Journal of Clinical Psychology* 62 (2006), 837–57; Karina L. Walters and Jane M. Simoni, "Reconceptualizing Native Women's Health: An 'Indigenist' Stress-Coping Model," *American Journal of Public Health* 92 (2002), 520–24.

13. See, for example, a key anthology in the field, Comas-Díaz and Griffith, *Clinical Guidelines in Cross-Cultural Mental Health.*

14. See Quimby, "Ethnography's Role in Assisting Mental Health Research and Clinical Practice."

15. Kleinman and Good, *Culture and Depression.*

16. O'Nell, *Disciplined Hearts.*

17. Holland, "The Last Word on Racism." See also her *The Erotic Life of Racism,* which was published while this book was in production.

18. Gilmore, *Golden Gulag,* 28.

19. It was hard to choose among the different possible archives for this chapter. Asian American studies, Mexican American studies, Latino/a studies, and postcolonial studies each provides rich bodies of theory and culture for thinking about the public feelings that circulate around contemporary migrations and displacements. In addition to work on racial melancholy cited earlier, scholarship on the relation between legal reform and emotional justice has been important to my project; see, for example, Eng, *The Feeling of Kinship;* Lowe, *Immigrant Acts;* and especially Lowe, "The Intimacies of Four Continents," which provides a model for the kind of integrated comparative studies that the project of connecting racism and depression entails. Jose Muñoz's ongoing work on racialized affect in *Disidentifications* and the forthcoming *The Sense of Brown* has also been foundational.

Mexican American studies work on the intersections of Catholicism and indigenous practices has been crucial to my efforts to think about the intersections of affect and spirituality. Indispensable texts include Anzaldúa, *Borderlands / La Frontera;* Sandoval, *Methodology of the Oppressed;* and the works of Moraga, including the indigenous focus of *A Xicana Codex of Changing Consciousness.*

For work on the intersections of African American and Native American studies, I have been inspired by the example of Holland and Miles, *Crossing Waters, Crossing Worlds.* My work at this crossroads has also been shaped by conversations with my aunt Celia Haig-Brown about the implications of Toni Morrison's failure to mention indigenous cultures in "Unspeakable Things Unspoken" and about resistance, within Canada at least, to the integration of indigenous studies with diaspora studies. I take this as one cautionary note among many about the challenges of making the connections here in a way that is useful. See Haig-Brown, "Decolonizing Diaspora."

20. See Farred, *What's My Name?*

21. Nella Larsen's novel *Passing* includes a number of incidents of what I call "emotional passing," another form of the more overt passing performed by Clare Kendry. In scenes such as the one where Irene witnesses Clare's husband make racist remarks, or where she jealously watches her husband dancing with Clare and breaks a tea cup, Irene Redfield covers her emotions in a veneer of politeness which is its own manifestation of the anger and rage that other forms of passing also disguise. A path not taken for this section was to explore the relation between so called depression and the everyday life of racism in affective performances of politeness that should be understood not

as "repressed emotion" but as different modes of emotional expression. See Larsen, *Quicksand and Passing*.

Anzaldúa, *Borderlands / La Frontera*; Kristina Wong, *Wong Flew over the Cuckoo's Nest*, performance at the Off-Centre Theatre, Austin, February 2008. For a discussion of "Neapolitan," see Bustamante and Muñoz, "Chat," and Muñoz, "Feeling Down, Feeling Brown," as well as "The Vulnerability Artist."

22. Harper, "The Evidence of Felt Intuition," 649, as well as the more general discussion of speculative reasoning and intuition throughout the essay. Harper argues that "minority existence itself induces such speculative rumination because it continually renders even the most routine instances of social activity and personal interaction as possible cases of invidious social distinction or discriminatory treatment" (643). He is talking more specifically about the methods of "black queer studies," and it is useful to remember that speculation, such as gossip, is also a frequent method of inquiry for queers. See, for example, Abelove, *Deep Gossip*, and Butt, *Between You and Me*.

23. Butler, interview. For another version of this story, see Rowell and Butler, "An Interview with Octavia E. Butler."

24. Melissa Harris-Lacewell, "Black Women's Depression and Resisting the Myth of Strength," paper presented at Depression: What Is it Good For? Conference, University of Chicago, 12 March 2004. Harris-Lacewell (now Harris-Perry) has used the informal genres of the blog and the conversation to address the ordinary and affective life of racism and racial politics. For her current work as a public intellectual, including her MSNBC television show, see melissaharrisperry.com.

25. Hartman, *Lose Your Mother*, 6. All further citations will be included in the text and refer to this edition.

26. The paradigmatic neo–slave novel is *Beloved*, but others include Gayl Jones, *Corregidora*; Butler, *Kindred*; Edward P. Jones, *The Known World*. Both slave narrative and neo–slave narrative have generated a vast body of criticism; important points of reference for my own thinking include Spillers, "Mama's Baby, Papa's Maybe"; Morrison, "Unspeakable Things Unspoken"; Gordon, *Ghostly Matters*, which includes a chapter on *Beloved*; Holland, *Raising the Dead*; Moten, *In the Break*; Hartman, *Scenes of Subjection*.

27. For further discussion of the difference between Hartman's more overt disappointment and that more covertly expressed by Maya Angelou and others, as well as the optimism of much slavery tourism, including that promoted by the Ghanaian government in, for example, the Joseph Project, see Commander, "Ghana at Fifty."

28. Interview with Saidiya Hartman, *Tavis Smiley Presents*, PBS, 27 January 2007. I thank my students in Oral History, Testimony, Memoir and other Genres of Public Feelings for bringing this interview to my attention.

29. See Best and Hartman, "Redress." For discussions of *Lose Your Mother*

that complement my own, see Gopinath, "Archive, Affect, and the Everyday," and Halberstam, *The Queer Art of Failure*.

30. Alexander, *Pedagogies of Crossing*, 287. Further citations will be included in the text and refer to this edition.

31. Some of the earlier essays in *Pedagogies of Crossing* take up this issue more directly in the context of exploring sexuality in a transnational context and refusing the construction of nations of the Global North as progressive in their attitudes toward sexuality as compared with a backward Global South. It is not a coincidence that Alexander's groundbreaking work on transnational sexualities should lead her to a reconceptualization of the relation between the sacred and the secular as well. Indeed, one way of characterizing the difference between her work and Hartman's might be that its embrace of the sacred manifests a queer sensibility.

32. Drawing from Yoruban spiritual traditions, Omi Osun Joni L. Jones articulates this concept as the premise for a jazz aesthetic that is a model for radical democracy. See Bridgforth, *Love Conjure/Blues*, introduction; Bridgforth, Jones, and Moore, *Experiments in a Jazz Aesthetic*. This lineage provides an alternative to the Western philosophical genealogies that provide the foundation for current interest in vitalism, such as Bennett, *Vibrant Matter*.

33. See Gordon, "Something More Powerful Than Skepticism."

34. Jacqui Alexander, "Sites of Memory: The Atlantic and Other Crossings," lecture, University of Texas, Austin, 20 November 2008.

35. See O'Nell, *Disciplined Hearts*.

36. See, for example, the work of Maria Yellow Horse Brave Heart (Oglala and Hunkpapa Lakota), founder of Takini Network, a nonprofit organization devoted to helping indigenous people heal from historical trauma: "The Return to the Sacred Path" and "From Intergenerational Trauma to Intergenerational Healing"; Yellow Horse Brave Heart and Deschenie, "Resource Guide." White Bison, a "Native American wellbriety and culture based community healing program," publishes the online journal *Wellbriety*, www.whitebison .org.

37. See Haig-Brown, *Resistance and Renewal*, as well as the video (made in collaboration with Helen Haig-Brown) *Pelq'ilq (Coming Home)*, which follows up on those interviewed for the original project and their children. For more information on Canada's Indian Residential Schools Truth and Reconciliation Commission, see its website at http://www.trc-cvr.ca/. See also Wilson and Yellow Bird, *For Indigenous Eyes Only*, especially the chapter "Relieving Our Suffering."

38. See Turner, *This Is Not a Peace Pipe*.

39. See Alfred, *Peace, Power, Righteousness*.

40. See also the queer indigenous discussions of sovereignty in Justice, Rivkin, and Schneider, "Nationality, Sovereignty, Sexuality"; Driskill, Finley, Gilley, and Morgensen, *Queer Indigenous Studies*.

41. See the list in note 14 in chapter 1.

42. Further references to these memoirs will be cited by page number in the text.

Another book that almost made it into this discussion because of its focus on the intersection of class, masculinity, and academia is Barber, *Songs from the Black Chair*. Barber is also the author of the recent critique of the medical model and pharmaceuticals, *Comfortably Numb: How Psychiatry Is Medicating a Nation*, mentioned in the previous chapter, but the latter book does not mention his earlier use of memoir to discuss the politics of mental health. Barber's account of his downwardly mobile trajectory after dropping out of Harvard raises interesting questions about the pressures of academia, particularly because he is the son of a professor, as is the high school friend whose suicide forms the emotional center of the book.

43. Indeed there is an uncannily direct connection because O'Brien mentions attending the MLA panel "Professors on Prozac" that my friend Lora Romero organized in 1996, the year before she died. I remember consulting with Lora about the call for papers for the panel, which was one of the offerings of the Popular Culture Division on whose Executive Committee we both served. O'Brien finds a disconnect between the experience of depression and the academic panel, suggesting that people "talk about Prozac because they are afraid to talk about depression" (258).

44. For a review of *The Family Silver* that makes similar claims about the book's scholarly merits, see Cahn, "Of Silver and Serotonin."

45. There are echoes here of Jane Tompkins's *A Life in School*, which also tracks the limits of success for a girl who is good at school even when she finds her way to feminism and theory; for Tompkins the way out is through forms of radical pedagogy that enable her to question the limits of the education system and the privileges of the Ivy League and other elite schools that also trouble O'Brien.

46. Compare, for example, with Stewart's complex ethnography of the post-industrial landscape of West Virginia in *A Space on the Side of the Road*, which presents the region as to the side of, not outside of, capitalism and deindustrialization. Southern Ohio, where Smith is from, is also the location of Toni Morrison's *Beloved*, which makes the history of the slavery central to this landscape.

47. Scheckel, "Traveling Nostalgia," for example, looks at how nostalgia, a medicalized disease not unrelated to melancholy, has its origins in colonial encounters and the loss of home not only by European travelers but by slaves and other displaced peoples (who are seen as crazy rather than just homesick). Smith's embrace of his rural and regional origins could also be productively read through the lens of critiques within queer studies of the privileging of the urban over the rural, such as Herring, *Another Country*, and Gray, *Out in the Country*.

48. On the history of the Eastern Band of Cherokees, see John R. Finger, *The Eastern Band of Cherokees, 1819–1900* (Knoxville: University of Tennessee Press, 1984) and *Cherokee Americans: The Eastern Band of Cherokees in the Twentieth Century* (Lincoln: University of Nebraska Press, 1991).

49. See Lowe, "The Intimacies of Four Continents."

50. I borrow this phrase from Miller and Hirsch, *Rites of Return*.

51. For more on queer attachments to land, including the representation of land as the site of wounded histories rather than pristine nature, see my discussion of Jan Zita Grover's *North Enough* (Minneapolis: Graywolf Press, 1996) in *An Archive of Feelings*.

52. For this question and many conversations about it, I am grateful to Celia Haig-Brown. See Haig-Brown, "Decolonizing Diaspora," the subtitle of which is "Whose Traditional Land Are We On?"

CHAPTER 3. THE UTOPIA OF ORDINARY HABIT

1. Stewart, *Ordinary Affects*, 52.

2. Stewart, *Ordinary Affects*, 2. For discussions of the ordinary in Stewart's work, see Highmore, *Ordinary Lives*, 7–9; Vogel, "By the Light of What Comes After."

3. Love, "Feeling Bad in 1963."

4. *Diagnostic and Statistical Manual of Mental Disorders: DSM-IV*. For a "major depressive episode," five or more of these symptoms must be present in a two-week period, and at least one of the symptoms must be either "depressed mood" or "loss of interest or pleasure." I'm suggesting here, though, that "depressed mood" is a blank and capacious category that warrants fuller description.

5. Brennan, *The Transmission of Affect*.

6. On Columbine as an example of ordinary affects surging into an event, see Stewart, "Teenagers Who Kill," *Ordinary Affects*, 74.

7. See Cvetkovich, *An Archive of Feelings*; Berlant, "I Hate Your Archive," *The Queen of America Goes to Washington City*, 10–15; Berlant, "On the Case"; Ahmed on "unhappy archives" in *The Promise of Happiness*; Love on the descriptive turn in "Feeling Bad in 1963." An ongoing inspiration for my thinking about the queer archive remains Muñoz, "Ephemera as Evidence," and my close relations with the artists about whom I'm writing also reflects Halberstam's discussion of the scholar critic as queer archivist in *In a Queer Time and Place*.

8. Highmore, *Ordinary Lives*.

9. Le Tigre's *Feminist Sweepstakes* album also includes the song "Keep On Livin'," which was featured in the opening of *An Archive of Feelings*.

10. The connection seems less than coincidental, given that, at this writing, Kathleen Hanna (formerly of Le Tigre and Bikini Kill) has been performing

with Kenny Mellman (formerly of Kiki and Herb) in a band called The Julie Ruin.

11. For a fuller account of Kiki and Herb's performances, see Vogel "Where Are We Now?"

12. Metzl, *Prozac on the Couch*.

13. Friedan, *The Feminine Mystique*, excerpted in Kolmar and Bartkowski, *Feminist Theory*, 198–203.

14. See Berlant, *The Female Complaint*, including, for the "juxtapolitical," 10, and for the "sentimental bargain," 20–23.

15. See Berlant, *The Female Complaint*, which offers an extended and much more detailed version of my discussion here. Berlant's analysis is particularly powerful because it spans work that began in the 1980s (with the essay "The Female Complaint"), encompassing the scholarship that has emerged since then, including a range of historical feminist studies, to explain the relevance of women's culture and the evolution of that work toward questions of the intimate public sphere and the politics of emotion. The earlier essays from which *The Female Complaint* developed have been formative for my ongoing thinking, but the book form also provides an important foundation for my discussion here, not only for its rich archive of the circulation and repetition of women's cultural texts but for its dazzling ability to set them in relation to theories of public feeling. Although my discussion may prove to be out of sync with Berlant's *Cruel Optimism*, which was published as this book was going to press, I am engaged here with the arguments of *The Female Complaint* as much as those of *Cruel Optimism* in order to underscore the feminist genealogy of Berlant's more recent analysis of political structures of feeling.

16. Berlant, *The Female Complaint*, 21.

17. Berlant, "Cruel Optimism," in Gregg and Seigworth, *Affect Theory Reader*, 110. See also the discussion of new forms of intimacy in her review essay about Leo Bersani and David Halperin, "Neither Monstrous nor Pastoral, but Scary and Sweet." On the "feminist killjoy," see Ahmed, *The Promise of Happiness*.

18. See Sedgwick, "Pedagogy of Buddhism," *Touching Feeling*, 153–81.

19. The full citation to this section's epigraph is Leslie Hall, "Craft Talk," from *Back to Back Palz*. See Leslie Hall's website, www.lesliehall.com. The video for "Craft Talk" can be found on YouTube.

20. Stitch is currently on hiatus. The Renegade Craft Fair began in Chicago in 2003 and now meets in Brooklyn, San Francisco, Los Angeles (www .renegadecraft.com), and other gatherings include Art vs. Craft in Milwaukee, Austin, and London, and DIY Trunk Show in Chicago (www.diytrunkshow .com). Although initially more grassroots and local affairs, many of these events now have corporate sponsorship, representing the same mix of DIY and capitalism that can be found in music festivals, such as Austin's SXSW, or gay pride celebrations.

21. See Levine and Heimerl, *Handmade Nation*, which surveys a range of artists and locations, as well as their documentary film, *Handmade Nation*.

22. For useful books on the history and theory of craft, see Adamson, *Thinking through Craft*; Alfody, *NeoCraft*; Risatti, *A Theory of Craft*. *Thinking through Craft* and *NeoCraft* are especially important for their refusal of the polarization of modernity and craft in favor of understanding craft as a constitutive category for modern art and vice versa.

New theory to accompany new forms of crafting has developed during the writing of this book. Recent books that share many of my concerns about the craft revival and the politics of craft are Adamson, ed., *The Craft Reader*, and Buszek, *Extra/Ordinary*.

23. See, for example, Somerson, "Knot in Our Name," which chronicles the knitting circle's move into activism. *Bitch* is prominent among the third-wave feminist publications that use print culture to promote crafting and other new forms of feminism activism. *Bust* magazine's founder, Debbie Stoller, for example, has gone on to a multimedia cottage industry inaugurated by the popular book *Stitch 'n Bitch*. See www.knithappens.com.

24. From Greer's website, www.craftivism.com, which also includes a visual archive of craftivism projects (accessed 15 March 2012). See also Greer, *Knitting for Good!* and "Craftivist History," in Buszek, *Extra/Ordinary*, 175–83.

25. See the surveys of artists in, for example, Hung and Magliaro, *By Hand*; McFadden, Scanlan, and Edwards, *Radical Lace and Subversive Knitting*, the catalogue for an exhibition at the Museum of Arts and Design in 2007; as well as Levine and Heimerl, *Handmade Nation*. *Radical Lace* showcases professional artists, *By Hand* combines artists and crafters, and *Handmade Nation* focuses more on those who have commercial craft practices, but these distinctions are fuzzy and a number of people show up in more than one of these books.

26. See, for example, ongoing debates about the history of feminist art practice in the exhibition catalogue by Butler and Mark, *WACK!*, and Phelan and Reckitt, *Art and Feminism*. For a discussion of feminist art and craft, see Adamson's discussion of Wilding and Chicago in the section titled "Feminism and the Politics of Amateurism," in *Thinking through Craft*, 150–58, which also argues that contemporary artists Mike Kelley and Tracey Emin embrace craft's abject status rather than trying to claim its equality with art.

27. They thus craft a very different relation between art and depression than that explored in Ross's *The Aesthetics of Disengagement*, which focuses primarily on artists whose work performs depression or melancholy rather than repairing it.

28. For documentation see the Fluent-Collaborative website, www.fluent collab.org, and Pepe's website, www.sheilapepe.com (both accessed 15 March 2012).

29. See Oliver, *Hand+Made*. Pepe's work is also featured in McFadden, Scanlan, and Edwards, *Radical Lace and Subversive Knitting*.

30. "The End of Ephemera," presentation at College Art Association Conference, 10–13 February 2010.

31. Gallery talk, Art House, Austin, 28 May 2009. For an online version of a gallery talk by Pepe, see *Blackbird Archive: An Online Journal of Literature and the Arts* 2, no. 1 (2003). See also Pepe's website at www.sheilapepe.com.

32. There was a major retrospective of Hesse's work at the San Francisco Museum of Modern Art in 2002, as well as one at New York's Jewish Museum in 2006, which enabled her work to be viewed by a new generation of scholars and artists. See Halberstam on Hesse in *In a Queer Time and Place*, and Reynolds on Hesse's relation to Ruth Vollmer and the New York art scene of the 1960s in "A Structure of Creativity."

33. For more on the Ladies Sasquatch, see the catalogue for the exhibition at McMaster University in 2009 curated by Carla Garnet, which includes my essay, "Touching the Monster: Deep Lez in Fun Fur," Mitchell, *Ladies Sasquatch*, 26–31, as well as Freeman, *Time Binds*, 85–93, and Moore, *Sister Arts*, 189–94.

34. The installation was at the National Textile Museum in Canada in 2008. Another version of *Hungry Purse* (from which the images here are taken) was installed at the Visible Vagina exhibition, David Nolan Gallery, New York City, 2010.

35. See "Deep Lez I Statement" (http://www.allysonmitchell.com) and in Mitchell and Cvetkovich, "A Girl's Journey into the Well of Forbidden Knowledge."

36. See Mitchell, Sorkin, and Quinton, *When Women Rule the World*, which was accompanied by the exhibition She Will Always Be Younger than Us, featuring craft work by Orly Cogan, Wednesday Lupypciw, Cat Mazza, Gillian Strong, and Ginger Brooks Takahashi.

37. For further discussion of Mitchell's relation to lesbian feminism and the 1970s as a form of queer temporality, see Freeman, *Time Binds*, 85–93.

38. *Menstrual Hut Sweet Menstrual Hut* was part of the exhibition FIERCE: Women's Hot-Blooded Film/Video at McMaster Museum of Art, January–March 2010.

39. Sedgwick, "Queer Performativity," 15. Hints of Sedgwick's own practice of textile arts appear in *Touching Feeling*, particularly in her discussion of the concept of "texture" in the introductory chapter, and it is on fuller display in *The Weather in Proust*.

40. See Dolan, *Utopia in Performance*.

41. Indeed, there is a huge popular literature that links knitting and spirituality. Titles include Susan Gordon Lydon, *The Knitting Sutra: Craft as a Spiritual Practice* (San Francisco: Potter Craft, 2004); Bernadette Murphy, *Zen and*

the Art of Knitting: Exploring the Links between Knitting, Creativity, and Spiritu-
ality (Avon, Mass.: Adams Media, 2002); Tara John Manning, *Mindful Knitting:*
Inviting Contemplative Practice to the Craft (Boston: Tuttle, 2004) and *Com-*
passionate Knitting: Finding Basic Goodness in the Work of Our Hands (North
Clarendon, Vt.: Tuttle, 2006); Betty Christiansen, *Knitting for Peace: Make*
the World a Better Place One Stitch at a Time (New York: Stewart, Tabori, and
Chang, 2006).

42. Muñoz, *Cruising Utopia*; Gordon, "Something More Powerful Than Skepticism"; Ahmed, ed. "Happiness," *New Formations* special issue, and *The Prom-*
ise of Happiness; Dolan, *Utopia in Performance*; Snediker, *Queer Optimism*. Halberstam's *The Queer Art of Failure* is another recent addition to queer theory's
meditations on the dialectical relations between utopia and its affective
others. For a perspective informed by Marxism and feminism, see also Passerini, *Memory and Utopia*, on utopian political desires, especially in feminism.

43. See Caserio, Dean, Edelman, Halberstam, and Muñoz, "The Antisocial
Thesis in Queer Theory."

44. Thus I would disagree with Michael Snediker's proposal, in making a
pitch for queer optimism, that queer studies has been characterized by a queer
pessimism in its focus on negative affects such as "melancholy, self-shattering,
shame, the death drive" (4), since so much of this work troubles distinctions
between positive and negative affects. Whether it's called queer pessimism or
queer optimism, though, I agree with the spirit of his call for an expanded vocabulary of affect that has greater specificity. See *Queer Optimism*, especially
12–15.

45. See Flatley, *Affective Mapping* for the notion of melancholy as a way of
making an affective map of the world and negotiating it as a sensory being.

46. See Gordon, "Something More Powerful than Skepticism," 196.

47. See especially material related to the unpublished fourth volume of *The*
History of Sexuality, "Confessions of the Flesh," some of which is in Foucault,
Religion and Culture. See also Carrette, *Foucault and Religion*; Halperin, *Saint*
Foucault.

48. For more on the films, see Bordowitz, *Drive*, the catalogue for an exhibition of Bordowitz's work at the Chicago Museum of Contemporary Art.
Bordowitz has been a regular participant in Public Feelings gatherings and
attended the initial "Depression, What Is It Good For?" conference at the University of Chicago. Berlant's *Cruel Optimism* also includes a reading of *Habit*
that overlaps with mine in ways that suggest our shared sense of the value of
Bordowitz's work for thinking about contemporary affective experience. See
Cruel Optimism, 55–63.

49. See his recent book of poem-questions, *Volition*.

50. The full citation to this section's epigraph is Gretchen Phillips, *I Was Just*
Comforting Her, music recording.

51. On matters of enchantment, see Bennett, *The Enchantment of Modern Life*.

52. See, for example, Carrette, *Selling Spirituality*.

53. For discussions of the concept and history of secularism, see for example, Asad, *Formations of the Secular*, which emerges from his work on the social production of the category of religion in *Genealogies of Religion*; Taylor, *A Secular Age*; Jakobsen and Pellegrini, *Secularisms*. This transformative work on the category of religion opens up room for new investigations of categories such as spirituality as well.

54. See, for example, Cobb, *God Hates Fags*, and Jakobsen and Pellegrini, *Love the Sin*.

55. See, for example, McGarry's *Ghosts of Futures Past*, which discusses nineteenth-century spiritualism, including its relation to queerness.

56. See, for example, Dolan's discussion of Deb Margolin's performance of *Oh Wholly Night and Other Jewish Solecisms* about the Jewish messiah in *Utopia in Performance*, 56–62.

57. See Flatley, *Affective Mapping*, on modernist aesthetics and forms of anti-depressive melancholy that are not transcendent.

58. See, for example, Chödrön, *When Things Fall Apart* and *The Places That Scare You*; Hanh, *The Heart of Understanding*; as well as Sedgwick's elegant fusion of Buddhism and critical theory in "Pedagogy of Buddhism," *Touching Feeling*, 153–81. Sedgwick's presence shadows these pages in ways difficult to acknowledge adequately or articulate fully.

EPILOGUE

1. Barry's use of the graphic narrative's combination of drawing and text to write about the creative process and the development of the artist resembles that of Alison Bechdel in *Fun Home*. See my "Drawing the Archive in Alison Bechdel's *Fun Home*." For a superb study of graphic narrative that features discussions of both Bechdel and Barry, including *What It Is*, see Chute, *Graphic Women*.

2. Barry, *What It Is*, 135.

3. See Zwicker, "Things We Gained in the Fire," for a discussion of burnout.

4. Barry, *What It Is*, 40.

5. The full citation to the source of this section's epigraph is David Foster Wallace, "Real Freedom?," commencement speech at Kenyon College, 2005, published in book form as *This Is Water*. Available online at www.humanity .org (accessed March 2011).

6. See, for example, Lim, "Queer Suicide," with essays by Jasbir Puar, Ann Pellegrini, Jack Halberstam, and others.

7. Jack Halberstam, "It Gets Worse . . . ," in Lim, ed., "Queer Suicide." For

Halberstam's writing with the Bully Bloggers, see http://bullybloggers.word press.com/, including Tavia Nyong'o's discussion of It Gets Better in "School Daze," 30 September 2010.

8. Tamar Lewin, "Record Level of Stress Found in College Freshmen," *New York Times*, 26 January 2011.

9. This account of ordinary life complements that of Wallace's more overt depiction of depression in his short story "The Depressed Person," which tracks the exhaustingly intricate and alienating mental logic of self-loathing. Unable to find any meaningful solace in conversation with either her therapist or a friend she calls on the phone, the depressed person's isolation suggests the failures of empathic connection or adequate forms of attention within therapeutic culture. The exploration of the ordinary life of the mind in Wallace's celebrated novel *Infinite Jest* (1996) also offers a valuable alternative to medical accounts of mental illness and addiction.

Explicit articulations of suicidal thoughts are far more prevalent in depression memoirs by men. See, for example, Hoagland, "Heaven and Nature," and Stringer, "Fading to Gray," in Casey, *Unholy Ghost*, which also includes an excerpt from Styron's *Darkness Visible*, as well as Mays's *In the Jaws of the Black Dogs*, in which he deals frankly with his suicidal impulses.

Wallace's accounts of ordinary life remind me of David Wojnarowicz's concept of the "preinvented world" in *Close to the Knives*. Perhaps the righteous indignation of queer rage about AIDS, even if it couldn't save Wojnarowicz from death, is a guard against suicidal depression.

10. Bornstein also made an It Gets Better video and had already used the phrase herself in her book, *Hello Cruel World*.

11. Lorde, "Poetry Is Not a Luxury," 37.

12. Myles, "Live through That?!," 219–20.

Bibliography

Abelove, Henry. *Deep Gossip*. Minneapolis: University of Minnesota Press, 2003.

Abramović, Marina, and Klaus Peter Biesenbach. *Marina Abramović: The Artist Is Present*. New York: Museum of Modern Art, 2010.

Abu-Lughod, Lila, and Catherine Lutz. *Language and the Politics of Emotion*. Cambridge: Cambridge University Press, 1990.

Adamson, Glenn. *The Craft Reader*. Oxford: Berg, 2010.

————. *Thinking through Craft*. Oxford: Berg, 2007.

Agamben, Giorgio. *Homo Sacer: Sovereign Power and Bare Life*. Stanford: Stanford University Press, 1998.

————. *Stanzas: Word and Phantasm in Western Culture*. Minneapolis: University of Minnesota Press, 1993.

————. *State of Exception*. Trans. Kevin Attell. Chicago: University of Chicago Press, 2005.

Ahmed, Sara. *The Cultural Politics of Emotion*. Edinburgh: Edinburgh University Press, 2004.

————. *The Promise of Happiness*. Durham: Duke University Press, 2010.

————. *Queer Phenomenology: Orientations, Objects, Others*. Durham: Duke University Press, 2006.

Ahmed, Sara, ed. "Happiness." Special issue of *New Formations* 63 (2008).

Alexander, M. Jacqui. *Pedagogies of Crossing: Meditations on Feminism, Sexual Politics, Memory, and the Sacred*. Durham: Duke University Press, 2005.

Alfody, Sandra, ed. *NeoCraft: Modernity and the Crafts*. Halifax: Press of the Nova Scotia College of Art and Design, 2007.

Alfred, Taiaiake. *Peace, Power, Righteousness: An Indigenous Manifesto*. Don Mills, Ontario: Oxford University Press Canada, 1999.

Allison, Dorothy. *Two or Three Things I Know for Sure*. New York: Penguin, 1995.

Anzaldúa, Gloria. *Borderlands / La Frontera*. 1987. 2nd ed. San Francisco: Aunt Lute, 1999.

Armstrong, Nancy. *Desire and Domestic Fiction: A Political History of the Novel*. New York: Oxford University Press, 1987.

Asad, Talal. *Formations of the Secular: Christianity, Islam, Modernity*. Stanford: Stanford University Press, 2003.

———. *Genealogies of Religion: Discipline and Reasons of Power in Christianity and Islam.* Baltimore: Johns Hopkins University Press, 1993.

Babb, Lawrence. *The Elizabethan Malady: A Study of Melancholia in English Literature from 1580 to 1642.* East Lansing: Michigan State University Press, 1951.

Baker, Samuel. *Written on the Water: British Romanticism and the Maritime Empire of Culture.* Charlottesville: University of Virginia Press, 2010.

Barber, Charles. *Comfortably Numb: How Psychiatry Is Medicating a Nation.* New York: Pantheon, 2008.

———. *Songs from the Black Chair: A Memoir of Mental Interiors.* Lincoln: University of Nebraska Press, 2005.

Barnes, Elizabeth. *States of Sympathy: Seduction and Democracy in the American Novel.* New York: Columbia University Press, 1997.

Barry, Lynda. *What It Is.* Montreal: Drawn and Quarterly, 2008.

Bechdel, Alison. *Fun Home: A Family Tragicomic.* Boston: Houghton Mifflin, 2006.

Benjamin, Walter. *The Arcades Project.* Cambridge: Belknap Press of Harvard University Press, 1999.

———. *Illuminations: Essays and Reflections.* Ed. Hannah Arendt. New York: Schocken, 1969.

———. "Left-Wing Melancholy." *The Weimar Republic Sourcebook*, ed. Anton Kaes, Martin Jay, and Edward Dimendberg. Berkeley: University of California Press, 1994. 304–6.

———. *Reflections: Essays, Aphorisms, Autobiographical Writing.* Ed. Peter Demetz. New York: Schocken, 1978.

———. *Selected Writings.* 4 vols. Ed. Michael W. Jennings, Howard Eiland, Marcus Bullock, and Michael W. Doherty. Cambridge: Belknap Press of Harvard University Press, 1999–2004.

Bennett, Jane. *The Enchantment of Modern Life: Attachments, Crossings, and Ethics.* Princeton: Princeton University Press, 2001.

———. *Vibrant Matter.* Durham: Duke University Press, 2009.

Bennett, Tony, Lawrence Grossberg, and Meaghan Morris, eds. *New Keywords: A Revised Vocabulary of Culture and Society.* Oxford: Blackwell, 2005.

Berlant, Lauren. *The Anatomy of National Fantasy: Hawthorne, Utopia, and Everyday Life.* Chicago: University of Chicago Press, 1991.

———. "Critical Inquiry, Affirmative Culture." *Critical Inquiry* 30 (2004), 445–51.

———. *Cruel Optimism.* Durham: Duke University Press, 2011.

———. "The Female Complaint." *Social Text* 19–20 (1988), 237–59.

———. *The Female Complaint.* Durham: Duke University Press, 2008.

———. "Neither Monstrous nor Pastoral, but Scary and Sweet: Some Thoughts on Sex and Emotional Performance in Intimacies and What Do Gay Men Want?" *Women and Performance* 19, no. 2 (2009), 261–73.

———. "On the Case." *Critical Inquiry* 33, no. 4 (2007): 663–72.

———. *The Queen of America Goes to Washington City: Essays on Sex and Citizenship*. Durham: Duke University Press, 1997.

———. "Slow Death (Sovereignty, Obesity, Lateral Agency)." *Critical Inquiry* 33, no. 4 (2007), 754–80.

———. "Starved." Janet Halley and Andrew Parker, eds. "After Sex: On Writing since Queer Theory." Special issue of *SAQ: South Atlantic Quarterly* 106, no. 3 (2007), 433–44, republished as *After Sex: On Writing since Queer Theory*. Durham: Duke University Press, 2011.

Berlant, Lauren, ed. *Compassion: The Culture and Politics of An Emotion*. New York: Routledge, 2004.

Berlant, Lauren, ed. *Intimacy*. Chicago: University of Chicago Press, 2000.

Berlant, Lauren, and Lisa Duggan, eds. *Our Monica, Ourselves: The Clinton Affair and National Public Interest*. New York: New York University Press, 2001.

Best, Stephen, and Saidiya Hartman, eds. "Redress." Special issue of *Representations* 92 (fall 2005).

Blackbridge, Persimmon. *Prozac Highway*. Vancouver: Press Gang, 1997.

Blazer, Dan G. *The Age of Melancholy: Major Depression and Its Social Origins*. New York: Routledge, 2005.

Blechner, Mark C. "Interaction of Social and Neurobiological Factors in Depression." *Contemporary Psychoanalysis* 44, no. 4 (2008), 571–80.

Bloomfield, Morton W. *The Seven Deadly Sins: An Introduction to the History of a Religious Concept, with Special Reference to Medieval English Literature*. East Lansing: Michigan State College Press, 1952.

Boler, Megan. *Feeling Power: Emotions and Education*. New York: Routledge, 1999.

Bordowitz, Gregg. *Drive: The AIDS Crisis Is Still Beginning*. Chicago: White Walls, 2002.

———. *Fast Trip, Long Drop*. 1993. Videotape.

———. *Habit*. 2001. Videotape.

———. *Volition*. New York: Printed Matter, 2009.

Bornstein, Kate. *Hello Cruel World: 101 Alternatives to Suicide for Teens, Freaks, and Other Outlaws*. New York: Seven Stories Press, 2006.

Boyarin, Daniel, and Elizabeth A. Castelli. "Introduction: Foucault's *The History of Sexuality*: The Fourth Volume, or, A Field Left Fallow for Others to Till." *Journal of the History of Sexuality* 10, nos. 3–4 (2001), 357–74.

Boym, Svetlana. *The Future of Nostalgia*. New York: Basic Books, 2001.

Breggin, Peter Roger, and Ginger Ross Breggin. *Talking Back to Prozac: What the Doctors Won't Tell You about Today's Most Controversial Drug*. New York: St. Martin's Press, 1994.

Brennan, Teresa. *The Transmission of Affect*. Ithaca: Cornell University Press, 2004.

Bridgforth, Sharon. *Love Conjure/Blues*. Washington, D.C.: Redbone Press, 2004.

Bridgforth, Sharon, Omi Osun Joni L. Jones, and Lisa L. Moore, eds. *Experiments in a Jazz Aesthetic: Art, Activism, Academia, and the Austin Project*. Austin: University of Texas Press, 2010.

Brison, Susan J. *Aftermath: Violence and the Remaking of a Self*. Princeton: Princeton University Press, 2002.

Brodzki, Bella, and Celeste Schenck, eds. *Life/Lines: Theorizing Women's Autobiography*. Ithaca: Cornell University Press, 1988.

Brown, Gillian. *Domestic Individualism: Imagining Self in Nineteenth-Century America*. Berkeley: University of California Press, 1990.

Brown, Wendy. "Neo-liberalism and the End of Liberal Democracy." *Theory and Event* 7, no. 1 (2003), 1–23.

———. "Resisting Left Melancholia." *Loss: The Politics of Mourning*, ed. David Eng and David Kazanjian. Berkeley: University of California Press, 2003. 458–65.

Bryant, Karl. "Making Gender Identity Disorder of Childhood: Historical Lessons for Contemporary Debates." *Sexuality Research and Social Policy* 3, no. 3 (2006), 23–39.

Burgett, Bruce. *Sentimental Bodies: Sex, Gender, and Citizenship in the Early Republic*. Princeton: Princeton University Press, 1998.

Burgett, Bruce, and Glenn Hendler, eds. *Keywords for American Cultural Studies*. New York: New York University Press, 2007.

Bustamante, Nao, and José Muñoz. "Chat." *The Way That We Rhyme*. Exhibition catalogue. San Francisco: Yerba Buena Arts Center, 2008. 10–13.

Buszek, Maria Elena, ed. *Extra/Ordinary: Craft and Contemporary Art*. Durham: Duke University Press, 2011.

Butler, Cornelia H., and Lisa Gabrielle Mark, eds. *WACK! Art and the Feminist Revolution*. Cambridge: MIT Press, 2007.

Butler, Judith. *Frames of War: When Is Life Grievable?* New York: Verso, 2009.

———. *Precarious Life: The Powers of Mourning and Violence*. New York: Verso, 2004.

———. *The Psychic Life of Power: Theories in Subjection*. Stanford: Stanford University Press, 1997.

Butler, Octavia. Interview. *Locus Magazine*, June 2000, online (accessed 8 September 2011).

———. *Kindred*. 1979. Boston: Beacon Press, 1988.

Butt, Gavin. *Between You and Me: Queer Disclosures in the New York Art World, 1948–1963*. Durham: Duke University Press, 2005.

Cahn, Susan. "Of Silver and Serotonin: Thinking through Depression, Inheritance, and Illness Narratives." *American Quarterly* 59, no. 4 (2007), 1225–36.

Cameron, Julia. *The Artist's Way: A Spiritual Path to Higher Creativity*. New York: Putnam's, 1992.

Carmody, Todd, and Heather K. Love. "Try Anything." *Criticism* 50, no. 1 (2008), 133–46.

Carrette, Jeremy. *Foucault and Religion: Spiritual Corporality and Political Spirituality*. London: Routledge, 2000.

———. *Selling Spirituality: The Silent Takeover of Religion*. London: Routledge, 2005.

Caruth, Cathy, ed. *Trauma: Explorations in Memory*. Baltimore: Johns Hopkins University Press, 1995.

———. *Unclaimed Experience: Trauma, Narrative, and History*. Baltimore: Johns Hopkins University Press, 1996.

Caserio, Robert L., Tim Dean, Lee Edelman, Judith Halberstam, and José Esteban Muñoz. "The Antisocial Thesis in Queer Theory." *PMLA* 121 (May 2006), 819–28.

Casey, Nell, ed. *Unholy Ghost: Writers on Depression*. New York: Harper Collins, 2002.

Cassian, John. [Joannis Cassiani]. *De Coenobiorum Institutis*. Patrologia Latina Database, Book 49. Alexandria, Va.: Chadwick-Healey, 1996. http://pld.chadwyck.co.uk/.

———. "The Institutes of John Cassian." *The Works of John Cassian. A Select Library of the Nicene and Post-Nicene Fathers of the Christian Church, Second Series, Book 11*, eds. Philip Schaff and Henry Wace. Translated from the Latin by Edgar C. S. Gibson. Buffalo: Christian Literature Publishing Company, 1894.

———. *The Institutes*. Trans. Boniface Ramsey. Mahwah, N.J.: Newman Press of the Paulist Press, 2000.

Chambers, Tod. "Prozac for the Sick Soul." *Prozac as a Way of Life*, ed. Tod Chambers and Carl Elliott. Chapel Hill: University of North Carolina Press, 2004. 194–206.

Chambers, Tod, and Carl Elliott, eds. *Prozac as a Way of Life*. Chapel Hill: University of North Carolina Press, 2004.

Charon, Rita. *Narrative Medicine: Honoring the Stories of Illness*. New York: Oxford University Press, 2006.

Cheng, Anne. *The Melancholy of Race*. New York: Oxford University Press, 2001.

Cherniavsky, Eva. *That Pale Mother Rising: Sentimental Discourses and the Imitation of Motherhood in 19th-Century America*. Bloomington: Indiana University Press, 1995.

Chesler, Phyllis. *Women and Madness*. Garden City, N.Y.: Doubleday, 1972.

Chödrön, Pema. *The Places That Scare You: A Guide to Fearlessness in Difficult Times*. Boston: Shambhala, 2007.

———. *When Things Fall Apart: Heart Advice for Difficult Times*. Boston: Shambhala, 2002.

Chute, Hillary L. *Graphic Women: Life Narrative and Contemporary Comics.* New York: Columbia University Press, 2010.

Clarke, Adele E., Laura Mamo, Jennifer Ruth Fosket, Jennifer R. Fishman, and Janet K. Shim, eds. *Biomedicalization: Technoscience, Health, and Illness in the U.S.* Durham: Duke University Press, 2010.

Clough, Patricia Ticineto, and Jean Halley, eds. *The Affective Turn: Theorizing the Social.* Durham: Duke University Press, 2007.

Cobb, Michael. *God Hates Fags: The Rhetorics of Religious Violence.* New York: New York University Press, 2006.

Cohen, Ed. *A Body Worth Defending: Immunity, Biopolitics, and the Apotheosis of the Modern Body.* Durham: Duke University Press, 2009.

Comas-Díaz, Lillian, and Ezra E. H. Griffith. *Clinical Guidelines in Cross-Cultural Mental Health.* New York: John Wiley, 1988.

Commander, Michelle D. "Ghana at Fifty: Moving toward Kwame Nkrumah's Pan-African Dream." *American Quarterly* 59, no. 2 (2007), 421–41.

Coole, Diana and Samantha Frost, eds. *New Materialisms: Ontology, Agency, and Politics.* Durham: Duke University Press, 2010.

Couser, G. Thomas. *Recovering Bodies: Illness, Disability and Life-Writing.* Madison: University of Wisconsin Press, 1997.

———. *Vulnerable Subjects: Ethics and Life Writing.* Ithaca: Cornell University Press, 2004.

Crimp, Douglas. *Melancholia and Moralism: Essays on AIDS and Queer Politics.* Cambridge: MIT Press, 2002.

Cvetkovich, Ann. *An Archive of Feelings: Trauma, Sexuality, and Lesbian Public Cultures.* Durham: Duke University Press, 2003.

———. "Drawing the Archive in Alison Bechdel's *Fun Home.*" *Women's Studies Quarterly* 36, nos. 1–2 (2008), 111–28.

———. *Mixed Feelings: Feminism, Mass Culture, and Victorian Sensationalism.* New Brunswick: Rutgers University Press, 1992.

———. "Public Feelings." Janet Halley and Andrew Parker, eds. "After Sex: On Writing since Queer Theory." Special issue of *SAQ: South Atlantic Quarterly* 106, no. 3 (2007), 169–79, republished as *After Sex: On Writing since Queer Theory.* Durham: Duke University Press, 2011.

Cvetkovich, Ann, with Allyson Mitchell. "A Girl's Journey into the Well of Forbidden Knowledge." *GLQ* 17, no. 4 (2011), 603–18.

Cvetkovich, Ann, and Ann Pellegrini, eds. "Public Sentiments." Special issue of *Scholar and Feminist Online* 2, no. 1 (2003).

Damasio, Antonio. *Descartes' Error: Emotion, Reason, and the Human Brain.* New York: G. P. Putnam, 1995.

———. *The Feeling of What Happens: Body and Emotion in the Making of Consciousness.* New York: Mariner Books, 2000.

———. *Looking for Spinoza: Joy, Sorrow, and the Feeling Brain.* New York: Mariner Books, 2003.

Danquah, Meri Nana-Ama. *Willow Weep for Me: A Black Woman's Journey through Depression*. New York: Ballantine, 1998.

Daston, Lorraine, and Peter Galison. *Objectivity*. New York: Zone, 2007, 2010.

Davidson, Cathy N. *Revolution and the Word: The Rise of the Novel in America*. New York: Oxford University Press, 1985.

———. *Thirty-Six Views of Mount Fuji: On Finding Myself in Japan*. Durham: Duke University Press, 2006.

Davidson, Cathy N., and Jessamyn Hatcher, eds. *No More Separate Spheres! A Next Wave American Studies Reader*. Durham: Duke University Press, 2002.

Deavere Smith, Anna. *Twilight: Los Angeles, 1992*. New York: Dramatists Play Service, 2003.

DelVecchio Good, Mary-Jo, Sandra Teresa Hyde, Sarah Pinto, and Byron J. Good, eds. *Postcolonial Disorders*. Berkeley: University of California Press, 2008.

Diagnostic and Statistical Manual of Mental Disorders: DSM-III. Washington, D.C.: American Psychiatric Association, 1980. Revised edition, *DSM-III-R*, 1987.

Diagnostic and Statistical Manual of Mental Disorders: DSM-IV. Washington, D.C.: American Psychiatric Association, 1994. Revised edition, *DSM-IV-TR*, 2000.

Dinshaw, Carolyn. *Getting Medieval: Sexualities and Communities, Pre- and Postmodern*. Durham: Duke University Press, 1999.

Dolan, Jill. "From Flannel to Fleece: Women's Music, Lesbian Feminism, and 'Me.'" Unpublished manuscript.

———. *Utopia in Performance: Finding Hope at the Theater*. Ann Arbor: University of Michigan Press, 2005.

Driskill, Qwo-Li, Chris Finley, Brian Joseph Gilley, and Scott Lauria Morgensen, eds. *Queer Indigenous Studies: Critical Interventions in Theory, Politics, and Literature*. Tucson: University of Arizona Press, 2011.

Dudley, William, ed. *Antidepressants (The History of Drugs)*. Detroit: Greenhaven, 2005.

Duggan, Lisa. *Sapphic Slashers: Sex, Violence, and American Modernity*. Durham: Duke University Press, 2000.

———. *The Twilight of Equality? Neoliberalism, Cultural Politics, and the Attack on Democracy*. Boston: Beacon Press, 2003.

Edelman, Lee. *No Future: Queer Theory and the Death Drive*. Durham: Duke University Press, 2004.

Ehrenberg, Alain. *La fatigue d'être soi: Depression et société*. Paris: O. Jacob, 1998.

———. *The Weariness of the Self: Diagnosing the History of Depression in the Contemporary Age*. Montreal: McGill–Queen's University Press, 2010.

Eng, David. *The Feeling of Kinship*. Durham: Duke University Press, 2010.

Eng, David, Judith Halberstam, and José Muñoz, eds. "What's Queer about Queer Studies Now?" Special issue of *Social Text* 84/85 (2005).

Eng, David, and Shin-Hee Han. "A Dialogue on Racial Melancholia." *Loss: The Politics of Mourning*, ed. David Eng and David Kazanjian. Berkeley: University of California Press, 2003, 343–71.

Eng, David, and David Kazanjian, eds. *Loss: The Politics of Mourning*. Berkeley: University of California Press, 2003.

Enterline, Lynn. *The Tears of Narcissus: Melancholia and Masculinity in Early Modern Writing*. Stanford: Stanford University Press, 1995.

Epstein, Stephen. *Impure Science: AIDS, Activism, and the Politics of Knowledge*. Berkeley: University of California Press, 1996.

———. *Inclusion: The Politics of Difference in Medical Research*. Chicago: University of Chicago Press, 2007.

Eyerman, Ron. *Cultural Trauma: Slavery and the Formation of African American Identity*. Cambridge: Cambridge University Press, 2001.

Farred, Grant. *What's My Name? Black Vernacular Intellectuals*. Minneapolis: University of Minnesota Press, 2003.

Felman, Shoshana, and Dori Laub. *Testimony: Crises of Witnessing in Literature, Psychoanalysis, and History*. New York: Routledge, 1992.

Flatley, Jonathan. *Affective Mapping: Melancholia and the Politics of Modernism*. Cambridge: Harvard University Press, 2008.

Foucault, Michel. *Religion and Culture*. Ed. Jeremy R. Carrette. New York: Routledge, 1999.

———. *"Society Must Be Defended": Lectures at the College de France 1975–76*. Trans. David Macey. New York: Picador, 2003.

François, Anne-Lise. *Open Secrets: The Literature of Uncounted Experience*. Stanford: Stanford University Press, 2007.

Franklin, Cynthia G. *Academic Lives: Memoir, Cultural Theory, and the University Today*. Athens: University of Georgia Press, 2009.

Franklin, Cynthia G., and Laura E. Lyons, eds. "Special Effects: The Testimonial Uses of Life Writing." Special issue of *Biography* 27, no. 1 (2004).

Freccero, Carla. *Queer/Early/Modern*. Durham: Duke University Press, 2006.

Freeman, Elizabeth. *Time Binds: Queer Temporalities, Queer Histories*. Durham: Duke University Press, 2010.

Freeman, Elizabeth, ed. "Queer Temporalities." Special issue of *GLQ* 13, nos. 2–3 (2007).

Friedan, Betty. *The Feminine Mystique*. New York: Norton, 1963.

Gallop, Jane. *Feminist Accused of Sexual Harassment*. Durham: Duke University Press, 1997.

Gilbert, Sandra M., and Susan Gubar. *The Madwoman in the Attic: The Woman Writer and the Nineteenth-Century Literary Imagination*. New Haven: Yale University Press, 1979.

Gilmore, Leigh. *The Limits of Autobiography: Trauma and Testimony*. Ithaca: Cornell University Press, 2001.

Gilmore, Ruth Wilson. *Golden Gulag: Prisons, Surplus, Crisis, and Opposition in Globalizing California*. Berkeley: University of California Press, 2007.

Gilroy, Paul. *Postcolonial Melancholia*. New York: Columbia University Press, 2005.

Glenmullen, Joseph. *Prozac Backlash: Overcoming the Dangers of Prozac, Zoloft, Paxil, and Other Antidepressants with Safe, Effective Alternatives*. New York: Simon and Schuster, 2000.

Goldberg, Natalie. *Writing Down the Bones: Freeing the Writer Within*. Boston: Shambhala, 1986.

Gopinath, Gayatri. "Archive, Affect, and the Everyday: Queer Diaspora Revisions." *Political Emotions*, ed. Janet Staiger, Ann Cvetkovich, and Ann Reynolds. New York: Routledge, 2010. 165–92.

Gordon, Avery F. *Ghostly Matters: Haunting and the Sociological Imagination*. Minneapolis: University of Minnesota Press, 1997.

———. "Something More Powerful Than Skepticism." *Keeping Good Time: Reflections on Knowledge, Power, and People*. Boulder: Paradigm Publishers, 2004. 187–205.

Gordon, James S. *Unstuck: Your Guide to the Seven-Stage Journey out of Depression*. New York: Penguin, 2008.

Gould, Deborah. *Moving Politics: Emotion and ACT UP's Fight against AIDS*. Chicago: University of Chicago Press, 2009.

———. "On Affect and Protest." *Political Emotions*, ed. Janet Staiger, Ann Cvetkovich, and Ann Reynolds. New York: Routledge, 2010. 18–44.

Gray, Mary L. *Out in the Country: Youth, Media, and Queer Visibility in Rural America*. New York: New York University Press, 2009.

Greenberg, Gary. Interview. *Leonard Lopate Show*. WNYC, 12 February 2010. Online (accessed March 2011).

———. "Manufacturing Depression: A Journey into the Economy of Melancholy." *Harper's*, May 2007, 35–46.

———. *Manufacturing Depression: The Secret History of a Modern Disease*. New York: Simon and Schuster, 2010.

Greenspan, Miriam. *Healing through Dark Emotions: The Wisdom of Grief, Fear, and Despair*. Boston: Shambhala, 2004.

Greer, Betsy. *Knitting for Good! A Guide to Creating Personal, Social, and Political Change, Stitch by Stitch*. Boston: Trumpeter, 2008.

Gregg, Melissa, and Gregory J. Seigworth, eds. *The Affect Theory Reader*. Durham: Duke University Press, 2010.

Grosz, Elizabeth. *Becoming Undone: Darwinian Reflections on Life, Politics, and Art*. Durham: Duke University Press, 2011.

———. *Time Travels: Feminism, Nature, Power*. Durham: Duke University Press, 2005.

Grover, Jan Zita. *North Enough*. Minneapolis: Graywolf Press, 1996.

Haacken, Janice. *The Pillar of Salt: Gender, Memory, and the Politics of Looking Back*. New Brunswick: Rutgers University Press, 1998.

Habermas, Jürgen. *The Structural Transformation of the Public Sphere: An Inquiry into a Category of Bourgeois Society*. Cambridge: MIT Press, 1989.

Haig-Brown, Celia. "Decolonizing Diaspora: Whose Traditional Land Are We On?" *Cultural and Pedagogical Inquiry* 1, no. 1 (2009), 4–21.

———. *Resistance and Renewal: Surviving the Indian Residential School*. Vancouver: Tillacum, 1988.

Haig-Brown, Celia, and Helen Haig-Brown. *Pelq'ilq (Coming Home)*. 2008. Videotape.

Halberstam, Judith. *In a Queer Time and Place: Transgender Bodies, Cultural Lives*. New York: NYU Press, 2005.

———. *The Queer Art of Failure*. Durham: Duke University Press, 2011.

———. *Skin Shows: Gothic Horror and the Technology of Monsters*. Durham: Duke University Press, 1995.

Hall, Leslie. "Craft Talk." *Back to Back Palz*, 2010. CD recording.

Halley, Janet, and Andrew Parker, eds. "After Sex: On Writing Since Queer Theory." Special issue of *SAQ: South Atlantic Quarterly* 106, no. 3 (2007). Republished as *After Sex: On Writing Since Queer Theory*. Durham: Duke University Press, 2011.

Halperin, David M. *Saint Foucault: Towards a Gay Hagiography*. New York: Oxford University Press, 1995.

Hanh, Thich Nhat. *The Heart of Understanding: Commentaries on the Prajnaparamita Heart Sutra*. Berkeley: Parallax, 1988.

Harper, Phillip Brian. "The Evidence of Felt Intuition: Minority Experience, Everyday Life, and Critical Speculative Knowledge." *GLQ: A Journal of Gay and Lesbian Studies* 6, no. 4 (2000), 641–57.

Harris, Thor. *An Ocean of Despair*. Austin: Monofonus Press, 2009.

Hartman, Saidiya V. *Lose Your Mother: A Journey along the Atlantic Slave Route*. New York: Farrar, Straus and Giroux, 2007.

———. *Scenes of Subjection: Terror, Slavery, and Self-Making in Nineteenth-Century America*. New York: Oxford University Press, 1997.

———. "Venus in Two Acts." *Small Axe* 12, no. 2 (2008), 1–14.

Harvey, David. *A Brief History of Neoliberalism*. New York: Oxford University Press, 2005.

Hawkins, Anne Hunsaker. *Reconstructing Illness: Studies in Pathography*. West Lafayette, Ind.: Purdue University Press, 1993.

Healy, David. *The Antidepressant Era*. Cambridge: Harvard University Press, 1997.

———. *The Creation of Psychopharmacology*. Cambridge: Harvard University Press, 2002.

———. *Let Them Eat Prozac: The Unhealthy Relationship between the Phar-*

maceutical Industry and Depression. New York: New York University Press, 2004.

——. *The Psychopharmacologists*. London: Oxford University Press, 2000.

Heilbrun, Carolyn G. *Writing a Woman's Life*. New York: W. W. Norton, 1988.

Hendler, Glenn. *Public Sentiments: Structures of Feeling in Nineteenth-Century American Literature*. Chapel Hill: University of North Carolina Press, 2001.

Herring, Scott. *Another Country: Queer Anti-Urbanism*. New York: New York University Press, 2010.

Hertz, Neil. *George Eliot's Pulse*. Stanford: Stanford University Press, 2003.

Highmore, Ben. *Ordinary Lives: Studies in the Everyday*. London: Routledge, 2011.

Hirsch, Marianne. *Family Frames: Photography, Narrative, and Postmemory*. Cambridge: Harvard University Press, 1997.

Hirsch, Marianne, and Nancy K. Miller, eds. *Rites of Return: Diasporic Poetics and the Politics of Memory*. New York: Columbia University Press, 2011.

Hirsch, Marianne, and Leo Spitzer. "'We Would Not Have Come without You': Generations of Nostalgia." *American Imago* 59, no. 3 (2002), 253–76.

Hoad, Neville. *African Intimacies: Race, Homosexuality, and Globalization*. Minneapolis: University of Minnesota Press, 2007.

Hoagland, Edward. "Heaven and Nature." *Unholy Ghost: Writers on Depression*, ed. Nell Casey. New York: Harper Collins, 2002. 44–59.

Hogan, Kristen. "Reading at Feminist Bookstores: Women's Literature, Women's Studies, and the Feminist Bookstore Network." Ph.D. diss., University of Texas, 2006.

Holland, Sharon Patricia. *The Erotic Life of Racism*. Durham: Duke University Press, 2012.

——. "The Last Word on Racism: New Directions for a Critical Race Theory." *South Atlantic Quarterly* 104, no. 3 (2005), 403–23.

——. *Raising the Dead: Readings of Death and (Black) Subjectivity*. Durham: Duke University Press, 2000.

Holland, Sharon P., and Tiya Miles, eds. *Crossing Waters, Crossing Worlds: The African Diaspora in Indian Country*. Durham: Duke University Press, 2006.

Horwitz, Allan V., and Jerome C. Wakefield. *The Loss of Sadness: How Psychiatry Transformed Normal Sadness into Depressive Disorder*. Oxford: Oxford University Press, 2007.

Horwitz, Allan V., and Jerome C. Wakefield. "Noonday Demons and Midnight Sorrows: Biology and Meaning in Disordered and Normal Sadness." *Contemporary Psychoanalysis* 44, no. 4 (2008), 551–70.

Huber, Cheri. *The Depression Book: Depression as an Opportunity for Spiritual Growth*. Murphys, Calif.: Keep It Simple Books, 1999.

Hughes, Holly, and David Roman, *O Solo Homo: The New Queer Performance*. New York: Grove, 1998.

Hung, Shu, and Joseph Magliaro, eds. *By Hand: The Use of Craft in Contemporary Art*. New York: Princeton Architectural Press, 2007.

Hustvedt, Siri. *The Shaking Woman, or A History of My Nerves*. New York: Picador, 2010.

Jackson, Stanley W. *Melancholy and Depression: From Hippocratic Times to Modern Times*. New Haven: Yale University Press, 1986.

Jakobsen, Janet R., and Ann Pellegrini. *Love the Sin: Sexual Regulation and the Limits of Religious Tolerance*. New York: New York University Press, 2003.

Jakobsen, Janet R., and Ann Pellegrini, eds. *Secularisms*. Durham: Duke University Press, 2008.

Jamison, Kay Redfield. *Exuberance: The Passion for Life*. New York: Alfred A. Knopf, 2004.

———. *An Unquiet Mind: Memoir of Moods and Madness*. New York: Alfred A. Knopf, 1995.

Jones, Edward P. *The Known World*. New York: Amistad, 2003.

Jones, Gayl. *Corregidora*. New York: Random House, 1975.

Joseph, Miranda. *Against the Romance of Community*. Minneapolis: University of Minnesota Press, 2002.

Justice, Daniel Heath, Mark Rivkin, and Bethany Schneider, eds. "Nationality, Sovereignty, Sexuality." Special issue of *GLQ 16*, nos. 1–2 (2010).

Kacandes, Irene. *Daddy's War: Greek American Stories. A Paramemoir*. Lincoln: University of Nebraska Press, 2009.

Kaplan, E. Ann. *Trauma Culture: The Politics of Terror and Loss in Media and Literature*. New Brunswick: Rutgers University Press, 2005.

Karp, David Allen. *Is It Me or My Meds? Living with Antidepressants*. Cambridge: Harvard University Press, 2006.

———. *Speaking of Sadness: Depression, Disconnection, and the Meanings of Illness*. New York: Oxford University Press, 1996.

Keenan, Thomas. "Mobilizing Shame." *South Atlantic Quarterly* 103, no. 2/3 (2004), 435–49.

Khalsa, Gurucharan Singh, and Yogi Bhajan. *Breathwalk: Breathing Your Way to a Revitalized Body, Mind, and Spirit*. New York: Broadway Books, 2000.

Khanna, Ranjana. *Dark Continents: Psychoanalysis and Colonialism*. Durham: Duke University Press, 2003.

Kirk, Stuart A., and Herb Kutchins, eds. *The Selling of DSM: The Rhetoric of Science in Psychiatry*. New York: A. De Gruyter, 1992.

Kirsch, Irving. *The Emperor's New Drugs: Exploding the Antidepressant Myth*. New York: Basic Books, 2010.

Kleinman, Arthur, Veena Das, and Margaret Lock, eds. *Social Suffering*. Berkeley: University of California Press, 1997.

Kleinman, Arthur, and Byron Good. *Culture and Depression: Studies in the Anthropology and Cross-Cultural Psychiatry of Affect and Disorder*. Berkeley: University of California Press, 1985.

Klibansky, Raymond, Erwin Panofsky, and Fritz Saxl. *Saturn and Melancholy: Studies in the History of Natural Philosophy, Religion, and Art.* London: Thomas Nelson and Sons, 1964.

Koestenbaum, Wayne. *Humiliation.* New York: Picador, 2011.

Kolmar, Wendy K., and Frances Bartkowski. *Feminist Theory: A Reader.* Boston: McGraw Hill, 2005.

Kramer, Peter D. *Against Depression.* New York: Viking, 2005.

———. *Listening to Prozac.* New York: Viking, 1993.

Kristeva, Julia. *Black Sun: Depression and Melancholia.* New York: Columbia University Press, 1989.

Kron, Lisa. *2.5 Minute Ride and 101 Humiliating Stories.* New York: Theatre Communications Group, 2001.

LaCapra, Dominick. *History and Memory after Auschwitz.* Ithaca: Cornell University Press, 1998.

———. *Representing the Holocaust: History, Theory, Trauma.* Ithaca: Cornell University Press, 1994.

———. *Writing History, Writing Trauma.* Baltimore: Johns Hopkins University Press, 2001.

Lamott, Anne. *Bird by Bird: Some Instructions on Writing and Life.* New York: Pantheon, 1994.

Lane, Christopher. *Shyness: How Normal Behavior Became a Sickness.* New Haven: Yale University Press, 2007.

Larsen, Nella. *Quicksand and Passing.* Ed. Deborah McDowell. New Brunswick: Rutgers University Press, 1986.

Latour, Bruno. *We Have Never Been Modern.* Cambridge: Harvard University Press, 1993.

Le Tigre. "Much Finer." *Feminist Sweepstakes.* Mr. Lady Records, 2001. Music recording.

Levine, Faythe, and Cortney Heimerl. *Handmade Nation.* 2009. Film.

Levine, Faythe, and Cortney Heimerl, eds. *Handmade Nation: The Rise of DIY, Art, Craft, and Design.* Princeton: Princeton University Press, 2008.

Leys, Ruth. *Trauma: A Genealogy.* Chicago: University of Chicago Press, 2000.

Lim, Eng-Beng, ed. "Queer Suicide: A Teach-In." *Social Text.* www.socialtextjournal.org.

Lochrie, Karma. *Heterosyncracies: Female Sexuality When Normal Wasn't.* Minneapolis: University of Minnesota Press, 2005.

Lorde, Audre. *The Cancer Journals.* San Francisco: Aunt Lute Books, 1980.

———. "Poetry Is Not a Luxury." *Sister Outsider.* Trumansburg, N.Y.: Crossing Press, 1984. 36–39.

Love, Heather K. *Feeling Backward: Loss and the Politics of Queer History.* Cambridge: Harvard University Press, 2007.

———. "Feeling Bad in 1963." *Political Emotions*, ed. Janet Staiger, Ann Cvetkovich, and Ann Reynolds. New York: Routledge, 2010. 112–33.

———. "Truth and Consequences: On Paranoid Reading and Reparative Reading." *Criticism* 52, no. 2 (2010), 235–40.

Love, Heather K., ed. "Rethinking Sex." Special issue of *GLQ: A Journal of Lesbian and Gay Studies* 17, no. 1 (2011).

Lowe, Lisa L. *Immigrant Acts*. Durham: Duke University Press, 1996.

———. "The Intimacies of Four Continents." *Haunted by Empire: Geographies of Intimacy in North American History*, ed. Ann Stoler. Durham: Duke University Press, 2006. 191–212.

Luciano, Dana. *Arranging Grief: Sacred Time and the Body in Nineteenth-Century America*. New York: New York University Press, 2007.

Lutz, Catherine. *Unnatural Emotions: Everyday Sentiments on a Micronesia Atoll and Their Challenge to Western Theory*. Chicago: University of Chicago Press, 1988.

Maitland, Sara. *A Book of Silence*. Berkeley: Counterpoint, 2008.

Manalansan, Martin. *Global Divas: Filipino Gay Men in the Diaspora*. Durham: Duke University Press, 2003.

Manning, Martha. *Undercurrents: A Therapist's Reckoning with Her Own Depression*. San Francisco: Harper San Francisco, 1994.

Marcus, Sara. *Girls to the Front: The True Story of the Riot Grrrl Revolution*. New York: Harper Perennial, 2010.

Martin, Emily. *Bipolar Expeditions: Mania and Depression in American Culture*. Princeton: Princeton University Press, 2007.

Massumi, Brian. *Parables for the Virtual: Movement, Affect, Sensation*. Minneapolis: University of Minnesota Press, 2002.

Mays, John Bentley. *In the Jaws of the Black Dogs: A Memoir of Depression*. New York: Harper Collins, 1995.

McFadden, David Revere, Jennifer Scanlan, and Jennifer Steifle Edwards. *Radical Lace and Subversive Knitting*. New York: Museum of Arts and Design, 2007.

McGarry, Molly. *Ghosts of Futures Past: Spiritualism and the Cultural Politics of Nineteenth-Century America*. Berkeley: University of California Press, 2008.

McLagan, Meg. "Introduction: Making Human Rights Claims Public." *American Anthropologist* 108, no. 1 (2006), 191–95.

———. "Principles, Publicity, and Politics: Notes on Human Rights Media." *American Anthropologist* 105, no. 3 (2003), 605–12.

McRuer, Robert. *Crip Theory: Cultural Signs of Queerness and Disability*. New York: New York University Press, 2006.

Merish, Lori. *Sentimental Materialism: Gender, Commodity Culture, and Nineteenth-Century America*. Durham: Duke University Press, 2000.

Metzl, Jonathan. *Prozac on the Couch: Prescribing Gender in the Era of Wonder Drugs*. Durham: Duke University Press, 2003.

Miller, Nancy K. *Bequest and Betrayal: Memoirs of a Parent's Death*. New York: Oxford University Press, 1996.

———. *But Enough about Me: Why We Read Other People's Lives*. New York: Columbia University Press, 2002.

———. *Getting Personal: Feminist Occasions and Other Autobiographical Acts*. New York: Routledge, 1991.

Miller, Nancy K., and Victoria Rosner, eds. "Writing a Feminist's Life: The Legacy of Carolyn G. Heilbrun." *Scholar and Feminist Online* 4, no. 2 (2006).

Miller, Nancy K., and Jason Tougaw, eds. *Extremities: Trauma, Testimony, and Community*. Urbana: University of Illinois Press, 2002.

Mitchell, Allyson. *Ladies Sasquatch*. Hamilton, Ontario: McMaster Museum of Art, 2009.

Mitchell, Allyson, and Ann Cvetkovich. "A Girl's Journey into the Well of Forbidden Knowledge." *GLQ* 17, no. 4 (2011), 603–18.

Mitchell, Allyson, Jennifer Sorkin, and Sarah Quinton. *When Women Rule the World: Judy Chicago in Thread*. Toronto: Textile Museum of Canada, 2009.

Montano, Linda M. *Letters from Linda M. Montano*. Ed. Jennie Klein. New York: Routledge, 2005.

Moore, Lisa L. *Sister Arts: The Erotics of Lesbian Landscapes*. Minneapolis: University of Minnesota Press, 2011.

Moraga, Cherríe. *Loving in the War Years: Lo que nunca pasó por sus labios*. Boston: South End Press, 1983.

———. *A Xicana Codex of Changing Consciousness*. Durham: Duke University Press, 2011.

Morrison, Andrew L. "The Discovery and Development of the First Modern Antidepressants." *Antidepressants (The History of Drugs)*, ed. William Dudley. Detroit: Greenhaven, 2005. 25–30.

Morrison, Toni. *Beloved: A Novel*. New York: Alfred A. Knopf, 1987.

———. "Unspeakable Things Unspoken: The Afro-American Presence in American Literature." *Michigan Quarterly Review*, Winter 1989, 1–34.

Moten, Fred. *In the Break: The Aesthetics of the Black Radical Tradition*. Minneapolis: University of Minnesota Press, 2003.

Muñoz, José Esteban. "Between Psychoanalysis and Affect: A Public Feelings Project." Special issue of *Women and Performance* 19, no. 2 (2009).

———. *Cruising Utopia*. New York: New York University Press, 2010.

———. *Disidentifications: Queers of Color and the Performance of Politics*. Minneapolis: University of Minnesota Press, 1999.

———. "Ephemera as Evidence: Introductory Notes to Queer Acts," *Women and Performance* 16 (1996), 5–16.

———. "Feeling Brown: Ethnicity and Affect in Ricardo Bracho's *The Sweetest Hangover (and Other STDs)*." *Theatre Journal* 52, no. 1 (2000), 67–79.

———. "Feeling Brown, Feeling Down: Latina Affect, the Performativity of Race, and the Depressive Position." *Signs: Journal of Women in Culture and Society* 31, no. 3 (2006), 675–88.

———. "From Surface to Depth, between Psychoanalysis and Affect." Introduction to special issue of *Women and Performance* 19, no. 2 (2009), 123–29.

———. *The Sense of Brown*. Durham: Duke University Press, forthcoming.

———. "The Vulnerability Artist: Nao Bustamante and the Sad Beauty of Reparation." *Women and Performance: A Journal of Feminist Theory* 16, no. 2 (2006), 191–200.

Murphy, Kevin P., and Jason Ruiz, eds. "Queer Futures." Special issue of *Radical History Review* 100 (winter 2008).

Myles, Eileen. "Live through That?!" *Live through This: On Creativity and Self-Destruction*, ed. Sabrina Chapadjiev. New York: Seven Stories Press, 2008. 219–24.

Nealon, Chris. *Foundlings: Lesbian and Gay Historical Emotion before Stonewall*. Durham: Duke University Press, 2001.

Newfield, Christopher. *Ivy and Industry: Business and the Making of the American University, 1880–1980*. Durham: Duke University Press, 2003.

———. *Unmaking the Public University: The Forty-Year Assault on the Middle Class*. Cambridge: Harvard University Press, 2008.

Ngai, Sianne. *Ugly Feelings*. Cambridge: Harvard University Press, 2005.

Norris, Kathleen. *Acedia and Me: A Marriage, Monks, and a Writer's Life*. New York: Riverhead, 2008.

O'Brien, Sharon. *The Family Silver: A Memoir of Depression and Inheritance*. Chicago: University of Chicago Press, 2004.

O'Leary, John V. "Putting It Together While Falling Apart: A Personal View on Depression." *Contemporary Psychoanalysis* 44, no. 4 (2008), 531–50.

Oliver, Valerie Cassel. *Hand+Made: The Performative Impulse in Art and Craft*. Houston: Contemporary Arts Museum, 2010.

O'Nell, Theresa D. *Disciplined Hearts: History, Identity, and Depression in an American Indian Community*. Berkeley: University of California Press, 1996.

Orr, Jackie. *Panic Diaries: A Genealogy of Panic Disorder*. Durham: Duke University Press, 2006.

Passerini, Luisa. *Autobiography of a Generation: Italy, 1968*. Trans. Lisa Erdberg. Middletown, Conn.: Wesleyan University Press, 1996.

———. *Memory and Utopia: The Primacy of Intersubjectivity*. London: Equinox, 2006.

Pensky, Max. *Melancholy Dialectics: Walter Benjamin and the Play of Mourning*. Amherst: University of Massachusetts Press, 2001.

Phelan, Peggy, and Helena Reckitt. *Art and Feminism*. London: Phaidon Press, 2001.

Phillips, Gretchen. *I Was Just Comforting Her*. Re-emergent Rascals, 2009. Music recording.

Pidduck, Julianne. "Queer Kinship and Ambivalence: Video Autoethnographies by Jean Carlomusto and Richard Fung." *GLQ* 15, no. 3 (2009), 441–68.

Probyn, Elspeth. *Blush: Faces of Shame*. Minneapolis: University of Minnesota Press, 2005.

Puar, Jasbir K. *Terrorist Assemblages: Homonationalism in Queer Times*. Durham: Duke University Press, 2007.

Quimby, Ernest. "Ethnography's Role in Assisting Mental Health Research and Clinical Practice." *Journal of Clinical Psychology* 62, no. 7 (2006), 859–79.

Radden, Jennifer. *The Nature of Melancholy: From Aristotle to Kristeva*. Oxford: Oxford University Press, 2000.

Radway, Janice. *Reading the Romance: Women, Patriarchy, and Popular Literature*. Chapel Hill: University of North Carolina Press, 1984.

Readings, Bill. *The University in Ruins*. Cambridge: Harvard University Press, 1996.

Reddy, William M. *The Navigation of Feeling: A Framework for the History of Emotions*. Cambridge: Cambridge University Press, 2001.

Reynolds, Ann Morris. *Robert Smithson: Learning from New Jersey and Elsewhere*. Cambridge: MIT Press, 2003.

———. "A Structure of Creativity." *Ruth Vollmer 1961–1978: Thinking the Line*, ed. Nadja Rottner and Peter Weibel. Ostfildern, Germany: Hatje Cantz, 2006. 48–57.

Risatti, Howard. *A Theory of Craft: Function and Aesthetic Expression*. Chapel Hill: University of North Carolina Press, 2007.

Romero, Lora P. *Home Fronts: Domesticity and Its Critics in the Antebellum United States*. Durham: Duke University Press, 1997.

Ross, Christine. *The Aesthetics of Disengagement: Contemporary Art and Depression*. Minneapolis: University of Minnesota Press, 2006.

Rowell, Charles H., and Octavia E. Butler. "An Interview with Octavia E. Butler." *Callaloo* 20, no. 1 (1997), 47–66.

Salecl, Renata. *On Anxiety*. New York: Routledge, 2004.

Samuels, Shirley, ed. *The Culture of Sentiment: Race, Gender, and Sentimentality in Nineteenth-Century America*. New York: Oxford University Press, 1992.

———. *Romances of the Republic: Women, the Family, and Violence in the Literature of the Early American Nation*. New York: Oxford University Press, 1996.

Sánchez-Eppler, Karen. *Touching Liberty: Abolition, Feminism, and the Politics of the Body*. Berkeley: University of California Press, 1993.

Sandoval, Chela. *Methodology of the Oppressed*. Minneapolis: University of Minnesota Press, 2000.

Schaffer, Kay, and Sidonie Smith. *Human Rights and Narrated Lives: The Ethics of Recognition*. New York: Palgrave, 2004.

Scheckel, Susan E. "Traveling Nostalgia." Paper delivered at the American Comparative Literature Association Meetings, 24–27 April 2008.

Schiesari, Juliana. *The Gendering of Melancholia: Feminism, Psychoanalysis, and the Symbolics of Loss in Renaissance Literature*. Ithaca: Cornell University Press, 1992.

Scott, Joan. "The Evidence of Experience." *The Lesbian and Gay Studies Reader*, ed. Henry Abelove, Michele Aina Barale, and David M. Halperin. New York: Routledge, 1993. 397–415.

Sedgwick, Eve Kosofsky. *Between Men: English Literature and Male Homosocial Desire*. New York: Columbia University Press, 1985.

———. *A Dialogue on Love*. Boston: Beacon Press, 1999.

———. "Queer and Now." *Tendencies*. Durham: Duke University Press, 1993. 3–19.

———. "Queer Performativity: Henry James's *The Art of the Novel*." *GLQ* 1, no. 1 (1993), 1–16.

———. "Teaching/Depression." *The Scholar and Feminist Online* 4, no. 2 (2006). www.barnard.edu/sfonline.

———. *Touching Feeling: Affect, Pedagogy, Performativity*. Durham: Duke University Press, 2003.

———. *The Weather in Proust*. Durham: Duke University Press, 2011.

Sedgwick, Eve Kosofsky, Adam Frank, and Irving E. Alexander, eds. *Shame and Its Sisters: A Silvan Tompkins Reader*. Durham: Duke University Press, 1995.

Seremetakis, Nadia. *The Senses Still: Perception and Memory as National Culture*. Boulder: Westview, 1994.

Shorter, Edward. *A History of Psychiatry: From the Era of the Asylum to the Age of Prozac*. New York: John Wiley and Sons, 1997.

Slater, Lauren. *Prozac Diary*. New York: Random House, 1998; paperback ed., New York: Penguin, 1999.

Smith, Jeffery. *Where the Roots Reach for Water: A Personal and Natural History of Melancholia*. New York: North Point Press, 1999.

Smith, Sidonie, and Julia Watson, eds. *Getting a Life: Everyday Uses of Autobiography*. Minneapolis: University of Minnesota Press, 1996.

Smith, Sidonie, and Julia Watson, eds. *Women, Autobiography, Theory: A Reader*. Madison: University of Wisconsin Press, 1998.

Snediker, Michael D. *Queer Optimism: Lyric Personhood and Other Felicitous Persuasions*. Minneapolis: University of Minnesota Press, 2009.

Solomon, Andrew. "Depression, Too, Is a Thing with Feathers." *Contemporary Psychoanalysis* 44, no. 4 (2008), 509–30.

———. *The Noonday Demon: An Atlas of Depression*. New York: Scribner, 2001.

Somerson, Wendy. "Knot in Our Name: Activism beyond the Knitting Circle." *Bitch* 34 (winter 2007), 36–41.

Soto, Sandra K. *The De-Mastery of Desire: Reading Chican@ Like a Queer*. Austin: University of Texas Press, 2010.

Spillers, Hortense. "Mama's Baby, Papa's Maybe: An American Grammar Book." *Diacritics* 17 (summer 1987), 65–81.

Spivak, Gayatri Chakravorty. "Can the Subaltern Speak?" *Marxism and the Interpretation of Culture*, ed. Cary Nelson and Lawrence Grossberg. Urbana: University of Illinois Press, 1987. 271–313.

———. *A Critique of Postcolonial Reason: Toward a History of the Vanishing Present.* Cambridge: Harvard University Press, 1999.

Squier, Susan. "The Paradox of Prozac as Enhancement Technology." *Prozac as a Way of Life*, ed. Tod Chambers and Carl Elliott. Chapel Hill: University of North Carolina Press, 2004. 143–63.

Staiger, Janet. *Perverse Spectators: The Practices of Film Reception.* New York: New York University Press, 2000.

Staiger, Janet, Ann Cvetkovich, and Ann Reynolds. *Political Emotions.* New York: Routledge, 2010.

Stengers, Isabelle. *Cosmpolitics I and II (Posthumanities).* Minneapolis: University of Minnesota Press, 2010, 2011.

Stern, Julia A. *The Plight of Feeling: Sympathy and Dissent in the Early American Novel.* Chicago: University of Chicago Press, 1997.

Stewart, Kathleen. "On the Politics of Cultural Theory: A Case for 'Contaminated' Critique." *Social Research* 58, no. 2 (1991), 395–412.

———. *Ordinary Affects.* Durham: Duke University Press, 2007.

———. *A Space on the Side of the Road: Cultural Poetics in an "Other" America.* Princeton: Princeton University Press, 1996.

Stockton, Kathryn Bond. *The Queer Child, or Growing Sideways in the Twentieth Century.* Durham: Duke University Press, 2009.

Stoller, Debbie. *Stitch 'n Bitch: The Knitter's Handbook.* New York: Workman, 2003.

Stringer, Lee. "Fading to Gray." *Unholy Ghost: Writers on Depression*, ed. Nell Casey. New York: Harper Collins, 2002. 105–13.

Sturken, Marita. *Tangled Memories: The Vietnam War, the AIDS Epidemic, and the Politics of Remembering.* Berkeley: University of California Press, 1997.

Styron, William. *Darkness Visible: A Memoir of Madness.* New York: Vintage, 1990.

Sue, Derald Wing, and David Sue. *Counseling the Culturally Different.* 3rd ed. New York: John Wiley and Sons, 1999.

Taussig, Michael T. *My Cocaine Museum.* Chicago: University of Chicago Press, 2004.

———. *The Nervous System.* New York: Routledge, 1992.

———. *What Color Is the Sacred?* Chicago: University of Chicago Press, 2009.

Taylor, Charles. *A Secular Age.* Cambridge: Belknap Press of Harvard University Press, 2007.

Terada, Rei. *Feeling in Theory: Emotion after the "Death of the Subject."* Cambridge: Harvard University Press, 2001.

———. *Looking Awry: Phenomenality and Dissatisfaction.* Cambridge: Harvard University Press, 2009.

Tompkins, Jane. *A Life in School: What the Teacher Learned*. Reading, Mass: Perseus, 1996.

———. *Sensational Designs: The Cultural Work of American Fiction, 1790–1860*. New York: Oxford University Press, 1985.

Torres, Sasha. *Black, White, and in Color: Television and Black Civil Rights*. Princeton: Princeton University Press, 2003.

Tougaw, Jason. "Aplysia californica." *From Boys to Men: Gay Men Write about Growing Up*, ed. Ted Gideonse and Rob Williams. Cambridge, Mass.: DaCapo Press, 2006. 287–302.

———. *Strange Cases: The Medical Case History and the British Novel*. New York: Routledge, 2006.

———. "Testimony and the Subjects of AIDS Memoirs." *Extremities: Trauma, Testimony, and Community*, ed. Nancy K. Miller and Jason Tougaw. Urbana: University of Illinois Press, 2002. 166–85.

Turner, Dale A. *This Is Not a Peace Pipe: Towards a Critical Indigenous Philosophy*. Toronto: University of Toronto Press, 2006.

Valenstein, Elliot S. *Blaming the Brain: The Truth about Drugs and Mental Health*. New York: Free Press, 1998.

Viso, Olga. *Ana Mendieta: Earth Body*. Ostfildern, Germany: Hatje Cantz, 2004.

Vogel, Shane. "By the Light of What Comes After: Eventologies of the Ordinary." *Women and Performance* 19, no. 2 (2009), 247–60.

———. "Where Are We Now? Queer World Making and Cabaret Performance." *GLQ* 6:1 (2000): 29–59.

Wallace, David Foster. "The Depressed Person." *Harper's Magazine*, January 1998, 57–64. Republished in *Brief Interviews with Hideous Men*. Boston: Little Brown, 1999. 37–69.

———. *This Is Water: Some Thoughts, Delivered on a Significant Occasion, about Living a Compassionate Life*. Boston: Little, Brown, 2009.

Warner, Michael. *Publics and Counterpublics*. Cambridge: MIT Press, 2002.

Weiner, Joshua J., and Damon Young, eds. "Queer Bonds." Special issue of *GLQ* 17, nos. 2–3 (2011).

Wenzel, Siegfried. *The Sin of Sloth: Acedia in Medieval Thought and Literature*. Chapel Hill: University of North Carolina Press, 1967.

Whybrow, Peter C. *American Mania: When More Is Not Enough*. New York: W. W. Norton, 2005.

———. *A Mood Apart: Depression, Mania, and Other Afflictions of the Self*. New York: Basic Books, 1997.

Williams, Raymond. *Culture and Society, 1780–1950*. Garden City, N.Y.: Doubleday, 1960.

———, ed. *Keywords: A Vocabulary of Culture and Society*. 1976. Revised ed. New York: Oxford University Press, 1983.

———. "Structures of Feeling." *Marxism and Literature*. New York: Oxford University Press, 1977. 128–35.

Wilson, Elizabeth A. *Psychosomatic: Feminism and the Neurological Body*. Durham: Duke University Press, 2004.

———. "Underbelly." *Differences* 21, no. 1 (2010), 194–208.

Wilson, Eric G. *Against Happiness: In Praise of Melancholy*. New York: Farrar, Straus and Giroux, 2008.

Wilson, Waziyatawin Angela, and Michael Yellow Bird. *For Indigenous Eyes Only: A Decolonization Handbook*. Santa Fe.: School of American Research, 2005.

Wojnarowicz, David. *Close to the Knives: A Memoir of Disintegration*. New York: Vintage Books, 1991.

Woodward, Kathleen. *Statistical Panic: Cultural Politics and Poetics of the Emotions*. Durham: Duke University Press, 2009.

Wurtzel, Elizabeth. *Prozac Nation: Young and Depressed in America*. New York: Riverhead, 1994.

Yagoda, Ben. *Memoir: A History*. New York: Riverhead Books, 2009.

Yellow Horse Brave Heart, Maria. "From Intergenerational Trauma to Intergenerational Healing." *Wellbriety* 6, no. 6 (2005). Online.

———. "The Return to the Sacred Path: Healing from Historical Trauma and Historical Unresolved Grief among the Lakota." Ph.D. dissertation, Smith College of Social Work, 1995.

Yellow Horse Brave Heart, Maria, and Tina Deschenie. "Resource Guide: Historical Trauma and Post-Colonial Stress in American Indian Populations." *Tribal College Journal* 17, no. 3 (2006). Online.

Young, Allan. *The Harmony of Illusions: Inventing Post-Traumatic Stress Disorder*. Princeton: Princeton University Press, 1997.

Young, James Edward. *The Texture of Memory: Holocaust Memorials and Meaning*. New Haven: Yale University Press, 1993.

Young, Kay. *Imagining Minds: The Neuro-Aesthetics of Austen, Eliot, and Hardy*. Columbus: Ohio State University Press, 2010.

Zunshine, Lisa. *Why We Read: Theory of Mind and the Novel*. Columbus: Ohio State University Press, 2006.

Zwarg, Christina. "Du Bois on Trauma: Psychoanalysis and the Would-Be Black Savant." *Cultural Critique* 51 (Spring 2002), 1–39.

Zwicker, Heather. "Things We Gained in the Fire: Burnout, Feminism, and Radical Collegiality." *Not Drowning but Waving: Women, Feminism, and the Liberal Arts*, ed. Susan Brown, Jeanne Perreault, Jo-Ann Wallace, and Heather Zwicker. Edmonton: University of Alberta Press, 2011. 107–20.

Illustration Credits

Page 29. Altar of rocks from Waterton Park, Alberta. Photo taken in Ithaca, N.Y., 1986. Personal collection of the author.

Page 43. Ann holding Virgen of Guadalupe by John Hernandez. Photo taken in Austin, 1988. Personal collection of the author.

Page 62. Ann and her father with fish. Photo taken in Campbell River, B.C., 1961. Personal collection of the author.

Figure 3.1. Page 155. Allyson Mitchell, *War on Worries*, 2001. Shadow boxes, 5" by 5". Collection of Ann Cvetkovich.

Figure 3.2. Page 162. Justin Bond and Kenny Mellman as Kiki and Herb, 2007. Photo by Liz Ligouri.

Figure 3.3. Page 170. Leslie Hall, Stargazer. Photo by Rena Hall.

Figure 3.4. Page 173. Lisa Anne Auerbach, *Body Count Mittens*, 2005. Photo courtesy of the artist.

Figure 3.5. Page 174. Lisa Anne Auerbach, *Take This Knitting Machine and Shove It*, installation at Nottingham Contemporary Museum, 2009. Photo courtesy of the artist.

Figure 3.6. Page 175. Magda Sayeg and Knitta Please, *Knitted Wonderland*, installation at Blanton Museum, Austin, 2011. Photo by Shawn P. Thomas.

Figure 3.7. Page 176. Betsy Greer, *These Are Dangerous Times*. Aida cloth and DMC thread. International Anti-War Graffiti Cross-Stitch Series: #2, Dublin, 2004. Photo courtesy of the artist.

Figure 3.8. Page 179. Sheila Pepe, *Lap*, 2001. Crocheted shoelaces, industrial rubber bands. Commissioned for Energy Inside, Faulconer Gallery, Grinnell College, Grinnell, Iowa.

Figure 3.9a and b. Page 180. Sheila Pepe, *Common Sense*, a collaboration with curator Elizabeth Dunbar, 2009. Yarn / audience participation. Solo exhibition at testsite/Fluent-Collaborative, Austin. Photos by Kate Watson courtesy of Fluent-Collaborative.

Figure 3.9c and d. Page 181. *Common Sense II*, 2010. Yarn, rope structure / audience participation. Included in Hand + Made, Contemporary Arts Museum, Houston. Photos by author.

Figure 3.10. Page 183. Faith Wilding, *Crocheted Environment (Womb Room)*. Rope and yarn, 9′ x 9′ x 9′. Womanhouse, Los Angeles, 1972. Photo courtesy of the artist.

Figure 3.11. Page 184. Allyson Mitchell, *55 Things That Tried to Kill Me*, 2000. Works on paper.

Figure 3.12. Page 187. Allyson Mitchell. *Menstrual Hut Sweet Menstrual Hut.* FIERCE: Women's Hot-Blooded Film/Video, McMaster Museum of Art, Hamilton, Ont., 2010. Photo by Jill Kitchener.

Figure 3.13. Page 195. Gregg Bordowitz, stills from *Habit*, 2001.

Page 203. Lynda Barry. *What It Is*, 130. Montreal: Drawn & Quarterly Press, 2008. Copyright Lynda Barry 2012. Courtesy Drawn & Quarterly Press.

Page 211. Lynda Barry. *What It Is*, 135. Montreal: Drawn & Quarterly Press, 2008. Copyright Lynda Barry 2012. Courtesy Drawn & Quarterly Press.

Plates appear after page 180.

Plate 1. Sheila Pepe, detail from *Gowanus*. Nautical towline, shoelaces, shopping cart. Commissioned for Two Women: Carrie Moyer and Sheila Pepe, Palm Beach Institute of Contemporary Art (PBICA), Lakeworth, Fla., 2004.

Plate 2. Sheila Pepe, detail from *Greybeard*. Yarn, silver thread, shoelaces. Included in Empire of This, Claire Oliver Gallery, New York City, 2008. Collection of the artist.

Plate 3. Sheila Pepe, *Mind the Gap*. Nautical towline, shoelaces, paint, hardware. Solo exhibition. University Gallery, University of Massachusetts, Amherst, 2005.

Plate 4. Sheila Pepe, *Under the F&G*. Crocheted shoelaces, paint, hardware. Visual Art Center of Virginia, Richmond, 2003.

Plate 5. Sheila Pepe, detail from *Your Granny's Not Square*. Crocheted yarn. Included in Color in 3D: Found, Applied and Readymade, Westport Arts Center, Westport, Conn., 2008. Collection of the artist.

Plate 6. Sheila Pepe, detail from *Terminal*. Nautical towline, tulle, silver thread, industrial rubber bands, shoelaces. Commissioned for Decelerate, Kemper Museum of Contemporary Art, Kansas City, Mo., 2006.

Plate 7. Sheila Pepe, *Mr. Slit*, 2007. Shoelaces, industrial rubber bands, yarn, hardware. 3.2 m x 2.1 m x .91 m. Collection of Lutz Hieber, Hanover, Germany.

Plates 8–11. Allyson Mitchell, *Hungry Purse: The Vagina Dentata in Late Capitalism*. Visible Vaginas, David Nolan Gallery, New York City, 2010. Photos by Tom Powel Imaging, New York. Courtesy David Nolan Gallery and Francis Naumann Fine Art, New York.

Plates 12–14. Allyson Mitchell, *Ladies Sasquatch*. McMaster Museum of Art, Hamilton, Ont., 2009. Photos by Cat O'Neil.

Index

Page numbers in italics refer to illustrations.

ANN CVETKOVICH
is Ellen C. Garwood Centennial Professor of
English and Professor of Women's and Gender
Studies at the University of Texas, Austin. She is the
author of *An Archive of Feelings: Trauma, Sexuality,
and Lesbian Public Cultures* (Duke, 2003) and *Mixed
Feelings: Feminism, Mass Culture, and Victorian
Sensationalism* (1992), as well as the editor of (with
Janet Staiger and Ann Reynolds) *Political Emotions*
(2010) and a former editor of *GLQ: A Journal of
Lesbian and Gay Studies.*

*Library of Congress
Cataloging-in-Publication Data*

Cvetkovich, Ann.
Depression : a public feeling / Ann Cvetkovich.
p. cm.
Includes bibliographical references and index.
ISBN 978-0-8223-5223-5 (cloth : alk. paper)
ISBN 978-0-8223-5238-9 (pbk. : alk. paper)
1. Queer theory.
2. Affect (Psychology)—Political aspects.
3. Depression, Mental.
4. Emotions—Political aspects.
5. Creative ability—Psychological aspects.
6. Autobiography.
I. Title.
HQ75.15C86 2012
616.85'27—dc23   2012011605